## What people are say

## Life Is a Song c

When Sally Patton speaks of a feminist revolution of the heart, she includes the need to leave behind the victim role. This is an important addition. With it, she acknowledges the "collective anger" being "felt, grieved and cleared" to allow women to come into "fierce love—first for ourselves and then for everyone." Sally grew, as many did, to be a caretaker of men's egos. Speaking of the message she "absorbed" from her mother, I could also identify. As she suggests, patriarchal values are dissolving as women share "our heroine's journeys." I also celebrate and witness, along with her, the beauty, support and power of the feminine in community.
**Mari Perron**, author of *A Course of Love* and *Mirari and Memoria: The Way of the Marys*

In *Life Is a Song of Love*, Sally Patton takes us on the winding path of the labyrinth into the healing of our heart womb and the restoration of our feminine power. Fiercely calling out the deceptions and distortions of patriarchy, she beckons us to face our own grief, anger and wounds in order to free ourselves to be the fullness of who we are: passionate advocates for love and powerful bearers of the New Earth.
**Patricia Pearce**, author of *Beyond Jesus: My Spiritual Odyssey*

Both scholarly and personal, Sally weaves a rich tapestry of her own lived mother-daughter experiences with myriad ancient feminine myths and truths. *Life Is a Song of Love* is a living book that invites the reader to turn within. No two readers will respond in the same way. Each will find the thread most resonant deep in their heart-belly-womb, follow where it leads, and be restored to themselves by all they discover.
**Christina Strutt**, CoCreating Clarity and Online Publisher of *A Journey Into the Unknown*

Sally Patton weaves together threads from wisdom teachings, her own spiritual path, many years of healing work, and stories from her own life into a sturdy cord that when followed can lead the reader through a landscape of patriarchal wounds and broken relationships to a place of insight, restoration and hope. She provides insights into relationships between mothers and daughters, demonstrating the difficulties caused by patriarchal conditioning. Sally shares her own pain and self-acceptance in ways that increase the possibilities for forgiveness and repair in the lives of others. Let her accompany you on your quest for deeper understanding and peace.
**Rev Jeanette Stokes**, Ex. Dir. Resource Center for Women and Ministry in the South. Author of three memoirs and three collections of essays, including *Just Keep Going: Advice on Writing and Life*

With tremendous vulnerability, tenderness and insight, Sally invites us to join her as she is guided on a labyrinthine mystical journey of self-love, integration and spiritual awakening. *Life Is a Song of Love* stays true to its intention of lovingly helping humanity to emerge from separation consciousness and weave its way back to wholeness. Even while taking a deep look at the roots of patriarchy and the many ways that patriarchal conditioning has affected humanity, Sally's tone is neither harsh nor full of blame. An important theme of the book is "forgiving the unforgivable and loving the unlovable" and Sally invites each of us to discover our own path to forgiveness and unconditional love.
**Sajit Greene**, soul guide and transformational coach informed by evolutionary astrology and years of experience facilitating somatic and expressive arts therapies.

*Life Is a Song of Love* powerfully and skillfully guides the reader from feelings of separation, lack and victimhood to an understanding and discovery of the innate love and abundance that resides in our core. From Sally's own life experience as a woman, daughter and mother, and from her extensive spiritual knowledge, she shares intimately about the process of facing her own wounding and trauma. The transformative healing journey that unfolds, with the grace of the Holy Mother, delivers her to greater empowerment, self-love, forgiveness and compassion for self and all others.

Sally is a visionary and presents a beautiful overview of a new Earth with the shift from a patriarchal "power-over" paradigm, to a feminine-based "power within" paradigm. This book is a rich treasure, a masterful and inspiring work that will benefit and serve women in their own healing and awakening journey. It lights the pathway and takes us home to the love that we truly are and to the sacred opportunity of creating a more peaceful and loving world.

**Suvani Stepanek**, clinical hypnotherapist, co-author of *Grow Your Healthy Relationship Cards*

*Life Is a Song of Love* is a deeply inspiring book that has the power to activate the remembrance of the Divine Self. The wisdom the author expresses cuts through the ego and touches the heart of the Soul. I appreciate that this book does not sugar coat or avoid addressing the wounds and trauma that we carry. Instead, it provides clear guidance for healing, transformation, and embodiment of our Highest Expression.

**Kandace Jones**, author of *From Stress to Peace: An Intimate Journal in the Journey from Living in Darkness to Living in the Light*

# Also by the Author

*Welcoming Children with Special Needs, A Guidebook for Faith Communities* ISBN 1-55896-479-7 (Out of Print. Available to read online at https://www.uua.org/files/documents/lfd/welcoming_children_specialneeds.pdf)

*Don't Fix Me I'm Not Broken, Changing Our Minds about Ourselves and Our Children* ISBN 978-1-84694-466-6

# Life Is a Song of Love

## A Woman's Spiritual Journey of the Heart and Womb

# Life Is a Song of Love

## A Woman's Spiritual Journey of the Heart and Womb

Sally Patton

BOOKS

Winchester, UK
Washington, USA

JOHN HUNT PUBLISHING

First published by O-Books, 2023
O-Books is an imprint of John Hunt Publishing Ltd., 3 East St., Alresford,
Hampshire SO24 9EE, UK
office@jhpbooks.com
www.johnhuntpublishing.com
www.o-books.com

For distributor details and how to order please visit the 'Ordering' section on our website.



ISBN: 978 1 80341 243 6
978 1 80341 244 3 (ebook)
Library of Congress Control Number: 2022909772



A CIP catalogue record for this book is available from the British Library.

Design: Lapiz Digital Services

UK: Printed and bound by CPI Group (UK) Ltd, Croydon, CR0 4YY
Printed in North America by CPI GPS partners

# Contents


**Prelude: We Begin** xvii

**Movement One: An Overture: The Heroine's Spiritual Journey** 1

**Chapter One: The Start of My Unique Song** 3

Inception 5

Shattering the Stone of Resistance 9

The Hero's Journey and the Heroine's Journey 12

**Chapter Two: The Labyrinth, A Symbolic Path into the Heart and Womb** 14

The Labyrinth's Story 16

Creating Labyrinths for Walking and Holding 18

Walking the Labyrinth 19

*Labyrinth in Snow: A Metaphor for Trusting Inner Guidance* 20

The Labyrinth as an Operating System 22

**Chapter Three: Simplify Your Journey: Follow Your Heart and Save Yourself** 24

The Difference between Self Love and Selfishness 28

**Chapter Four: Myths and Stories Transcend and Inform My Spiritual Path** 32

Balancing Masculine and Feminine Energies 34

*David's Father* 35

*The Paper Bag Princess* 37

*Jane and the Dragon* 38

*Lady Ragnell and Sir Gawain* 40

**Chapter Five: Embracing the Wildness in Our Soul** 43

Men's Journey into Their Hearts 45

Creating the New 46

**As Within So Without Meditations, The Gift of a Question** 49

**Movement Two: The Mystic's Song of Truth** 53
**Chapter One: What Is a Mystic?** 55
Mystics Hold the Myths of Divine Truths 61
Listening to the Voice of Love 62
**Chapter Two: Mystical Teachings** 68
Contemporary Mystical Teachings Influencing My Heroine's Journey 71
Mystical Truths in a Time of Reason and Scientific Proof 75
**Chapter Three: Women as Mystics, the Old and the New** 79
Women Mystics Who Fill My Heart with Gratitude 81
*Hildegard of Bingen* 82
*Julian of Norwich* 83
*Thecla Who Saves Herself Over and Over Again* 85
*Contemporary Women Mystics* 88
**As Within So Without Meditations, The Gift of a Question** 89

**Movement Three: I Am Lilith, Hear My Song** 91
**Chapter One: Lilith and Sexuality** 93
Lilith's Story, the Good, the Bad and the Ugly 95
Lilith's Story Symbolizes Her-Story Within the His-Story of Humanity 99
**Chapter Two: Lessons from Lilith** 105
Lilith as First Woman Is the Black Goddess of Air and Night 105
Lilith's Spirit Animals 107
Lilith as a Sexual Woman and the First Mom 108
Lilith as Shadow Woman of Grief and Anger 113
Lilith as a Witch Who Burns and Uses Magic 115

Lilith Is a Woman of Power Out of Exile 117
**Chapter Three: The Song of Lilith's Expression in Me** 119
Snake Medicine Within Me 119
The Owl as My First Spirit Guide 122
**Chapter Four: Lilith's Legacy** 125
The Tantric Path 125
Can We Forgive Adam? 127
The Cosmic Egg 129
**As Within So Without Meditations, The Gift of a Question** 133

**Movement Four: Healing the Mother Daughter Patriarchal Wound** 135
**Chapter One: The Wound of Separation** 137
Healing Our Own Core Wound of Separation 142
Loving Our Inner Child to Forgive Ourselves and Other Women 146
*Visualization* 147
The Perpetrator, Victim, Savior Triad 148
*We Are Not Victims* 151
Freedom from Suppression of the Feminine 152
**Chapter Two: Healing Our Sacred Core Wound** 157
Recognizing Divine Masculine Energy as Our Spiritual Foundation 159
Symbols of Sacred Union 163
Repressed Anger 165
The Soul's Pre-Planning Process 169
**Chapter Three: The Mother Daughter Relationship** 171
Relationship with My Grandmothers 172
*My Maternal Grandmother* 172
*My Fraternal Grandmother* 173
Relationship with My Mother 175
*My Story as Daughter* 178

Sarah and My Stories as Mother and Daughter 180
*The Silent Scream* 187
*The Gift of Depression* 188
Crawling Inside the Wound Becomes Total Surrender to What Is 194
**Chapter Four: Forgiving Mothers, Daughters, Sisters and Ourselves** 197
The Feminine Archetypes 204
Mothers and Daughters Are Constantly Searching and Finding Each Other 206
**As Within So Without Meditations, The Gift of a Question** 215

**Movement Five: The Siren Song of Anger** 219
**Chapter One: Transmuting Anger into Fierce Love** 221
My Story of Anger 224
*My Journey of Dissolving Anger* 229
The Story of Kali Ma and Shiva 234
*Why This Story Speaks to Women's Anger* 235
The Dragon Doesn't Live in Me Anymore 238
Healing Dis-Easement of the Body 239
**Chapter Two: Forgiving the Unforgivable and Loving the Unlovable** 242
Power-Over Transformed into Power of Love 244
Forgiveness and Surrendering to Divine Innocence in Ourselves and Others 248
**As Within So Without Meditations, The Gift of a Question** 255

**Movement Six: The Divine Sophia's Song of Beauty** 257
**Chapter One: Walking in Beauty and Remembering My Song** 259
The Power of Song 262

**Chapter Two: When the World Tried to Sever the Divine Mother from God** 268
The Fall from Grace 269
*When the World Forgot How to Hug* 274
*Embracing Indigenous Roots* 278
*The Marys Shine the Divine Feminine Light* 281
**Chapter Three: Womb Healing and Awakening** 283
The Wise Woman Returns 285
Universal Grandmothers' Chorus of Love 288
*Dissolving the Ties That Bind* 290
*Wisdom Weavers Co-Creating the New Earth* 293
*Wisdom Weavers as Charismatic Adults* 296
Whirling Rainbow Prophecy 298
**Chapter Four: When Children Are Safe and Loved, Everyone Is Safe and Loved** 300
Unconditional Listening Creates a Song of Love 304
**As Within so Without Meditations, The Gift of a Question** 309

**Movement Seven: The Great Tuning to Love** 311
**Chapter One: A Time to Flourish** 313
**Chapter Two: The Process of Transformation and Resurrection** 317
Howling at the Moon 318
Removing Myself from the Cross 319
Grief Allows Love to Bloom 322
Forgiving the Unforgivable and Loving the Unlovable 324
*Stories of Forgiveness* 325
*Personal Forgiveness* 328
**Chapter Three: All the Traditional Systems Are Dissolving and Transforming** 334
Lack Consciousness 335

**Chapter Four: A Vision of the New Earth Created with Compassion** 340
Can We Create a World Where All Children Are Safe and Well? 343
Creating Intentional Communities in Devotion to Life's Song of Love 346
Being Authentic 348
The Will of Sophia God Is Our Will 352
Atonement and the Time of Christ 353
God Exists in the Details, in Ordinary Everyday Events 355
The One Source Light of Creation 360
Completion 362
**As Within So Without Meditations, The Gift of a Question** 364
*Visualization* 364
**Finale: We Begin Where We End** 368

Endnotes 372
Acknowledgments 377
About the Author 378
For More Information 380

I dedicate *Life Is a Song of Love* to my daughter Sarah for her courage, clarity of purpose, and her infinite kindness and compassion, and to mothers and daughters everywhere.

# Prelude: We Begin

*The song of my heart*
*Blossoms into Love*
*All life embraced as sacred.*

I begin this spiritual journey of the heart and womb by feeling without any doubt that my song of the heart is blossoming with the writing of this book. It is a beautiful experience. I have come to realize that this is a sacred, intensely courageous human journey to remember my Truth as a divine, beloved, holy child of the Mother Father Sophia God. This journey toward human sovereignty has no end and in essence leads each of us full circle to our God Self which we never left. The process of forgiving and falling in love with ourself is the transformation to being fully human and fully divine.

I begin with this still point of awareness in this lifetime of the personal self called Sally. I turned 69, 70, and 71 while writing this book. I thought I had already made my heartfelt contribution to the world. I thought I could live on the top of my mesa in northern New Mexico quietly embodying my divinity in this incarnation. The gradual awareness that service to the Cosmic Mother Father does not recognize age or retirement and is in essence never ending is part of this journey of the heart and thus the content of this book.

As I begin, I do not know where the writing of this book will ultimately lead me. It is a journey of remembering and fulfilling my unique purpose in union with God, a journey that is not a destination but an expression of expanding love. As we come to know the unknown mysteries of the Beloved One Source Light of Creation we are drawn again into the unknown. There are no absolute endings, only beginnings and the infinite expansion of the love; that's all there is. I like the idea of an infinite divine existence filled with stopping points or sign posts indicating and leading to more astounding adventures of the heart. This helps in understanding and allowing this current life to be filled with the grace of Sophia God.

The fall into separation consciousness coincided with humanity's concerted movement to try and erase all traces of the Holy Mother from the face of God. We became disconnected from our hearts and the divine feminine essence which houses our nurturing, intuitive, imaginal and creative abilities. I describe how this imbalance destructively played out in women and men for thousands of years, wounding women in our wombs and men in their hearts. The female wound created from patriarchal conditioning, what I call the Mother Daughter Patriarchal Wound, is felt by all women. With the more recent rise of the sacred feminine, we are now able to heal this imbalance and usher in a time of Unity/Christ/Buddha Consciousness. We are in the midst of a planetary awakening, the Great Tuning to Love. The blessing is that we are co-creating heaven on earth, co-creating becoming divinely human—something that has not been created before. We are co-creating a new species of human. And thus we add to the variety, diverseness and richness of the Holy Mother Holy Father Sophia God's multidimensional, infinite ever-expanding realities.

This is a book about weaving together the various spiritual truths and paths that merge into my journey. The heroine's spiritual journey is mystical and organic, not linear. Linear is the separated ego. Linear thinking has been helpful in navigating this dense, low-energy 3D world and even starting us on our return to Unity consciousness. However, it is constricting and keeps us from an awareness of who we are as limitless beings, always creating and expanding God's love. I learned to think logically, to plan, to write outlines, to provide proof of my views. Yet, they were a straitjacket to keep my divine feminine essence from embracing the whole that follows tangents of ideas and weaves it all together into the new. Thus, the labyrinth became a metaphor for the heroine's journey into the heart and womb of the Holy Mother and her daughter, Mother Gaia.

This is a book for women, although I hope some men will read it. It is for women because we've been forced into the patriarchal hero's journey—which is to overcome many obstacles in order to transcend the body. This type of hero's journey is wedded to the patriarchal power-over paradigm of force and dominance. The heroine's journey is inward and embraces the feminine paradigm of power within.

God is genderless, with masculine and feminine resonance joined as One. However, on earth within separation consciousness, gender has divided us—with a focus on our bodies. Women have been treated for eons as the second sex, demeaned, violated, suppressed and persecuted, creating a wound in our wombs. In the process men lost the ability to feel their emotions, creating a wound in their hearts. These wounds need to be healed and dissolved in order for humanity to move into wholeness and become divinely human. Pretending the trauma of suppression and annihilation of the feminine divine does not exist only allows it to fester and grow. Hence there is immense benefit in bringing the words, energy and essence of both the sacred feminine and sacred masculine into our awareness to return balance to humanity. The deep anger, grief and unworthiness needs to be acknowledged, seen and felt before it can be released.

Writing about the patriarchal paradigm and its harmful effect on women may seem as if I'm dumping on men and blaming them. I have done that at times in my life, but I no longer carry that energy. The book's purpose is to understand how patriarchy as a tool of the separated ego has greatly programmed both men and women's lives to the point of unconscious adherence to the doctrine of power-over. Both men and women have their own unique paths to waking from this illusion of separation from our Beloved Source. His-story is the result of men's hearts being closed off so that they lost their connection to emotions and their Soul. His-story is the story of colonization and the suppression and elimination of anyone embodying the feminine energy of creation, birth and deep connection to the sacredness of Mother Earth's web of life. Women, indigenous communities, people of color and Jews have been consistently and violently targeted for thousands of years. Our heroine's spiritual journey is freeing us to remember the time before the fall from grace when we were intimately connected with all life enfolded in the embrace of the Holy Mother.

This is a book for women to help access eons of womb trauma from the brutal suppression of the feminine. As we acknowledge, feel, heal and dissolve this trauma, we love ourselves into freedom from the human ego of separation, into our divine sovereignty. This helps women to empathize with the wound men carry from the trauma of eons of carnage, unspeakable pain and destruction on the battlefields of conflict and war. Both the feminine and masculine divine must be honored and embraced individually and collectively to return us to balance and wholeness. Men are released from their own patriarchal constraints as women awaken to model for men how to access their own inner feminine in order to heal their distorted and wounded masculine energy. The Mother aspect of God has returned to her rightful place as the Creatrix of all there is, enfolding the Holy Father. Therefore, this is a book about remembering and returning to Unity Consciousness which does not separate or divide according to race and gender differences. We are the One in the many and the many in the One—difference and individuation within union and relationship.

It became apparent early in the writing process that this book is writing and birthing me. Therefore, I stopped trying to plan and organize. Awareness came when needed. The unfoldment of this story came with seven movements like sections with multiple melodies or chapters within each. In many ways they feel like movements in a symphony with many tones, songs, sounds, vibrations and rhythms weaving together in harmony within the symphony of creation. The Overture introduces the themes for the rest of the book. Without any conscious attempt on my part, the pivotal movement of the book is Healing the Mother Daughter Patriarchal Wound. Three movements prepare us for it and three movements evolve from it. My divine guidance was strong throughout the writing. I had no sense of the significance of having seven movements until I was guided to research the spiritual meaning of the number seven.

Seven is associated with intuition, mysticism, inner wisdom and deep inner knowing. It means everything is flowing. Seven is the first of what is known as the higher vibrational numbers. Seven is associated with the search for Truth that knows reality is hidden behind the veil of illusion. Seven is the number of completeness and perfection. It is tied directly to God's creation of all that is. It is important in Hinduism, Islam and Judaism. In Christianity, God created the earth in 7 days. I am humbled and so grateful for the divine guidance that orchestrated this book and seven beautifully summarizes my writing process.

I write about themes central to our heroine's journey: forgiving and loving ourselves free to return to Unity consciousness; enfolding our wild creative feminine selves in balance with the support, discernment and clarity of our masculine energy; healing the mother daughter wound perpetuated by patriarchal conditioning; embracing the Universal Grandmother's basket of love for all humanity; healing sexism and racism to co-create a world where all children are cherished. And through it all is the ever-present melody of forgiving the unforgivable and loving the unlovable. We are ushering in the age of compassion, co-creating the New Earth as fully human and fully divine beings.

There are many names for the One God. No name is better than the other. God does not care what it is called. Under patriarchy, the feminine essence of God was suppressed almost to extinction. This created our seriously dysfunctional world of separation. Therefore, it is important to use the divine feminine names in order to repair the idea that God the Father contains only masculine energy. Father God has been used to justify the idea that women are lesser beings of the divine. Continuing to use only patriarchal language of the past keeps us recycling separation consciousness.

I use many names for the feminine face of God: Holy Mother, Divine Mother, Mother Earth, Universal Mother, Cosmic Mother, Immanent Mother, Great Mother and Holy Mother Sophia God. Sometimes I join Her with the Holy, Divine, Universal, Cosmic Father. Sometimes I use Mother/Father/One or the Beloved, Creator and the Source of All that Is. There is no pattern to when I use one over the other. I use whatever seems to flow with what is being revealed as I write.

I use Jesus' Aramaic name Yeshua because it frees me from negative associations to organized patriarchal Christianity's Jesus. I also interchangeably use the words: God Self, I Am Presence, Higher Holy Self, Sacred Self, Soul Self and Christ Self. The word Christ comes loaded with the patriarchal Christian Church's distortion of the word. It means anointed by God and was not meant to refer only to Jesus/Yeshua. Christ is Oneness, Unity or Buddha as the inner divine essence in everyone. Within Unity is individuation and differentiation. Within separation consciousness we use individuation to separate and divide. Christ is a bridge to our direct relationship with God and thus relationship with all individuated or differentiated beings because all beings exist in and of God. If Christ pushes your buttons, use another word until you can claim the word as your own. Many mystics sourcing from other faith traditions use the word Christ. In Oneness, faith traditions or religions disappear in the Unity of All there Is, although the rich cultural heritage remains.

I draw on stories and myths to illustrate and help us go deep into our shadow to shine a light on all the shame, blame and anger we want to suppress. Myths and stories can open our hearts in ways that feel less threatening, enlightening us in ways not previously imagined. Myths and stories often bypass logical reasoning, allowing our hearts to lead our self-inquiry and healing.

This book is about my evolving mystical heroine's journey. *Some of what I describe may resonate and some may not. Take what works for you and leave the rest.* Each one of us is on our own unique heroine's journey into the heart and womb. *There are immutable Truths in everyone's journey of awakening where there are intersections of shared experience and deep knowing.* We all return Home to our Soul Selves in harmony and unity, how we get there may differ. It is what's so breathtaking and awe inspiring about Sophia God's infinite creations. I write about what sings to me on my path to embody Christ in this life time. Everyone is co-creating the New Earth to ascend together into the fifth dimension, where the stillness of music within the multiverse is always heard. Beyond silence and within stillness is Song, our unique love song of life. Meet me here in Love and Oneness. Life is a song of love. Blessed Be.

# Movement One

# An Overture: The Heroine's Spiritual Journey

## Chapter One

# The Start of My Unique Song

*My voice joins with you*
*We create a choir*
*Singing a new world of love.*

Music is a multidimensional language. All creation carries sound, resonance, vibration and tone. When in relationship with all that is, we hear our unique song. Each song combined with others becomes a choir that seamlessly joins as One in harmony to become a symphony of color and sound that generates joy, peace and infinite love. This is the music of the soul, the language of the heart that is tied to the Source of all creation, joining the physical heart and the holy heart together to create a new world symphony. The cadence, rhythm and pulse of each song, together, is the breath and heartbeat of planet earth. The song of the universe and the multiverse is all these rhythmic patterns resounding together.

The earth, the sun, the galaxies, the stars, light frequencies—all God's creations—are singing in a sea of the oceanic presence of Sophia God's heart womb. It is all a natural flowing symphony of song in which everything is in harmony even if our earthly eyes and ears can't see it or hear it. When we tune to our own unique song, we tune to all that is. The earth's ley lines are vibrational tunes aligning the earth to the symphony of the multiverse interdimensionally and within multiple realities. Everything breathes and sings with Sophia God.

The songs of the high desert resonate with my own heart song. When I'm hiking or walking my labyrinth, I hear earth's heart beat in the raucous crows and the chirping birds, in the bellowing of cows, the coyotes' howl, the buzzing of bees and the scurrying of lizards. Most of all I hear it in the silence of desert flowers, piñon pines, junipers, cactus and the astounding colorful rocks of the high desert of New Mexico. Many of us have a place on Mother Earth that sings to us. Where is yours? Is it by the ocean, in the forest, on the plains, on a mountain, or in the city? If we listen, we can hear the music of the heart wherever we are, even during these polarizing times.

As we listen to the music of love, God speaks to us in a myriad of ways. We are called to pay attention. When we listen with our whole bodies, our whole hearts, then we can hear the music of love even during these destructive times of confusion, dense energy and unloving acts. Especially there, where love is needed, we can hear the faint heart music and our loving attention helps it gain power to dissolve the perception of darkness.

I am embraced within Sophia God's music. It flows through me, around me, in harmony with my own breath and heartbeat. Let me always listen. Let me always open my heart to the singing of mother earth, the song of the universe and the song of the multiverse. The angelic choir is constantly singing. The Sky Grandmothers weave all the unique melodies of the Holy Mother's creations into a symphony and chorus with one purpose—to constantly rejoice and sing the love, joy and peace of the Holy Mother Holy Father. As Mystical Soul Sisters and Wisdom Weavers we listen unconditionally to the music of love emanating from all that is and magnify the music till it vibrates clearly from all sources to join in one magnificent sustained symphony of life. It is flowing, changing, full of variations in tempo and unique melodies all harmoniously woven together in one long symphony of love.

My God Self is the conductor of my orchestrated life's song. Any mistakes or discordant notes are woven into my life's song with one purpose: to sing with the angels. No matter how many discordant notes occur, my God Self continues to conduct because Sophia God only hears my divinely perfect song. There are no discordant or wrong notes in the symphony of the multiverse because our miscreated notes only exist in this dream of separation. Being a beloved child of God means that we represent the continuity of creation and the acceptance and fulfillment as divine sovereign beings. The discordant notes are part of the process of learning to accept our true inheritance. Yeshua says in A Course of Love (ACOL):

> This could as easily be stated as you being a Song of God. You are God's harmony, God's expression, God's melody. You, and all that exist with you, form the orchestra and chorus of creation. You might think of your time here as that of being apprentice musicians. You must learn or relearn what you have forgotten so that you can once again join the chorus. So that you can once again be in harmony with creation. So that you can express yourself within the relationship of unity that is the whole of the choir and the orchestra. So that you can realize your accomplishment in union and relationship. So that you can join your accomplishment with that of all others and become the body of Christ.[1]

## Inception

When did it begin, this woman's journey of the heart and womb to knowing fully life as a song of love that has always been a song of love? Did it begin when I received the message to write this book or did it begin when I actually started it? Or did it begin over 40 years ago when my intuition led me to read *Dear Heart Come Home* by Joyce Rupp? That book answered a dormant longing and launched me on a spiritual journey into my heart that continues today. But wait, maybe it goes even further back, to my birth on my mother's birthday. Between myself and my mother there was always something special, something mystical about being born on her birthday. Maybe it started with the radiant child who had all this music within her so that I rocked and swayed all the time. Perhaps it goes back before my birth to the soul planning for this life, choosing my parents, brothers, husband, children, friends and experiences that would be part of my soul's journey as I would be part of their souls' journeys. Oh yes, I feel it starts even before this, with the many incarnations I've experienced on earth all happening in the eternal now. And yes, all the way to the very beginning of life when a light that was uniquely my soul was birthed within the primordial dark unconditional loving space of the Divine Mother's womb and ushered into being with the clarity and sacred purpose of the Divine Father.

Okay then: maybe there is no beginning, maybe it just is, this longing to experience earth and create something new, to become divinely human. Maybe the beginning always starts in the heart. In this place called earth with its dense energy of separation consciousness, we go in and out of listening to our heart. Our heroine's journey encompasses the process of being led by our heart and then occasionally being pulled into the habits of the separated ego until more and more we stay in the heart—until that's all we know. Until all we hear within is the voice of our God Self. That is what is meant by the second coming of Christ—when everyone on earth remembers to listen to the inner voice of Love that always was and always will be. When each one of us claims, I Am the living Christ!

As I write these words, I am in my heart, listening to my God Self and the words flow. This has been my struggle: to be in my heart long enough to write. It comes in spurts and starts because I am still living my heroine's journey of going in and out of my heart. My life is a continuous prayer to stay totally within my heart space, to listen only to the voice of Love. My voice of Love comes from many sources: my Higher Holy Self or I Am Presence, which is my God Self; and my light family which includes Yeshua, Mother Mary, Mary Magdalene, Kali Ma, Quan Yin, White Buffalo Woman, St Germaine and many more. Love wisdom also comes from my spiritual sisters and brothers, my family, friends, brief encounters with seeming strangers and heartfelt conversations with the people that flow in and out of my life.

I am not sure when I stopped believing any spiritual guidance could come from outside of me. It lessened over time as I dropped more and more often into my heart. Eventually without making note of it, I started knowing in my heart the words "we are all One in Union with our Beloved Source of All that Is." I started feeling it deep within the driest and darkest recesses of this body. The thirst for solace and mercy eventually allowed the waters of forgiveness to quench the thirst for my God Self—to allow this body, this chalice of the Holy Mother's love, to fill up and overflow. Even the sense of unworthiness cannot remain along with the gratitude I feel for the uncompromising, unconditional love of my True Self in union with the Holy Mother Holy Father Sophia God. My heroine's journey to this awareness in my elder wisdom years is still ongoing. I am still living this journey while I write as well as stop. I still occasionally get triggered by people and experiences. Only now I accept how I'm feeling instead of stuffing or ignoring the feelings. I am quicker to feel anger because I no longer bury the anger until it points to what still needs to be dissolved into wholeness.

We exist in Oneness. When we are within our heart hearing only the many voices of Love, we know Oneness. We know we are equal within Oneness. The voice of Yeshua, Mother Mary, Buddha, Kali Ma, or whoever you feel most closely aligned, speak within us, because we are One with all of God's multifaceted, multidimensional, multitudinous creations. When we abide in our hearts, we hear the wondrous music—God's orchestra and chorus of creation in Oneness. The more we stay in our heart space, the more we hear only the Voice of Love in its variety of forms. Staying within the spacious self, what I call the "heart womb space," allows us to always lead with our heart's intuition, with our mind following to provide clarity and support for action. I equate heart with the sacred feminine, and mind with the sacred masculine. In balance, we are invincible and whole, we are divine sovereign creators.

When I finally said Yes and started writing this book after several years of resistance, I realized I was still in the process of embodying what was being revealed in my inner work. While the crippling lower back and neck pain was healed by going inward and recognizing all the anger I'd buried, the pain in my upper back and hips occasionally resurfaces. I have been frustrated when some pain returns, allowing myself to go into fear that I'm a failure at this healing thing, that the crippling pain will return. Then I return to accepting my feelings instead of burying them, which is the cause of the pain. This allows my heart to open again with gratitude and wonder.

Pain in my body is a bellwether that immediately reminds me that I'm out of my heart. I am learning to be grateful for this reminder that healing occurs when the body is embraced with gratitude for showing, through pain or disease, what feelings need to be recognized, felt and accepted. It is not easy to be grateful when in pain, yet I've found it is the only way healing occurs. Gratitude leads to remembering we are the light, the way and the Truth. While writing this book, all is being dissolved as I continue to love Sally. This Sally who always does the best she can with the love and awareness she's feeling in each moment. *This is important for all of us to remember: everyone is always doing the best they can with the love and awareness they are currently holding in each moment.* I am loving myself with all my scars, wounds and feelings of unworthiness. My heart blossoms into Oneness within my Soul, my God Self.

## Shattering the Stone of Resistance

Writing this book about the heroine's journey of healing and transformation has paradoxically sped up and slowed down my journey. When I received a message from my God Self to write another book titled *Life Is a Song of Love*, I first said No Way. Yet the seed was planted and it started to grow despite my resistance. We've all seen plants growing in cracks in the pavement or rocks in seemingly arid places. This is what it felt like, that I was birthing and growing something despite my arid and rock-like resistance. Literally, the flower that was growing from my heart was shattering the hard shell of my resistance.

I came to trust the process of growing the flower of my heart which became this book. It was not always easy. I am an outline type of person. While in school I learned to write an outline before completing essays or writing research papers. I struggled with yes or no questions because many times I felt there was no right or wrong answer. Essays and papers I'd write well because I followed an outline. This has proven helpful all my life. I became an accomplished proposal writer for nonprofit organizations because I followed the outlines of the giving institutions—and included the heart in my writing. So following an outline, which is a type of map, was reinforced. However, at some point on our heroine's spiritual journey, we have to throw away the map because it is no longer useful for the flower of our soul to shatter the stone.

Outlines worked for my first two books. Both outlines came from the inspiration of my God Self. I thought this book would flow the same way. It did not. I knew I was to create for the divine feminine what I'd done for children with special needs labels while seeing past the labels to the whole divine child. OK, I thought, we create wholeness by freeing and honoring the divine feminine energy, thus freeing the shadow masculine into wholeness. That is as far as I got.

Fairly early I did receive that some of the content of the book would be about creating a container of love for the awakening heart of humanity called the Universal Grandmother archetype. How, however, was left unanswered. This pattern continued for several years while I was coming to understand that there was much for me to dissolve and heal before the writing could start and flow. The process of learning what at the time was unknown was demonstrated by the many emanations of what would be the second part of the book's title that clarifies in a few words what the book is about. I'd think I knew and then eventually realize I didn't.

Each change of the title brought experiences, awareness and a call to go even deeper to dissolve old habits, self-judgments and co-dependent attachments of the separated self. And each time the flower of my heart womb opened more. The realization that buried anger and rage for lifetimes and decades was manifested in severe back and neck pain was profoundly life-changing and finally started the process of dissolving a hard block of resistance around my heart. It literally felt as if the flowering of my heart was shattering this long-held ball of rage. I felt my world fall apart. Then the flower began to flourish and heal all those angry wounded places I'd buried deep in the dark recesses of the unconscious. This was the wound I carried in my womb. I began to understand how anger can point the way to embracing the fierce love of the sacred feminine.

What landed completely in my heart is that we are always coming to know the unknown. The awakening journey has no end because we have no end and we are always expanding, creating and being love. Each one of us is a unique vibration of the Cosmic Mother containing the Cosmic Father, the Source of all that is.

The flower of inspiration was shattering the stone of my resistance. I realized I've always been on a heroine's journey and that, yes, I can claim I'm a modern-day mystic. Books and stories came into my life about women on their own unique mystical heroine's journeys which shared immutable truths and interconnections with my unique journey. I continue to realize with the mystic soul sisters in our co-creator's group that sharing with each other our unique spiritual journey of the heart and womb is necessary for awakening. It is an individual quest as well as a communal quest. We need each other. I open more and more to the beauty of both women and men's unique path and song of remembering the divine Truth of who we are. I breathe into my heart and trust I'm only being led by love. Deep within my womb I feel that every place I stand is holy ground.

I received message after message indicating that the path I'm on is not linear and there is no outline to follow; that I should write whatever comes up, whatever knowing comes through, start to type without regard to where it will fit in the book. Yes, you'll repeat what's already been written. Yes, you'll not know where it will go. Yes, all this jumble will turn into a whole and complete book. Yes, you may need to re-write, combine and throw out. The process is teaching you to trust what's coming through. You do not need to know the ending first. Yeshua says in ACOL:

> This is the first transition, the transition in which you really "get it" that the unknown cannot be taught, laid out on a map, or shown to you by another.[2]

This idea of writing without a map, without an outline, without a book's instructions telling me what to do was very scary. I realize this need to have it all neatly fit together is a residual compulsion of the separated self, the part of me that needs order and control in my life. Letting go to trust that my God Self already knows the shape and content of the book in many ways is what this book is about. I felt confident that I was writing about my own heroine's journey and how it intersects and holds truths for each woman's spiritual journey. So, what exactly are the stages in a heroine's journey? I know they are different from the patriarchal hero's journey. I had a glimmer that perhaps there are no set stages.

## The Hero's Journey and the Heroine's Journey

It is beneficial to understand what is considered the hero's journey. Within the structure of patriarchy, which is an effective manifestation of the separated state, we idealize the hero's journey. A hero must experience the travails of darkness and overcome great obstacles in order to become a man, to feel alive, to find happiness and maybe win the love of a woman. The patient, long-suffering woman always seems to be waiting for the hero to return whole and complete. The archetypal hero's journey is often considered to be Odysseus and his men trying to return home after the Trojan War as described by Homer in *The Odyssey*. They sail on their ship and encounter a series of trials and tribulations crafted to test their resolve. And Odysseus's wife, Penelope, waits patiently for his return from war and the sea. In fact, she so distrusts the gods, she does not initially believe the man claiming to be her husband is actually Odysseus.

Ah yes, the drama, we must pay for our fleeting chance at happiness. And for women it has been and often still is defined by the men in our lives. Just as Penelope waited years for Odysseus' return, the divine feminine has waited patiently for twelve thousand years to rise and for the divine masculine to heal and merge with her into Oneness. Now that Odysseus has returned to the feminine energy of Penelope, he has the opportunity to take the journey inward into his heart. This opportunity is currently being presented to all men.

The patriarchal hero's journey is not my song. Yet, I still wanted to know what is the heroine's journey? I googled and discovered an actual book, *The Heroine's Journey*, by Maureen

Murdoch, which answered my question. Perfect, I thought—there's a circle diagram describing the stages and everything. But while I loved her book, which reminded me much of what I already knew, I still felt I was missing something. I returned to my contemplative practices: meditating in the bath; singing and praying while hiking; listening to music; and walking my labyrinth. Walking the labyrinth, that's it! The heroine's journey, the woman's journey of the heart and womb, is like walking the labyrinth! With the awareness that the labyrinth provides a heart-opening symbol of women's spiritual path, the stone of resistance to writing this book was completely shattered.

## Chapter Two

# The Labyrinth, A Symbolic Path into the Heart and Womb

Labyrinths are a symbol of the Earth Mother. They emerged from her-story before patriarchy became the dominating social, religious and governmental structure. Labyrinths are often mistakenly used as a synonym for mazes. The difference is that mazes are multicursal and are created to confuse the walker with many entrances, exits and cul-de-sacs. Mazes appear in many myths and contemporary stories with traps that often kill. Mazes are a product of the power-over paradigm.

The labyrinth's path is circular like the spiral. However, it includes folds in the circular path that take one in and out. As you get close to the center, it folds and takes you out until it folds again to go inward. This repeats until the folding of the path ends in the center. This is the same pattern as you follow the path out from the center, it folds and takes you inward before folding and taking you outward over and over again until you emerge. It is this unicursal path leading into the center which renders the labyrinth appropriate as a walking meditation and a perfect spiritual metaphor for the heroine's spiritual journey.

Our journey gradually takes us into our hearts supported by our abdomen or womb. Therefore, we can consistently lead from our spacious heart empowered by the intuitive strength of our womb. It may feel circular but it's rarely been direct. It contains elements of movement and expression. Like walking the labyrinth, we move in and out of our womb space while always going inward toward the center of our heart. Then we bring love's expression into the world by moving outward and inward to reflect the inner knowing we've felt in our hearts. It is a dance and song of movement continuously flowing. There are no obstacles to overcome, nothing to achieve, just the in and out movement of our inner work and inner wisdom to enliven our world.

These elements of movement and expression sometimes take us into the unconscious feelings we've denied, such as anger, unworthiness, shame, blame, guilt and grief. While we are in the darkness, we are afraid, often feeling as if we are in the dry desert wilderness of no beginning and no end, thirsty for the healing waters of our soul. Or we feel lost in the deep dark forest, unable to see our path. There is no way to be lost in the labyrinth of our God Self, there is no maze to deliberately cause us to get lost. We weave in and out constantly, experiencing what we need to experience to awaken. We fold in and out of forgiveness, in and out of self-love, in and out of compassion for ourselves and others. Walking into the Divine Mother's loving primordial womb, warmth and life becomes the labyrinth of our soul. We trust that we will always emerge refreshed, balanced and once again in our heart space. We fold in on ourselves and then move out to bring our knowing into a world that constantly changes according to our movement and expression into knowing the unknowable. And we begin again.

I am blessed to have a labyrinth out my front door. I am blessed to live in a place of big sky, lots of sun, and open space on a mesa surrounded by other mesas and mountains. The spaciousness of my environment gives a tangible reminder of my spacious Self. When we moved to this beautiful spot in the high desert, I fell in love with the gorgeous multi-colored rocks of northern New Mexico. Anytime I hike, I constantly notice the variety of colors and patterns of the rocks and sometimes a stone says, take me home. These are the rocks that I used to create my labyrinth modeled on the eleven-fold labyrinth at Chartres Cathedral in France. Sometimes I walk the labyrinth every day, sometimes every week and sometimes after several weeks. It often depends on the weather. Even when I'm not actually walking the labyrinth it stays as a constant reminder of the sacred feminine within me. I have grounded this labyrinth energy with Mother Gaia's blessing. Wherever I go I bring the labyrinth of my God Self with me.

Writing this book is like walking the labyrinth. I folded in out of awareness of what was to be written. It became a dance of love and expression constantly weaving in and out of the chapters without finishing any one of them until the book was complete. For example, when the writing started to flow, I had no idea that a central theme was to be the story of Lilith, the first woman strong in her sacred sexual life force and power. Writing this movement or section on divine sexuality helped with understanding the shape and content of the entire book. The movement on the mother daughter patriarchal womb was also a total surprise. Until my daughter started sharing her sacred womb of abandonment, I never realized there was a universal mother daughter patriarchal wound. It became the pivotal movement. With all movements leading to it and from it, I felt the book folding in and out, always leading into my heart and womb and then out again as written expression.

## The Labyrinth's Story

Labyrinths are ancient, universal and archetypal symbols of the Universal Mother's primordial womb of creation. They can be traced back within the 5000 years of entrenched patriarchy, the beginning of recorded his-story, although we know within our hearts that the labyrinth existed earlier in matrifocal times when we still worshipped the Mother God. Labyrinths can be found in many different cultures all over the world. The Hopi in North America created a seven-fold labyrinth similar to the classical seven-fold labyrinth found in Europe. It is the symbol for Mother Earth, which re-creates the sacred spiraling form found throughout nature. We can find labyrinths and spirals in ancient puebloan petroglyphs.

There were labyrinths built into the floors of several medieval cathedrals. One of the most famous is at Chartres Cathedral in France, constructed in the thirteenth century over an ancient pagan sacred site of worship to the Holy Mother. There is also an ancient Roman well maintained in the basement of the cathedral. The patriarchal Christian church co-opted the pagan design in order to bring Goddess worship ritual into Christianity. Medieval labyrinths were used as a substitute for an actual pilgrimage to Jerusalem. These medieval labyrinths are what is called classical design and are generally circular in nature. According to Lauren Artress, author of *Walking the Sacred Path*, labyrinths are a subset of the mandala, the Sanskrit word for circle. Mandalas are often used as spiritual tools to help one's inward journey into the Sacred Self.

There are many labyrinths built by people in their back yards, in churches of all faiths, at retreat centers and in public spaces all over the world. My dear childhood and life-long friend Rev Jeanette Stokes made an eleven-fold labyrinth out of canvas that can be taken apart and folded so she can cart it around to churches. She gives labyrinth workshops and opens the church space to the public so they can walk the labyrinth. Jeanette sparked my interest and eventually my passion for the labyrinth. Jeanette says:

> When I first walked the Grace Cathedral labyrinth in San Francisco, I felt like I was walking into the middle of myself. When I reached the center, I sat down to meditate. I felt received and blessed as though by the warm love of a mother's arms. I did not want to leave. I did not want to leave myself. I felt certain that I could return to that place.
>
> The labyrinth turned out to be a path that actually took me places. It took me to a medieval understanding of God as the center of everything. It taught me about a time in Europe before the Reformation and the Enlightenment when

> the cycles of life and the seasons of the year were central metaphors. It introduced me to aspects of the feminine divine.[3]

I have walked many labyrinths I found in churches while conducting my workshops about seeing the wholeness in atypical children. I walked a labyrinth Jeanette's friends had made out of leaves. I walked a labyrinth at a home in the woods of New Hampshire while my friend attended a therapy session. At a retreat in New Hampshire with my Unitarian Universalist Church (UU) in Massachusetts, we created a temporary eleven-fold labyrinth out of leaves and pine needles. I even walked the labyrinth at Chartres Cathedral after the church closed to the public and they removed the chairs that usually are placed on top of their beautiful labyrinth. Besides my home labyrinth, there is an eleven-fold labyrinth at the education and retreat center called Ghost Ranch in Abiquiu, NM. I walked this labyrinth many times before I completed my labyrinth.

## Creating Labyrinths for Walking and Holding

When I moved to Abiquiu, New Mexico from Massachusetts in 2011, I fell in love with the variety of multi-colored rocks in northern New Mexico. I discovered so many gorgeous rocks I felt Mother Gaia speaking through them. Anytime I hike, I constantly notice the variety of colors and patterns of rocks, and sometimes a stone says: take me home.

Spirit led me directly to the land on which we built our home. Rick and I were visiting the casita we were going to rent while building our house. As we were driving, I heard a voice say: go to the top of that mesa. We did and it felt like home, with gorgeous views. We learned the next day that the lot had gone on the market the day before. Instantly we knew to buy it. Fortunately, Spirit also arranged for someone to buy the lot where we thought we were going to build.

Our home is on top of a mesa overlooking Abiquiu Lake and the red cliffs and mesas of Ghost Ranch to the north and the mountain Cerro Pedernal to the south. This area is often referred to as the artist Georgia O'Keefe's country. One of her famous sayings was that God told her Cerro Pedernal was hers if she painted it enough.

In one of those moments of pure knowing, I realized I was to build a labyrinth facing south under the presence of Cerro Pedernal. I had a very intuitive friend tell me I created the labyrinth on top of a site where the ancient Hopi shamans held their ceremonies. This resonates with me as I sense their guardianship and presence as I walk. I placed an old cedar stump in the center to sit on and meditate while gazing at Cerro Pedernal. I began to call her Mother Mountain. It is whispered on the wind that the ancient Navajos who used to live in the area now covered by Abiquiu Lake referred to her as Changing Woman. This resonates in my heart and feels right. I have the iconic flat-topped view of Cerro Pedernal. If one travels west, the flat top changes and turns into a point. Also, the clouds and breathtaking light of this area are always changing the face of the mountain.

I realize labyrinths are not readily accessible for everyone; however there are labyrinths available in community spaces and churches in most cities, and in retreat centers. A google search usually reveals those that are open to the public. If none of the above is practical or available to you, there are hand-held labyrinths you can buy. I have a metal labyrinth I hold and use a stick to follow the path. Using drawings available on the internet, you can create your own, adding colors and symbols that speak to you. Then use your finger or a crystal to follow the path in meditation.

## Walking the Labyrinth

There is no right or wrong way to walk the labyrinth. It is about silently and meditatively walking a sacred path to our own inner guidance, going inward for healing, self-knowledge and creativity. The interior process of walking is about releasing worries and fears, receiving guidance as we walk the circular path to our center, and returning into the world replenished. For women it can be a healing practice of returning to the wisdom of our wombs connecting directly to Mother Gaia's primordial womb energy.

The labyrinth can be a symbolic pilgrimage of your own design and choosing. Some people ask a question of their inner Self for revelation. Some use the walk as a process of meditation, purely as a tool to calm the mind. Some use a chant as they walk, some pray throughout the walk. I use all these approaches depending on my needs, including singing and sometimes drumming to the earth's heartbeat. I always set an intention and pray before starting to walk, and usually sit in the center to meditate, pray, and talk with the Holy Mother. I often walk the labyrinth focusing on the rocks and their color and beauty. It calms my mind and brings peace. Sometimes I have revelations. Sometimes nothing happens, just a feeling of being centered. My strongest advice is to have no expectations of outcome. Once we decide we need something from the labyrinth the separated self takes over, which is a certain way to ensure that nothing happens. If we learn this while walking the labyrinth, it obviously helps with all of life's experiences.

### *Labyrinth in Snow: A Metaphor for Trusting Inner Guidance*

Even at our high altitude of about 7000 feet, it does not snow much in northern New Mexico. When it does, it usually melts quickly under our bright sun. The day after a storm in which it snowed eight inches, I wandered out to look at my labyrinth to see if I could walk it. It was buried with none of the rocks that delineate the complex unicursal path visible. My first reaction was: Okay not today, I'll wait till the snow melts. I paused and thought this would be an interesting experiment in trusting that I can find the path without the rocks to guide me.

As I stood at the entrance gazing at the snow and setting my intention to let go and walk, I noticed very slight indentations in the snow that looked as if they were in the center of the path. I started walking very slowly, thoroughly present, for the indentations were very faint. It required releasing any doubts that surfaced about whether they were actually pointing the way. In the beginning, I kept hesitating and second-guessing the slight indentations and temporarily allowing myself to get confused. Then I just let go and trusted. I felt such peace and love to be present in this moment to walk my prayer in the beauty of the snow.

When I arrived at the center, I thought how often we believe that the process of trusting our inner guidance is difficult. We question what we are receiving. I have heard people say that the ego speaks first. Yet when I let go, I realize that everything is always perfect, each experience is exactly as it should be for remembering our Oneness with God. With this understanding, I stopped worrying whether or not it was the ego speaking first and started to trust that the inner guidance from my Holy Self is always present and always directing what is for my highest good. It is immensely freeing. Walking the labyrinth in the snow reinforced trust that my Holy Self is always present guiding me.

Once in the center, I felt deep peace, love and direct relationship within the womb of Mother Earth. I looked around and of course the path out was clearly marked by my footprints in the snow. I realized that walking out of the labyrinth following my own footsteps, my own guidance, is a metaphor for weaving my spiritual journey into my everyday life. I take my guidance out into the world. Trusting and following my own footsteps and inner guidance creates an unshakable pathway to embracing my I Am Presence.

The next day while I was not at home, a friend came and walked the labyrinth. The snow in the labyrinth had not melted much and he found my footprints very helpful for leading the way. At one point he was unsure whether or not I had strayed from the correct path, but he continued to follow my footsteps and was pleased to arrive at the center. His comment was that I must be very familiar with the path. Of course, it is both physically as well as spiritually familiar. Trust frees us to be intimate with our inner spiritual guidance, our direct relationship with the Mother/Father/One, even if it seems we have strayed. When everyone joins in Union with God at the same time as having a unique relationship with God, we learn by following each other's footsteps.

## The Labyrinth as an Operating System

The labyrinth is also a metaphor for our soul's operating system. When we begin this spiritual journey within separation consciousness, we're not very aware of the operating system of our God Self. It is faint and very much in the background. However, as the inner path folds in and out, we gain awareness until we receive an upgrade. Then our labyrinth starts over at a higher resonance, and we fold in and out on our journey until we receive another upgrade in the operating system of our God Self. We start over with another labyrinth, only at a higher vibration. During this process our awareness is such that everything we experience becomes symbolic, is seen as meaningful, even the seemingly small daily tasks. At this stage we can still get triggered by the separated ego with irritation, anger, physical pain, etc. Yet we are able to enfold all of this easily and return to our heart and the strength and wisdom of our womb. Eventually, we reach a place when we are very much existing in the operating system of our Christ Self.

Walking the labyrinth over and over again with the many upgrades in our operating system creates a pathway to our multidimensional selves. I visualize labyrinths one on top of the other connected in the centers by a beam of the golden white light of All that Is, following the rainbow path of the vast variety of the Universal Mother's never-ending creations that weave all of God's diverse creations together in Oneness as we move in and out within the heart womb of the Cosmic Mother.

The labyrinth upgrades are the process of our carbon-based DNA changing into our crystalline DNA needed to create the new earth in the fifth dimension. When we are fully in union and relationship with God, all the labyrinth upgrades collapse into each other since they'll no longer be needed. There will be a total absence of fear with only love remaining. We'll know absolutely with no residual questions that we are in and of God and God is in and of us.

## Chapter Three

# Simplify Your Journey: Follow Your Heart and Save Yourself

Once I was able to visualize the woman's spiritual journey as a labyrinth rather than stages, I opened to receive messages from my God Self in a different way. All the information I wanted to include in this book started to mold and fold like the labyrinth. Despite the necessity for the labyrinth to have an entrance and an exit, it is a circle and circles have no beginnings and no endings. Trust is what the labyrinth is about. Trust that as I write it will all flow into where it is supposed to be. And I heard the words, "It is really very simple, not the complex arrangement of information that you feel warrants an outline or map."

The guest of a friend came to walk the labyrinth. I was working at my computer, which is by a window looking out at the labyrinth. I glanced up periodically and noticed the woman was hopping from one circular path to another, stopping, looking confused and then trying again. I guessed she thought the labyrinth was a maze so that when she came to a fold in the path, she thought it was a trick to confuse her. I stopped to put on shoes and a coat. By the time I started outside to help her, she had left. If she had been paying attention, centering herself at the entrance of the labyrinth, I think she would have noticed the path's direction only went to the center.

Whenever we are confused, conflicted or doubtful, we are in the thought pattern of the separated self. These egoic mental conditions have become a red flag for me. Have you ever started a conversation to share something meaningful but at some point, after lots of questions, you are frustrated and confused? What seemed so meaningful is now lost in a morass of confusion. If

I pause and breathe into my heart, I realize I've slipped back into the habit of the separated self. The woman walking the labyrinth tricked herself into believing that the labyrinth was a puzzle containing obstacles to deceive, frustrate and confuse. Of course, she stopped walking—she gave up what appeared to be too difficult. That is life within separation consciousness: we try to figure out life's maze, overcome the obstacles and try to control getting confused or lost. We either stop or doggedly continue to live our life at this lower vibration. Sometimes we just give up and stop living. Or we notice the still small voice within saying there has to be a better way than this game of chance with few rewards and lots of suffering.

Reaching this place for women is a blessing, although it may not feel like it at the time. We have been living within patriarchy for thousands of years. We bought into the patriarchal hero's outward journey that says life is a series of obstacles to overcome, and then bam—leave the body behind, go vertical and ascend. Saving myself meant do it all: birth and raise children; work hard and have a career; have my own autonomy even if married; fix all problems that come my way; exercise, meditate, read books and watch the Red Sox baseball team win; spend quality time with my children, my husband and my friends; go on outings and vacations with the family; manage the household and the children's schedules; and volunteer at my UU Church in my free time, etc. Simply writing this now makes me feel tired.

The feminist revolution freed women to be either a mom or not, and also have a career, work all the time, and be the most successful we possibly could be—but on men's terms. We are expected to conform to the male values of success. What we need deep in the recesses of our heart does not matter because they are opposite to the dominant patriarchal values. We ignore our feelings and the call of our soul, stuffing them deep into our unconscious until some sort of event or crisis compels us to start listening to our heart's song.

In contrast, the heroine's journey is an inward journey. And like the labyrinth's path, we weave in and out, experiencing many dark nights of the soul. There truly is always a light at the end of the dark tunnel. We can trust this because we know our inward path always leads into the heart of our being. There is no way to get permanently lost.

When my children were small, I decided I wanted them to experience going to church, to have help with their spiritual life. Rick, a burnt-out Catholic who wanted no part of organized religion, was agreeable to leaving the decision with me. I was brought up in the Presbyterian church by a mother who was comfortable with her children finding their own faith. We were never forced to attend Sunday School. This was highly unusual, especially in Tulsa, OK and Houston, TX where I grew up. What I loved about church was the music, so I'd sing in the choir and occasionally attend Sunday School. However, the message never felt right, and fairly early I developed an uneasiness with a male God. The sermons were boring and felt too restrictive and irrelevant. I realized later I was rejecting the church's patriarchal teachings of Jesus. By high school I gave up on church and became an agnostic. I threw Jesus out with the bath water. In my forties after reading several metaphysical texts I allowed Jesus back in my life. Part of what helped was to call him by his Aramaic name: Yeshua ben Josef.

Having children stirred something within me for spiritual direction. The Unitarian Universalist (UU) denomination fit my needs. This church used gender neutral language, taught from many different religious perspectives and cared about social justice issues. It became a blessed community for my family, including Rick at times. I sang in an excellent choir, and the sermons usually spoke to a yearning in my soul. Eventually UU churches offered a receptive audience for my ministry to change people's minds and hearts about atypical children, those we label as "special needs."

What does this have to do about keeping it simple? At some point the UU Association launched a campaign to simplify what it means personally to be a UU. They called it the elevator speech. You are on the elevator and have a brief moment to explain to someone what Unitarian Universalism is. I actually struggled with this—my feelings felt way too complicated to explain in a few words. By this time, I'd written my book, *Welcoming Children with Special Needs, a Guidebook for Faith Communities*, and was traveling all over the country giving workshops. Several years later, I knew the answer and it was simple. Being UU meant freedom, freedom to follow my own spiritual path within the church community's loving embrace.

The simple message I was receiving over and over again while writing this book was to lead from my heart and save my Self. I capitalize the S in self because it refers to our God Self or our Higher Holy Self rather than our personal self. Our God Self or I Am Presence is the part of our soul that remains in Oneness. The Divine Mother would never leave us alone without a way to return Home. The God Self is the bridge between our dream of separation and our Over Soul. Ultimately this means: stay within your heart womb space to receive messages from your I Am Presence to remember and embrace your divine sovereign power.

Saving your Self does not mean pick yourself up by your boot straps and go it alone—that is the hero's journey. Saving your Self happens in relationship with the Holy Mother and all her creations. We cannot be anything but in relationship with the Holy Mother Holy Father Sophia God because God is in us and we are in God. Everything else is an illusion. We can only pretend separation from God. Pretending does not make it real. We created the perception of separation—however it is a perception and not real. It is a dream. The heroine's journey is to remember we never left the Holy Mother's embrace.

## The Difference between Self Love and Selfishness

Both men and women are conditioned to believe doing something just for ourself is being selfish. I allow myself to be confused by this, especially when I'm with a man or woman who always does exactly what they want so that others are forced to compromise if they want to be with them. For me, it is more difficult to handle with men because within patriarchy there's always been the underlying unconscious agreement that men lead and women follow. I have been caught in this belief and then felt miserable being in a relationship with a man whose expectation was always to do what he wanted to do. After all, it is their life—and I am being required to join it, according to patriarchal conditioning.

If I want to be successful, then become more like a man. Remember in the movie *My Fair Lady*, Rex Harrison as Henry Higgins sings the song *Why Can't a Woman Be More Like a Man*, despite Audrey Hepburn as Eliza Doolittle having done everything possible to learn to be a proper lady to please him. But when she wants Higgins to see her as other than his puppet, he thinks she's being emotional. In other words, he doesn't want Eliza to feel with her heart but wants her to conform to the male ideal of being a woman: look beautiful, dress and speak properly, and never say no.

This is often the woman's dilemma. It is an either-or-situation, but neither one answers her heart's calling. With the feminist revolution, women were given the chance to be more like a man. We wore ourselves out and realized that emulating men was not serving the longing deep within our souls. It is a Catch 22. When women become more like men, we lose our intuitive knowing, and then are rejected for not acting as the idealized woman. When women mold ourselves into the expectations of men by being malleable, dutiful and physically attractive, we trigger possessiveness and deny our heart's calling.

Self-love is learning to say No to what no longer serves us as women, with saying No coming out of a healed and strong heart womb. This is very relevant for our relationships, especially with the men in our lives. I have a tendency to say I'm sorry first when I'm not sorry: it is an apology for speaking from my heart. Authenticity is so important to actually loving myself. Do I love myself enough to actually say No without apologies to what does not nourish me? I don't do this anymore, even if it's the polite thing to do. When it comes from the heart, it is self-love. My heart tells me to say No, even if the person I'm saying No to thinks I'm being selfish. I have noticed, however, that when I say No from my heart space, the person often feels the love behind it and does not take offense. When we can say No to what does not serve us, then we can say Yes to life—Yes, I am divinely human. Yes, I am living my prayer. Yes, I am co-creating the new earth. Yes, I am the living Christ.

No longer caretaking men's egos means no longer feeding the hungry wolf's need to control. As a caregiver instead of caretaker we can provide comfort when needed. We can say I'm sorry you are experiencing pain, without feeding or taking on another's pain. It lets people know they've been heard with love. Caretaking exists within the separated state. It is when we take on the responsibility for another's suffering, thus perpetuating the pain. Caregiving comes from a compassionate heart that knows giving and receiving are one.

Those who are being selfish are coming from the need to be in control, thinking that if they don't take what they need, they'll never have what they deserve. They believe in the separated ego's dog-eat-dog world. I can have compassion for a person acting from this unloving place, because it must be terrifyingly lonely, exhausting and precarious.

Self-love as self-compassion comes from looking at all those places held deep within that you dislike about yourself, all those places within the shadow where you feel anger, shame, guilt, grief or fear of losing control. This is your inner child holding your uncensored emotions. We tenderly hold our inner child by accepting our feelings rather than burying them or projecting them onto others. We do not have to like a hurtful experience in order to accept what we are feeling about it. We do not have to like people whose actions are unloving, instead we are asked to forgive our judgments. We first must lovingly embrace and accept our wounded inner child before we can unconditionally love the Christ in ourself and then in others. Loving ourself is not being selfish, it is saving ourself, allowing the Divine Mother's love to wash us clean. When we do this, we see with the uncompromising love of the Holy Mother Father. Lama Sing channeled by Al Minor said:

> There is no thing that you have ever done or failed to do that has not been forgiven. In fact, God's Love for you is so omnipotent that before you could think of an act or failure to act, His love has gone before to make the way not only passable for you to emerge and forgive yourself but to heal all those who are involved in same.[4]

*Visual Meditation*: Wrap your arms around you. Hold yourself tenderly as if you are an innocent baby. Take a deep breath into your womb, feeling it inflate like a balloon. Feel the golden energy of Mother Gaia's womb filling, healing and strengthening your womb. Then feel her breath's energy flow into your heart. Love yourself like you've never loved before. Let the waters of the Holy Mother's compassion and grace fill all those dry, bruised, wounded places within you. Feel the depth of the Holy Mother's all-encompassing love blooming inside your womb and your heart. Let the energy of this love fill you up until your body becomes the divine feminine chalice overflowing to bless every person around you and everyone in the world. We have enough love within us to float the world.

Allow the divine masculine's gentle strength, protection and clarity to join with this abundance of love, until you always know within your heart that you are a beloved child of God and thus a divine being. This is the process of saving your Self. This is Self-Love and Self-Compassion.

## Chapter Four

# Myths and Stories Transcend and Inform My Spiritual Path

I believe as we experience this momentous time of humanity's awakening, more and more people are accepting wisdom from many spiritual paths and faith traditions. We've begun to realize the esoteric non-dual truths existing in all paths and faiths. Thus, the Universal Mother Father is speaking to us in endless variety as we fashion our own unique way of remembering our Divine Sovereignty. No longer is one faith tradition the exclusive right of its followers. Spiritual teachers, elders, wisdom keepers, ministers, rabbis, yogis and shamans from many faiths and spiritual traditions are sharing their spiritual gifts and insights with the world. This creates an awareness of everyone existing in Oneness, the many in the One and the One in the many.

There is abundance of wisdom gained from the esoteric mystical truths of all these spiritual paths. While my lineage comes from Yeshua, Mary Magdalene and Mother Mary, I've benefited and gained awareness from many other spiritual paths and faith traditions. My God Self speaks to me in any way that captures my attention and my heart, all wrapped in the embrace of the Universal Mother.

The patriarchal world view taught us to dismiss stories and myths as being false imagination with no logic or scientific proof. The stories of many ancient Eastern faith traditions and indigenous spirituality of the First Nations are demeaned by patriarchal Christianity as myth, inferior compared to the science and reason of Western culture. Both Hinduism and indigenous people's spiritual expressions are fertile ground with the many faces of both the Holy Mother and Holy Father.

Paula Gunn Allen, a Native American of the Laguna Pueblo and Sioux heritage, in her book *The Sacred Hoop, Recovering the Feminine in American Indian Traditions* wrote about the universal intelligence of the Holy Mother:

> This spirit, this power of intelligence, has many names and many emblems. She appears on the plains, in the forest, in the great canyons, on the mesas, beneath the seas. To her we owe our very breath, and to her our prayers are sent blown on pollen, on corn meal, planted into the earth on feather-sticks, spit onto the water, burned and sent to her on the wind. Her variety and multiplicity testify to her complexity; she is the true Creatrix for she is thought itself, from which all else is born. She is the necessary precondition for material creation, and she, like all of her creation, is fundamentally female—potential and primary. She is also the spirit that informs right balance, right harmony, and these in turn order all relationships in conformity with her law.[5]

The Mother breathes into all life infinitely, and we often use myths and stories to understand and convey her magnificent all-encompassing love which has no opposite. Women are reclaiming these stories to understand and own our divine feminine power. The power of myth enables us to see past the constructs of separation and his-story to rediscover our inner wisdom that exists beyond our limited personal perceptions to the reality of our divine inheritance.

I offer and expand on many stories and myths speaking deep to our inner knowing of the Divine Mother aspect of God. These stories and myths help us transcend our dense third-dimensional ego-based human program, igniting our souls' desire to remember our truth as interdimensional beings held within the embrace of the Cosmic Mother.

## Balancing Masculine and Feminine Energies

We have lived within patriarchy's cultural and religious power and control system approximately twelve thousand years. Patriarchy thrives on the imbalance between the feminine and masculine energies. Both masculine and feminine energies have been separated, wounded, distorted, repressed and misunderstood. Consequently, there are plenty of wounded and damaged men and women who then take it out on their children. Women unwittingly pass down these wounds felt in our wombs to our children. We lost an understanding of these energies to the point where we are conflicted, confused and doubt ourselves. I have friends whose mothers were abusive and toxic. I have friends whose fathers were abusive and raped them. And of course, all of us were born to mothers and fathers who were struggling with their own issues resulting from the false perception of separation from God. Therefore, some women have more difficulty reconciling with the sacred feminine and some women have more difficulty reconciling with the sacred masculine. Whichever it is for you, it is vitally important to dissolve your misperceptions so you can love your Self.

The sacred masculine has been difficult for me to understand. We have lived a long time with the damaged masculine of patriarchy, so I considered all energies of love, nurture and compassion to be the divine feminine. How can I reconcile the masculine and feminine energies within me if I think all masculine energies are destructive? The sacred union of the masculine and feminine requires embracing and loving both aspects of the divine. For this to occur, I needed to understand what the sacred masculine is. This in turn allowed the feminine resonance of God to rise, thus freeing the masculine resonance to merge in union within.

As I was absorbing the advice to keep it simple, I was reminded of three children's books I'd read to my children, Sarah and Tyler, when they were young. Two by Robert N. Munsch,

*David's Father* and *The Paper Bag Princess*, are very small-sized books (3 ½″ square) with very simple messages. *David's Father* illustrating positive masculine energy, and *The Paper Bag Princess* illustrating positive feminine energy are delightful and humorous. My re-telling does not do justice to Munsch's humor and ability to tell stories that connect to children's feelings and hearts. *Jane and the Dragon* by Martin Baynton is another delightful tale of a girl who follows her heart, loves the dragon and saves her Self. It is interesting that these books were written by men. To me it's an example of the divine masculine providing support and clarity to the feminine energy.

### *David's Father*

In *David's Father*, Julie is out walking and notices someone moving in next door to her house. The movers are hauling enormous utensils for eating, and immediately she is frightened and runs home and hides under her bed. The next day she meets David who asks if she wants to play. He seems normal enough, so she agrees. At five o'clock her mother yells for her to come home and David's father yells for him. Frightened by his big voice, Julie turns around in three circles and runs home to hide again in her room.

The following day Julie again agrees to play with David, as he still looks like a regular boy. He asks Julie if she wants to come home with him for dinner. Julie remembers all the huge utensils and says No. David says they are having cheeseburgers and chocolate milkshakes which Julie loves, so she agrees. They enter the kitchen and Julie sees a small table with cheeseburgers and milkshakes, and an enormous table set with utensils the size of a pitch fork and a flag pole. Julie asks who the table is for and David replies it's for his father. BOOM, BOOM, BOOM, David's dad enters. He is a giant. While Julie and David eat, David's father eats snails, and octopuses, and bricks covered in chocolate. He offers some to Julie. She declines, but bravely asks for another milkshake, and the giant kindly makes her one, bowing down with a smile to give it to her.

Julie quietly says to David that he does not look like his dad. He replies that he's adopted but his father is great, come and see. They go shopping, and when they can't cross a busy street because of the traffic, David's father walks to the middle and stops the cars. When they are in a grocery store and the store owner does not want to serve them because they are children, David's dad sticks his head in and says, THESE KIDS ARE MY FRIENDS. Immediately they get served lots of food to take home. Then a bunch of older kids start taking their food until David's father yells BEAT IT. Julie's elbow gets scraped in the melee of kids running around. David's father puts a large bandage around her elbow, smiling sweetly at her. Julie tells David that he has a very nice father, but he's kind of scary. And David replies with a smile, wait till you meet my grandmother.[6]

Re-reading *David's Father* reminded me that the sacred masculine is about protection, clarity, discernment, gentle inner strength and the power of love within. David demonstrates that masculine energy can be our friend. We've been conditioned to be scared of the masculine energies, to symbolically hide under the bed or get so confused we run around in circles. The distorted masculine energy of control and power of the logical mind, which at times leads to violence and destruction, can be very scary. The arrival of the giant grandmother shows that feminine energy can also be scary. We are often afraid of our own feminine power for it requires being courageous in a world distrustful of powerful spiritual women. If the story had gone further, I bet the grandmother would have been powerful in her loving kindness. I love the idea of my masculine energy being a loving giant ready to protect and serve my feminine energy. I love the idea of powerful grandmother energy.

### *The Paper Bag Princess*

*The Paper Bag Princess* delightfully illustrates what happens when a girl leads with her heart. Elizabeth is a beautiful princess soon to marry a prince named Ronald. One day a dragon comes and burns the castle to the ground and abducts Ronald. Elizabeth decides to save Ronald, but her dress is scorched and all her clothes burned. She finds a paper bag to use for a dress.

Elizabeth travels to the dragon's cave and bangs the knocker on the door. The dragon opens the door and says he'd love to eat her; however, he's eaten a whole castle and is too full and tired— she should come back in the morning, and closes the door in her face. Elizabeth persists and asks the dragon if it is true that he is the smartest dragon in the world. He says Yes. Elizabeth asks him to show how smart he is by demonstrating his mighty powers. The dragon proceeds to burn down hundreds of forests till he is out of fire. Then he flies around the world in 10 seconds, over and over again, till he is so tired he lies down and falls sleep. Elizabeth goes into the cave to get Ronald. But Ronald is appalled by her appearance: tangled hair, smelling like smoke and dressed in a paper bag. He tells her to come back dressed like a real princess. Elizabeth responds that he looks like a real prince but he is a bum, decides not to marry him and then dances off on her own.[7]

In my interpretation, the dragon represents the separated ego and the distorted, destructive patriarchal masculine. Trying to prove he's smart, he became scary, violent and devouring. Under patriarchy, many believe a show of violence is a smart idea. Elizabeth goes within to access her own strength and wisdom. She exhausts the monster, thus saving Ronald and herself. When Ronald doesn't want to be saved by a woman in her powerful wildness, Elizabeth sees with clarity that she no longer wants to be a bride to the distorted masculine. She leaves the restrictiveness of the male gaze, leaving the prince in the cave, trusting that with the dragon asleep Ronald can find his own way out. This is important.

Following your heart and saving yourself is the sacred feminine in expression. As we stay true to our heart, we know and trust that men are on own their own sacred journey to save themselves. We do not have to do it for them. We've been taught to caretake the wounded masculine energy of patriarchy. As we save ourselves and come into our own divine sovereignty, we do not have to do that anymore.

### *Jane and the Dragon*

*Jane and the Dragon* tells the story of a noble-born girl who hates sewing. Jane watches the knights practicing swordplay while she practices her stitching. Jane tells her mother, father, the King, the young prince and also the knights that she wants to be a knight. They all laugh and tell her that it is nonsense. Her mother says she is to be a lady-in-waiting and her father says only boys can be knights. Everyone else makes fun of her. Jane tells the court jester who does not laugh. He listens and understands. He tells Jane that he also wanted to be a knight, but he is too small, although he still sometimes dreams about it. He gives Jane his armor, saying he'd never be brave enough but that she should dream of being a knight for him. Jane starts watching, learning from the knights practicing with their swords. Whenever the knights chase the King's enemies, Jane puts on her armor and practices swordplay, horseplay and giving victory speeches.

One day while the knights are away at a jousting carnival, an enormous green dragon flies to the castle and steels the prince. The king and queen are afraid since there is no knight left to save their son. To their surprise a small knight saddles the prince's pony and gallops away to find the dragon. Jane follows the dragon to his mountain lair and demands the prince be released. The dragon laughs and scorches her helmet's plume with his hot breath. Jane draws her sword and a long and dreadful battle ensues with both the dragon and Jane having opportunities to hurt each other, but they do not. Eventually too exhausted to continue to fight, they sit down on the cave floor.

Both the dragon and Jane admit they could have killed each other. Jane asks the dragon why he did not kill her. The dragon tearfully replies that he does not like to hurt people and says he only abducted the prince because it was expected of him. Jane tells him to do the unexpected and takes off her helmet. The dragon is amazed she is a girl and says he could fry her for breakfast. She replies that would be too easy, just as it would be easy for her to be a lady-in-waiting because people expect it. But she wants to be a knight. What do you want, she asks? The dragon sobs and says he wants to be loved, so Jane puts down her sword, kisses him, and tells the dragon she loves him. Jane says she has to take the prince home so the king and queen will not worry any longer. The dragon asks if she will visit him. She promises she'll visit every Saturday, then hugs and kisses him one more time.

When Jane arrives back at the castle the king and queen are overjoyed to see their son, but want to know who is the mysterious knight. When Jane takes off her helmet, everyone gasps. Her father stands with his mouth wide open and her mother faints gracefully. In gratitude the King writes a contract to make Jane a knight with every Saturday off to visit a friend. That night the king gives a royal ball. Jane's parents are now very proud of their fearless daughter. With Jane the guest of honor, the king asks her to choose a partner to lead the first dance. Among all the handsome young men, Jane chooses the jester as her partner. "Thank you for the armor," says Jane. "Thank you for the dream," says the jester. And together they dance and dance and dance.[8]

What I love about this story is not only did Jane follow her heart despite ridicule and opposition, but she befriended the dragon with love and saved herself, the prince and the dragon. Her heart told her to ask the unhappy dragon what he wanted. Everyone wants to be loved and have a friend. The jester represents the kind and supportive masculine energy. The dragon or monster we fear inside of us is actually our friend willing to be tamed and loved. For me this fiery fierce dragon energy is my protective masculine energy calling me to clarity of purpose, courage and uncompromising love for myself and others. Do we have the courage to love ourselves so completely that we know we are One with absolutely all of God's creations?

### *Lady Ragnell and Sir Gawain*

The following is a powerful allegory about the sacred union of the divine masculine and feminine energies. I was guided again to re-read the story I had read many years ago about King Arthur, his knight Sir Gawain, and Lady Ragnell. It is described in *Ladies of the Lake* by authors Caitlin and John Matthews, and also re-told in Murdoch's *The Heroine's Journey*. There are several versions of this story, however its essence remains the same. While King Arthur is hunting in the woods, he encounters a fully-armed man named Gromer Somer Jour who threatens to take Arthur's life for giving Gromer's lands to Sir Gawain. He agrees to spare Arthur's life if he returns to the same spot in one year's time with the answer to the question: what do women want above all else?

King Arthur tells Sir Gawain what happened and the two independently search the land for an answer to Gromer's question. They search for a long time, but neither of them are happy with the answers they receive. While searching, Arthur meets Lady Ragnell, a woman large and grotesque. She convinces Arthur that all the answers he's received are useless, and she has the only correct answer. She tells him that if Sir Gawain agrees to marriage, she will give it to him. Arthur replies he can't do this unless Gawain agrees. Arthur tells Gawain what has occurred and Gawain, from the goodness of his heart and his desire to save his king, readily agrees to marry Lady Ragnell no matter how hideous she is.

Arthur and Gawain return to Lady Ragnell and she gives Arthur the answer. What women want most is their own sovereignty—the right to make their own decisions. Arthur travels to meet with Gromer. Desperate to save his knight Gawain from a marriage to a grossly ugly woman, he repeats all the other answers he's been given. When they are gleefully rejected by Gromer, Arthur finally gives him Ragnell's answer. Gromer is furious because he knows only his stepsister could have given Arthur the correct answer.

Sir Gawain honors his promise and marries Lady Ragnell in a grand ceremony, attended with dismay by the people in King Arthur's court, who feel sorry for Gawain having to marry such an ugly woman. That night, after the wedding, Lady Ragnell asks Gawain to kiss her. When he does, she turns into a beautiful woman. Ragnell explains that her stepbrother Gromer hated her because she was bold, defied him and refused his sexual advances, so he cursed her with his sorcery turning her ugly and undesirable. This is symbolic of women who follow their own heart instead of bowing to the wishes of men who often see them as castrating bitches and thus ugly and grotesque.

Ragnell explains the curse is only partially broken. She can either be a beautiful woman at night and ugly during the day, or beautiful during the day and ugly at night. That is some choice to make, to have his male friends only see her ugly form or to have her beautiful at night for their love making. Sir Gawain, true to his wise, kind and compassionate nature, kneels, touches Lady Ragnell's hand and tells her the choice has to be hers and he'll support what she decides. Ragnell is filled with joy and tells Gawain the curse is now completely broken because he gave her the free will to make her own choice, to have sovereignty over her life.

The curse Lady Ragnell is under is the patriarchal spell which convinces women that following our hearts somehow makes us less desirable and ugly in men's eyes. I find it interesting that Gromer believed Lady Ragnell's answer to what women want. Many men are aware of this, but have been conditioned to believe giving women their own power to decide will end in chaos. Yet Lady Ragnell had the courage to follow her heart despite the consequences, even being turned into an ugly woman. She convinces Arthur and Gawain she has the answer to Gromer's question and then convinces Gawain to marry her, thus saving Arthur's life and herself by breaking the curse. She loved herself enough to save herself. Sir Gawain provides clarity and purpose as the supportive masculine energy by giving Lady Ragnell the choice to decide her own fate.

Sir Gawain and Lady Ragnell enter into a sacred marriage which heals both the distorted masculine and the wounded feminine. It portrays beautifully what happens when the divine feminine (the heart) is allowed to lead and the divine masculine (the mind) supports the heart. In one telling of the story, Ragnell asks Arthur to forgive her stepbrother and he does. For me this is what it's all about, the courage to see through the illusion of the separated ego in order to embrace the unconditional love of the Holy Mother Father who forgives.

The process of remembering we are whole and divine asks forgiveness of the feminine and masculine wounded energies to be reconciled into union. The alchemy which occurs when these energies are joined in harmony creates a world where all the unique mystical paths come together in Oneness.

## Chapter Five

# Embracing the Wildness in Our Soul

When I read *Women Who Run with the Wolves: Myths and Stories of the Wild Woman Archetype,* by Clarissa Pinkola Éstes, I was stunned. I so resonated with what she wrote. It was the first time anyone had named this longing in my soul for wildness and freedom from the restrictive patriarchal masculine views of what a woman should be. There is a divine feminine: I'm not crazy, only longing to express what I'd buried in the shadow. Published in 1996, it is now a classic. Almost all of my women friends read the book and were affected by it in some way. I've discovered women writers much younger than me who still refer to the book when they are writing their own books about the divine feminine. My daughter has read it.

Divine feminine energy is intrinsically chaotic. Because we've been conditioned by patriarchy for so long, it can feel unsafe, frightening and dangerous to our lives. Yet this is where women's power resides: within the chaos of unlimited potentialities, the wildness of our soul. The distorted, wounded masculine energy existing within men is afraid of the powerful intuitive chaotic feminine energy and automatically wants to control it.

Embracing the wildness in my soul occurs gradually as I continue the process of shedding my reliance on outside influences that originate from my false sense of self. As illustrated by Lady Ragnell's story, wild women are often seen as crazy, insane, ugly, lacking in feminine graces, abhorrent and should be shut away. Ronald saw Elizabeth as wild, with her messy soot-filled hair and her paper bag dress. It takes lots of courage to go against convention. We are called to embody the divine feminine wildness that frees us from the dragon of self-hatred. This allows the dragon as monster to be transformed into the dragon as divine masculine energy of protection, discernment and uncompromising truth that love is all there is. The masculine energy of clarity and purpose becomes the foundation within our womb, our strength and sustenance.

> *He drew a circle that shut me out, Heretic, rebel, a thing to flout.*
> *But love and I had the wit to win.*
> *We drew a circle that took him in.*
> Edwin Markham from the poem *Outwitted*

Edwin Markham was an American poet (1852-1940). The language he uses in this poem is old fashioned, yet it still speaks to me. Women who stay true to their inner feminine knowing were and still are often considered heretics and rebels, someone to silence and often labeled as insane in order to shut us away. What we represent is anathema to the separated ego in the guise of the patriarchal structure of reason, logic and control, devoid of influence from the heart. Most often through history we've been kept out of the circle. Now women are healing in vast numbers in their heart womb space, embracing their divine feminine power. We are gaining the strength to draw a circle of love around all those who wish to maintain the dense patriarchal energy. Love always has "the wit to win." Love is the truth, the way and the light. Love is and always has been. It is the light force of the multiverse. We are dissolving the veil of forgetfulness to co-create Nova Earth born in love and ruled by love.

The symbol of the dragon as divine protection instead of monster coalesced when I read *The Sophia Code* channeled by Kaia Ra. In this living transmission from Sophia God, the Sophia Dragons are introduced as the highest angelic order, known as the seraphim, and they assist Sophia God in birthing Divine Sovereign Creators. I started realizing that this dragon energy of rage that I held within my womb was misunderstood, that I'd made it into a monster to fear rather than my masculine energy trying to get my attention. I realize I've always had this knowledge within me to access whenever I was ready to follow my heart.

## Men's Journey into Their Hearts

Of course, there are men lightworkers, loveholders and wayshowers who are on their own spiritual journey into the heart. I am not dismissing them in writing about the heroine's journey. They are on their own unique path to remembering they are One with all that Is. Within patriarchy men are the dominant gender, thus a man's journey differs from a woman's journey. In many ways the man's journey into his heart is more challenging. Men have been conditioned to deny their feelings. Letting go of the outward patriarchal hero's journey of overcoming obstacles can be difficult. It is so ingrained in our culture. Eventually their journey will lead inward to embodiment and trusting wholeheartedly their Oneness with the Holy Mother Holy Father.

As I watched some of the Kavanaugh hearings to appoint him as a US Supreme Court Justice, I felt my dwindling anger turn into compassion for the grumpy, angry, power-hungry old white men and many women who are clueless as to what is happening. I began to understand and have compassion for how patriarchy/separation consciousness has also suppressed and violated men. I heard a young male spiritual teacher say that patriarchy is an equal opportunity oppressor. Men have been taught to disregard feelings, to never cry because vulnerability is not manly. Sometimes men feel comfortable enough to be vulnerable with their wives or partners, and if this does not happen, they have nowhere else to turn. Critical judgment, abuse or violence often results. Being vulnerable with a male friend shows weakness. If a man wants to be vulnerable with a woman other than his wife or partner, it can easily be mistaken for sexual attraction, which can result in guilt and anger for being vulnerable outside of marriage. Many women are complicit in this and are uncomfortable with men who cry or share their feelings. We've all been influenced by patriarchal conditioning.

It is through vulnerability, being radically honest and transparent that we become invulnerable and remember we are divinely perfect, innocent and holy. As we purge everything unlike love, what remains is our Compassionate Self. This is the awakening heart of humanity. As women stop playing victim and realize our power lies in being vulnerable and honest about decades of abuse, not only do we heal the fear of seeing men being vulnerable, we free men to embrace their own vulnerability. This allows the emergence of the divine feminine and the release of the divine masculine to join in Oneness within every single person on earth. This is a holy calling. This has been the Mother's plan since the dawn of earth's time.

*The separated ego in the guise of left-brain intellectual reason and logic tries to suppress the divine feminine at all costs because it knows that a woman in her full power of balanced feminine and masculine energy will dissolve separation consciousness permanently.* A woman in her full power of love frees the divine masculine from the shackles of the wounded and distorted masculine energy of patriarchy. Men are freed to embrace both their feminine energy and their heart, able to join women as equals in being fully human and fully divine.

## Creating the New

This book is my heroine's journey of the heart and womb to remembering life can only be a song of love. When we choose to remember this, the veil of illusion disappears. The heroine's inward journey is the process of becoming divinely human. It is co-creation. It asks us to stay in our spacious heart space, keep it simple and abide in the Oneness that is our inheritance.

When we walk the labyrinth of the Holy Mother's spacious primordial womb, we return to the Holy of Holies within. As we walk, we breathe into our wombs' connection to the heart and to the earth. We breathe over and over again feeling lasting peace and love residing within our heart. Resting in the center of the labyrinth, we sit neutrally and ask the Holy Mother for inspiration. Then we wait in surrender and trust.

Light workers and mystics are being called to be loveholders of the Holy Mother's ocean of love flowing over the planet. As we embrace the Universal Grandmother's archetype, we become wisdom weavers for the awakening heart of humanity. We are emissaries of the Sky Grandmothers who are constantly weaving our many lifetimes into the fabric of this pivotal current life that returns all of humanity to love.

While it may feel as if I'm writing contradictions, on a soul level we've crossed through the doorway into the fifth dimension, the New Earth. We cannot return to the old paradigm of separation consciousness. What is left is the transition time. We are in the space of the threshold where old habits of separation consciousness still remain. We feel as if we have one foot on the new earth and one foot on the old earth. This transition is the process of transforming consciousness. It is what I call the Great Tuning to Love.

*Life Is a Song of Love* is my heroine's journey of the heart and womb, my spiritual journey to remembering my true divine inheritance igniting the sacred fire of the divine feminine and masculine in balance. I practice my song over and over to once again be in harmony with all of creation. When I burn with desire, it is the desire for the Holy Mother in union with the Holy Father. I want to feel this fire in my body. It is this desire for union that is the whole of the choir and the orchestra. I can realize my accomplishment within this heroine's journey which dissolves the separated self. You and I are the ones we've been looking and waiting for. I am the voice and song I've been hearing. I am the lover I've been seeking. The God I seek is within me. We exist in relationship with each other. There is nothing outside of us. Sophia God is not outside of us. We are of God and God is of us. We are in God and God is in us. We cannot separate, we can only dream we are separate. Within the relationship of Oneness exists the wondrous, unlimited variety of All that Is. The Source Light is Love.

# As Within So Without Meditations

## The Gift of a Question

*She remembers who she is and the world quakes.*

"As within, so without" is a phrase often used in the dialogue section of *A Course of Love* (ACOL). It simply means that as we listen to the voice within, our God Self, we begin to create the world outside of us from love. As we transform ourselves within, the world outside is transformed. As we become fully human and fully divine, we create the new earth. This is an inward movement first that shapes our love to manifest in the outer world.

This interior work of falling in love with Self involves self-inquiry that explores the shadow places where we hide what we don't like about ourself, the place where we bury shame, guilt, anger and grief. We save ourself, rather than look for saviors in someone or something outside of ourself. Inquiry work involves giving ourself the gift of a question to ignite inward dialogue and contemplation. When we invite help from our God Self, breathe deeply to relax and empty our mind of thoughts, then intuition, inspiration and imagination are ignited. Sometimes it happens immediately, sometimes it comes later. Byron Katie's self-inquiry process called "The Work" explained in her book, *Loving What Is,* describes four questions which help with this self-inquiry process. The methods of contemplation that work for me in conjunction with questions to Self are: walking the labyrinth, taking a bath, singing and listening to music, meditating, hiking and reading passages from metaphysical texts and poetry. What works best for you?

These "as within so without" meditations and questions are offered after every Movement. I provide the general theme of the inquiry work, which begins with "She remembered who she is and…" I encourage writing down your thoughts and feelings in your journal. I am guessing you already have a contemplative practice. I always center myself before doing inquiry work. Do this till you feel your thoughts drift away and you feel centered and in peace. You can use the following practice, or use whatever works best for you.

Take a few breaths, filling your belly first and then your chest.

On the in breath: Say silently "God breathes me."
On the out breath: Say silently "I breathe God."
On the in breath: Say silently "Love breathes me."
On the out breath: Say silently "I breathe love."
On the in breath: Say silently "Life breathes me."
On the out breath: Say silently "I breathe life."

Please start with the two following questions before beginning your inquiry process then read the additional questions. Try to write down whatever arises without judgment or editing what you don't like. Most importantly ask your guides/light family to help with your inquiry work.

Can I love myself enough to forgive myself?
Can I forgive myself enough to love myself?

### *Additional Questions*

Like Lady Ragnell, do you believe you are under a spell (a self-limiting belief) that keeps you from loving, saving yourself and claiming your divine sovereignty? What is the self-limiting belief(s)?

What can you do to release these self-limiting beliefs?

As with the children's stories, does your masculine energy feel like a monster ready to devour you or a friend?

Or is it your feminine energy you most fear, perhaps believing it makes you ugly and loathsome?

Envision then describe yourself as a beautiful woman powerful in her loving kindness.

Are you connected to your feminine wildness, your intuitive creative abilities? If yes, how would you describe this wildness?

Are you afraid of your wild longings? If yes, what are you afraid will happen if you express your wild intuitive knowing?

Return to the first two questions about loving and forgiving yourself.

This is the final surrender.

# Movement Two

# The Mystic's Song of Truth

# Chapter One

## What Is a Mystic?

> *Mysticism is the pursuit of a spiritual and intangible quest; the finding of a "way out" of illusion or a "way back" to absolute truth. It is an intimate personal adventure. Mysticism is the art of arts. It is the most romantic of adventures.*
> Evelyn Underhill, *Mysticism*

Mysticism is the journey into remembering our Truth as divine beings. A mystic is someone who has ineffable experiences of transcending separation consciousness into the heart of the Mother/Father/One God. Mystics continually pursue the truth of God which often results in non-dual mystical texts teaching their divine inspiration. Our world religions started from mystics such as Buddha, Yeshua, Mohammed and Lao Tzu. Most organized religions have lost an intimate understanding of the mysticism from which they grew. However, there are many mystics who still exist within all religions. The contemporary metaphysical channeled texts which inform this book plus many others have helped birth legions of modern-day mystics.

There are more modern-day mystics than there have ever been before. We are called lightworkers, wayshowers and loveholders. If you are reading this book, you are already on a mystical path. We come from all walks of life and from all corners of the world. We include people of all ages who choose to listen from their hearts to God's call. During this pivotal time the mystical truths are known within our cells, within our very being. If your awareness has wakened you to God's loving presence within, then you are a mystic. Mystics speak and sing in many tongues, yet teach the same truth: love is the only force in the multiverse, all else is the illusion of fear.

Even though I've been on a spiritual quest to remembering and knowing my Truth more than half of my life, I never thought of myself as a mystic. I'm still reluctant at times to claim this. We've been taught in this dream of separation from our Beloved God that only a very few men have been or are mystics, and even fewer women. The mystic always seems to be someone else, someone to look up to but certainly a title that does not apply to me. Claiming to be a modern-day woman mystic smacks of hubris. Doesn't it?

When I was ready to claim myself as a mystic, I began to wonder why. Why do I feel I am a mystic now at this point in my spiritual journey? What is different? I realize:

- God infuses my life—a constant presence and awareness.
- I am actively engaged in a deep inner dialogue with my God Self to cleanse and heal my shadow of shame, blame, anger, hatred and grief.
- I am devoted to seeing beyond the falsity of separation to the Truth of my divine sovereignty.

This book about my spiritual journey of the heart is my claim to being a mystic. It is definitely a spiritual, intangible, intimate personal journey. Most of the time I feel it has been an awe-inspiring journey into the labyrinth of my heart and womb. Those times when my heart sings, it feels like a marvelous adventure. Without a doubt, it has taken an enormous amount of personal courage over and over again to continue on this path of reuniting with the Source of All that is, the Holy Mother Father. I've come to realize everyone at their core is a mystic. We are spiritual beings having a physical experience. Some people have yet to understand this, remaining stuck in the collective dream that reinforces separation from God. Yet at any moment they can have an experience which ignites the spark of the divine within to open and walk the mystic's path.

On this journey we are constantly in the process of coming to know the unknown. There is no end point or a time when we've arrived because we are always expanding and expressing God's love in multiple realities and dimensions. As we awaken in these earthly bodies we start to realize and remember our Soul's interdimensional existence. Therefore, I add to my list of mystical characteristics:

- I embrace my multidimensional interdimensional Self.

Yet something is still missing, at least for me. It is the passion, the burning in my heart for the Divine Mother. I want to be consumed by the love of the Cosmic Mother for all her creations. As Underhill says, "It is the most romantic of adventures." I'm on a heroine's journey, not a hero's journey. For too long, the masculine idea of mysticism has been to meditate, clear your mind, deny your body, and ascend vertically. Men over the eons have built temples, towers, cathedrals and skyscrapers, all with the thought of transcending the body. Women tend the hearth, family, community and the earth. We plant and grow things with our hands, imaginations, and spiritual longing and connections. Some of us give birth and nurture our children. All of us are honoring our creative energy in a myriad of ways. We are constantly creating and birthing the new earth. Meinrad Craighead, a contemporary mystic and visual artist of the Immanent Mother, wrote:

> Whether or not a woman actually conceives, she always carries the essence of the germinative ocean within her, the flux of the energy in formless potential. It is a spiritual fertility, full from within, a woman's inheritance, not dependent on

> external catalyst. So too, the artist is always pregnant from within, a container of endless potential transformations, abandoned to the fertilizing powers of the imagination, actualizing unknown faces parthenogenetically.
>
> In solitude our deepest intuitions of an indwelling personal God Spirit are confirmed, the Mothergod who never withdraws from us and whose presence is our existence and the life of all that is.[9]

The sacred feminine is about embodying the divine enfoldment of the Holy Mother's love. Therefore, I add a fifth and sixth characteristic to being a mystic that is applicable for both men and women.

- I am consumed by the creative, luminescent life force of the Holy Mother aspect of God.
- I constantly seek to forge, within, a joining of the sacred feminine and masculine energies into compassionate harmony for creation of heaven on earth.

Andrew Harvey in *The Essential Mystics, The Soul's Journey into Truth* writes that all beings on earth are vibrant with the light and love of the forgotten Mother and that we are not here to escape and transcend earth but to embody her love—to be here in full presence and gratitude.

> The universe, as many mystical traditions tell us, is the "child" of a sacred marriage between the feminine and masculine forces within the One, what Taoists call yin and yang, what Hindus' name Shiva and Shakti; it is the constantly self-transforming expression of their eternal mutual passion. For the human race to have a chance to survive, this cosmic sacred marriage has to be mirrored and enacted in our being at every level.[10]

Yes, yes, yes, every cell in my body resonates with this message! Reclaiming the divine feminine within allows me to feel the fire in my belly to unequivocally choose to be One with the Divine Mother. When the masculine energy of gentle strength, protection and clarity merges with the primordial feminine energy of birth and divine embodiment, it creates the alchemy of fierce passion to bring love into action to create heaven on earth. This is my mystic's song of Truth.

There are many names for lightworkers and mystics from many different spiritual paths. They are: wisdom keepers, loveholders, shamans, spiritual elders, ministers, imam, rabbis and wisdom weavers. We are birthing a spiritual revolution to embrace the return of the Divine Feminine returning the Holy Mother to the face of God. As I write about the characteristics of a mystic or lightworker, it feels as if I'm describing what Yeshua refers to as "the elevated Self of form" in *A Course of Love* (ACOL) when we accept both our human self and our divine Self as our divine inheritance:

> Life, your humanity, is the variability. Spirit, your oneness, is the constant. Life is oneness extended into separation and variability through experience. The elevated Self of form will be the expression of new life lived within the constant wholeness but continuing to experience the variability of separation. This is what you practice as you gather on the mountain top while remaining on level ground.[11]

Mystics are people who experience their Truth as divine daughters and sons of God while still living within separation consciousness. We've been to the mountain top through metaphysical teachings and our own divine guidance. However, we are encouraged to bring our knowledge of the Oneness of life down to level ground where separation consciousness still exists. The elevated Self of form or our Mystical Self is a level of awareness that prepares us to leave separation consciousness and become divinely human.

In Buddhism the term bodhisattva is used to describe people who have wakened their heart mind and wish to become enlightened not only for themselves but also to benefit others. This feels similar to what I'm referring to as a mystic and also the elevated Self of form. Mystics, bodhisattvas, lightworkers, wayshowers, loveholders and elevated Selves of form are the transition place in the process of becoming awakened. We are almost there; however, we are still needed to be the bridge for others between the old and the new, between separation consciousness and Christ consciousness. Bodhisattvas become Buddhas who are fully awakened human beings. Mystics, lightworkers and elevated Selves of form become fully human and fully divine.

While we reside as mystics in our elevated Self of form, we will experience what many refer to as liminal space, the experience of being between the known and the unknown. Often we are propelled into the liminal realm as the result of a crisis such as the loss of a loved one, a life-threatening disease or a moment when all life feels hopeless and useless. In liminal space I had an ineffable feeling that there had to be a better way to live and parent my children, especially my atypical son. Caring and fighting for my son Tyler propelled me into liminal space which led to my ministry for children with special needs labels. My daughter Sarah propelled me into liminal space with the need to heal the mother daughter wound. Liminal space is where our spiritual journey is ignited.

These moments continue to occur while on our journey. We follow the labyrinth of our soul into the center of our heart and suddenly we pause at one of the folds unable to go forward or backward. This darkness is actually full of promise and revelation which compels us into liminal space where we are open to infinite possibilities. Liminal space is where the sacred feminine and masculine join in union. Medieval women mystics such as Julian of Norwich, Teresa de Avila, and Hildegard of Bingen resided in the liminal realm continuously. Much of this book is being written while in liminal space.

The great pause and reset caused by the coronavirus pandemic is liminal space for all of humanity. Some will recognize this place of being between the known and the unknown as an opportunity to go inward to listen to the still small voice within. Some will be unable to hear as they are not ready yet. All is wrapped in the embrace of the Holy Mother Sophia God. All is perfectly orchestrated for our awakening.

## Mystics Hold the Myths of Divine Truths

Myths are divine truths told in the form of a story. Mystics use myths as part of their inner spiritual journey of transcendence. The many faces of the Goddess are preserved in the stories and myths running through all religions, faith traditions, spiritual paths and cultures. His-story has tried to re-write and distort these myths to serve their power—destroying Her-story as being fantasy, not logical, unproven by scientific truth. So myths began to be seen as nonsense, fairy tales told by the ignorant, primitive and uneducated. This occurred in an effort to repress imagination, which is our connection to the divine. All is designed with the intent to confuse and keep people from an inner spiritual journey of the heart leading to awakening from this dream of separation from our Beloved Source.

Mystics devote time in contemplation and inner journeying into their God Self. Inevitably we are led to embracing myths as part of our awakening path. I draw on children's stories and the Arthurian legend of Lady Ragnell as myths pointing to divine truths of balancing masculine and feminine energies. The divine feminine, the Immanent Mother of all life, is held in the myths and stories of Goddesses. We'll be drawn to the Goddess that speaks the divine truths to us, and she will change depending where we are on our wakening journey. As we encounter the labyrinth's folds on our path into the heart womb, our awareness changes and another Goddess may appear with wisdom we are able to receive. These Goddesses become overseeing spirit guides for our journey into Christ consciousness.

I write about and mention Lilith, Kali Ma, Shakti, Isis, Green Tara, Mother Mary, Mary Magdalene, Quan Yin, White Buffalo Woman and Changing Woman/Grandmother Spider. Many more may emerge as I write. Their resonance as wise spiritual ascended masters are accessible if we ask and open to receive. Hundreds of Gods and Goddesses aspects of the One from different cultures and faith traditions are not mentioned in this book, and several may make an appearance during your spiritual journey of the heart and womb. Honor whoever shows up to guide you in the mysteries of the multiverse. The divine truths these myths hold have kept the sacred feminine from oblivion. Both men and women mystics will eventually encounter stories about the transcendent Mother on their inner journey into the heart. These myths set us free from the perception of separation. They free the Cosmic Mother, the Creatrix of all Life that contains the Cosmic Father to once again reign in our hearts.

## Listening to the Voice of Love

Before exploring contemporary mystical teachings there needs to be an understanding of what is meant by channeled teachings. Initially I was confused; however my understanding has expanded over the years. *A Course of Miracles* (ACIM) was my first foray into a contemporary channeled text, and this shaped my initial understanding. I thought only special people with a special connection to an ascended master such as Yeshua or Mother Mary could channel.

I now believe any of us, aligning with our Higher Holy Self, receive God's message in the manner that speaks most strongly to us and these messages are constantly streaming to us. All we need is a little willingness to receive. I have consistently received personal messages through a variety of ways. Yet I doubted myself when it came to receiving verbal messages. I've always suspected the verbal messages I think I receive from Yeshua as not very eloquent and sounding suspiciously like me. During a time when I was feeling especially open and in tune with Yeshua, I asked: "Why do I trust various ways you send messages, but not the dialogue in words." This is what Jeshua replied:

> *I can only use the words you would use yourself. This is why the content is the same but the wording is different from one person to the next. By wanting my words to be more eloquent you have slipped into believing that I am outside you. In fact, this is part of the Trust you are re-learning. You and I are the same, and truly I come from within your Sacred Self, the part of you that knows it's not separate. Trust in your Sacred Self equates to Trust in me and therefore you and I as One.*
>
> *So I use the words coming from your heart. When you question that I'm using your words, you are distrusting our Oneness. You are worthy. You are a child of God. We are both creations of God, extensions of Her Love. You can be nothing less. I can be nothing less. Therefore, we can have this conversation continually. What happens is when you ask for help with a specific problem, you are so wrapped up in your past behavior that you distrust any words coming through. You begin to stop listening as your heart freezes with fear and the ego mind takes over. Yet even in those times, you've been open enough to hear in other ways: music, dreams, animal spiritual guides and downloads of knowing.*

(Yeshua then refers to a specific ongoing struggle with a relationship, and says I stop listening and believe Yeshua has stopped talking because I'm afraid he will ask me to do something I do not want to do.)

*I would never tell you to do something, especially something you do not want to do, because anything done in fear is the separated ego. And telling you to do something negates your free will. I can feel you questioning this, as if you feel I've done that in the past. Have I? Because you and I are One, anything you end up doing has to be a joint decision emanating from love. I take whatever experience you are having and join with you for the most benevolent outcome for all involved. To repeat what you know deep down: every experience is perfect for your awakening. Your Holy Self has created it in Oneness with me for your highest good. And what can be your highest good but a return to Christ consciousness in form.*

*So take up your pen and let's have these written dialogues with no censoring because you think something can't be my words. Just write as you've done here. Do you feel because you've not been a literary genius that means we are not conversing as One? Do not worry that the ego slips in every once in a while. It is Okay because you have yet to abide fully as the Christ you are. Yet you do know the Truth and the words that point to the Truth. So let's release once and for all the idea that if I was truly dialoguing with you, the words would sound different. I Am in you, a part of you, One with you. I'm in joy at this opening of your heart. It's been closed to this form of communication because you fear not being worthy of my support and of moving forward, as manifested by the pain in your hip and back.*

*Yes, we will work through this together as One. It's your free will that brings you to me and the desire to create together in order to return to your Holy Self. And because you asked, I will assist you in every way possible with joy in our joining. Welcome home, sister.*

*And So, It Is*

*Blessed Be and Amen*

I received this communication several years ago before opening more fully to receiving messages from Divine Feminine Christ Ascended masters such as Mother Mary, Mary Magdalene,

Quan Yin, Kali Ma and White Buffalo Woman. My heroine's journey involved allowing Yeshua back into my life and healing the deep anger I'd felt. I thought he'd betrayed the divine feminine by allowing patriarchy to exist. Pretty funny when I finally realized that this is impossible. Yeshua's messages in ACIM, *Way of Mastery* (WOM) and ACOL are about only love is real and the rest we made up during this dream experience of being separate from God.

I held this crazy mixed-up idea that what I wrote was not true channeling for many, many years. Yet when I've re-read some of what I've written in my first two books and my blog, I sometimes wonder, wow, this was inspired, it came directly from my heart and feels wonderful. It is very clear what doesn't feel inspired because my heart does not sing with love. Inspiration means being guided by the divine, with the heart and mind joined in wholeheartedness. When we are inspired or in-Spirit, it is channeling, nothing special about it. It is our Truth in Oneness speaking to us. It is our intuition and inspiration. We are channeling in a variety of ways emanating from our Unity with the Divine Mother Father. Recognizing what we receive comes from our union with Sophia God, we welcome into our hearts the awareness that all ascended masters, archangels and spiritual teachers are the voice of Oneness heard from within. We cease to feel there is anything or any being outside of us and our world changes from one of separation to one of union. Thus, Terra Nova is co-created into being. Yeshua says in ACOL:

> What you allow yourself to receive and what you do with what you receive is all that matters. You realize now that life itself is a channel and that you are constantly receiving. You will perhaps think in terms of receiving meaning that there is something given from a source beyond the Self, but this is the "thought" that has to change. If giving and receiving are one, then giver and receiver are also one.[12]

Everyone receives the unceasing messages from Spirit through their own personal lens or way of perceiving the world. Sometimes these messages are influenced by the separated ego. The separated ego, our false sense of self, is the part of us that believes we can be separate from God. Before we opened to receive our mystical path, we resided almost full time with our separated self. We may still slide back into the separated ego at times, only now we have the spiritual tools to return to peace and Oneness. Being aware of this helps to avoid falling into the trap of believing our spiritual path is the one true path. There are many paths to remembering our Truth as a divine sovereign being.

With my total dismissal of organized patriarchal Christian religion, I carried the belief that anyone, including ministers, priests and people who worshipped in these churches did not understand the True teachings of Yeshua as revealed in contemporary channeled texts. Therefore, I steadfastly refused to read authors whose understanding of Christianity came from the Bible, believing they could not possibly access the Truth this way. With this belief I judged anyone who had not read the contemporary channeled texts as being unable to access their wisdom and inner knowing.

The separated ego is very slippery, I did not realize how utterly ridiculous and judgmental I was being and how it contradicted everything I was learning. The divine message I receive over and over again is that everyone, absolutely everyone, has the ability to go within and hear the Truth of their divine sovereignty from their God Self, and that Truth comes in many forms: from teachers, from ministers, from books, poetry, videos and movies, from visions, visual art and from music that resonates within one's heart. This judgment began to soften and dissolve as I read some of Father Richard Rohr's meditations and Cynthia Bourgeault's book, *The Meaning of Mary Magdalene*. Much more of my judgment dissolved when I read Mirabai

Starr's book, *Wild Mercy: Living the Fierce and Tender Wisdom of the Women Mystics*. Starr introduced women mystics of the past and modern-day women mystics who have followed a different path from mine. The Shekinah, the indwelling spirit of the sacred feminine that I have carried within all my many lives was set ablaze.

## Chapter Two

# Mystical Teachings

I am not a scholar of the many ancient mystical teachings. I trust my God Self to lead me to what I need to know. I have borrowed from many faith traditions' revealing truths without becoming a devoted student. What has remained constant is the sense that they all lead to the same place. We are created in the image of God and are in essence divine beings. We chose to experience this perception of separation from God. Because it is impossible to separate from an All-Loving God, all we experience with these bodies is an illusion or a dream. God is all-encompassing love with no opposite, therefore the suffering and pain we experience is not from God but was created by us through the mistaken perception of separation consciousness. The mystic's journey is to remember that only love is real and re-awaken to our divine sovereignty.

There are many paths and religious traditions leading us to this Truth because God teaches in a variety of ways, depending on one's culture, country, aspirations, ways of learning and being. As we are becoming the song of our heart, the many paths to remembering our divinity are merging and vibrating to speak to each one's unique heart song. Lilith, as first woman created equally with Adam, made a surprise visit to return sexuality as the innocent life force of creation and lead this book to wholeness. The Hindu Goddess Kali Ma is resonating and singing to me. I know little about Hinduism, yet Kali Ma came to me and provides a focus for moving through rage and transmuting anger into fierce love for all of humanity. This fierce love is a hallmark of the Universal Grandmother archetype.

The indigenous teachings of Native American people have a special place in my heart. I find the simple yet profound way of experiencing the Great Mystery and the Great Spirit within the mystery sings to me in ways I finally comprehend. I am grateful their way of life infused by the Great Mystery was not completely destroyed, and that many wise women, shamans, grandmothers and grandfathers have come forward to teach humanity with their spiritual wisdom. They provide an example of a way to live in harmony as we co-create Nova Earth. The wisdom and inherent power of women is not lost. The Sky Grandmothers and original thirteen clan mothers' wisdom and love for all living beings creates the Universal Grandmother's archetype.

Even though I resonate with other faith traditions, my spiritual lineage comes from Yeshua, Mother Mary and Mary Magdalene. I dislike using the word Christianity because several hundred years after the life of Yeshua, a bunch of power-hungry men gathered with the intent of controlling the populace, especially women, through religion. This patriarchal governing council for the newly forming Christian religion within the Roman Empire systematized early Christian Church doctrine into a unifying religion that became the Roman Catholic Church. They appropriated the Greek word *Christos* to designate Yeshua as the one and only Christ. *Christos* originally was used to describe someone who has been anointed to sacred service. The Hebrew word *messiah* also means anointed. And so Yeshua was re-created several hundred years after his life as the only anointed Messiah who became known as the one and only Christ. Then they grounded all Christian doctrine in the false concept that every person is born with original sin. Only Jesus was born free of sin. Thus church fathers taught that only through them Jesus could save one's soul if we sacrificed enough of our earthly desires. The Roman Catholic Church blamed and persecuted Jews for denying Jesus was the foretold messiah and then executing him which became a central message of colonization. And the Catholic Church's doctrines and hatred of the Jews was transmitted into Protestant Christianity. Instead of all life being sacred, all life became a means for dominance and exploitation.

In 325 AD, early church fathers at the Council of Nicaea created the Christian Creed that is still used today in Christian churches all over the world. This is also when the four gospels—Matthew, Mark, Luke and John—were chosen for the New Testament. The gospels of Mary Magdalene, Thomas, Philip and Judas were left out and ordered destroyed. Also included for destruction were *The Thunder, Perfect Mind,* which praised the divine feminine, and *The Acts of Paul and Thecla,* which described women as being divinely equal to men. (Many of these Christian and Gnostic texts were discovered near Nag Hammadi, Egypt in 1945.) This created a religion in which people were taught the only way to Yeshua "the Christ" or salvation was through intermediaries such as priests. This effectively taught that God was not found within but existed outside of us, judging and deciding who could be saved and who could not be saved.

Christianity eventually became the religion of choice for European countries involved in empire building. Christianity to save the heathens justified colonization to dominate people of different faiths and spiritual practices in places such as India and the indigenous and tribal people in the Americas, Canada, Australia, New Zealand and Africa—all aiming for the patriarchal goal of power and control by trying to suppress any faith teaching that all creatures on earth are divine and have a direct connection to our Beloved Source.

Mystics and metaphysical teachings and texts in all world religions have always pointed us in the direction of our inner knowing of our divinity. Even though the world's organized religions have been influenced and dominated by the separated ego's tool of patriarchy, the mystical teachings have remained and are regaining strength within many faith traditions. Separation consciousness will never be able to entirely suppress the message of the Holy Mother's all-encompassing love existing within. I appreciate how Andrew Harvey describes the mystics' voices of the main world religions: indigenous voices of the first world, Taoism as the way of the Tao (reality, universe and authentic human life), Hinduism as the way of presence, Buddhism as the way of clarity, Judaism as the way of holiness, Ancient Greece as the way of beauty, Islam as the way of passion and Christianity as the way of love in action.[13] In our heroine's journey we are being called to bring into wholeness all the mystics' voices of all the world's faith traditions.

## Contemporary Mystical Teachings Influencing My Heroine's Journey

Motherhood sparked my spiritual journey. I wanted a daughter and the Holy Mother blessed me with Sarah. As fairly common for first-time mothers, my relationship with Sarah gave me the first taste of fierce love. I suddenly realized I would do anything to protect Sarah. Then I gave birth to my son Tyler and that fierce motherly love was put to an even greater test. It became evident by age five that Tyler was different from the "norm" and it was soon determined he had a learning disability. I've documented my spiritual journey with Tyler in two books. My fierce mother's love led to a heart ministry of teaching and facilitating workshops on seeing past the labels we give atypical children to the whole divine child.

As I explained in Movement One, the Unitarian Universalist (UU) faith tradition fit my needs for a spiritual home because I wanted my children to learn from many faith traditions. Two UU principles especially spoke to my values: the inherent worth and dignity of every person, and the respect for the interdependent web of all existence of which we are part. It is with the UUs that I started my ministry for atypical children with labels.

The first book I can remember that chipped at my wall of resistance to the divine within was *Dear Heart, Come Home, The Path of Midlife Spirituality* by Joyce Rupp. I cried all the way through the book. She spoke to my very soul, reaching those deep dry places I'd denied for too long. I realize now that she described reclaiming the sacred feminine, even though she called it midlife yearning. She wrote a poem about the old maps we've been following that no longer work, yet we are frightened about throwing them out and exploring on our own. We walk into the dark night and trust the stars' light shining in our souls to guide and lead us home.[14]

This poem spoke directly to letting go of that which no longer serves us. While I felt this at a deep level, it was not until writing this book that I finally let go to trusting my inner wisdom, which needs no map. Our yearning for the sacred feminine answers our longing for God the Beloved and is often found in the dark recesses of the soul. This is not the dark we were taught to fear. The patriarchal masculine dark is full of terror and those who can harm us. The heroine's journey calls us to be brave and venture into the dark, and once there we feel the sacred feminine spark that has never gone out waiting for us to set it ablaze. This is the dark of the welcoming primordial womb of the Divine Mother. This dark enfolds us in an all-encompassing love surpassing all understanding. It fills us with the blazing light of our divinity and we become one of the stars guiding ourselves home.

The written word has always been and continues to be the most powerful way for me to access my inner knowing. Life changed when I read non-dualistic mystical channeled teachings such as: ACIM, ACOL, WOM and *The Sophia Code*. All these teachings, as well as a myriad of other metaphysical texts, have influenced my process of awakening and inform the writing of this book.

While writing this book, my dear mystical soul sister Christina Strutt of Co-Creating Clarity partnered with Rick Greathouse to publish online his channeled metaphysical text *A Journey into the Unknown*. This text continues to expand

and clarify Yeshua's teaching in ACIM and ACOL. Yeshua in *Journey into the Unknown* says that ACIM as the first text of this trilogy introduces Christ Awareness, ACOL as the second text introduces Christ consciousness, and *A Journey into the Unknown* as the third text introduces Christ transformation. Mari Perron, the first receiver of ACOL, published her channeling of Mother Mary called *Mirari, The Way of the Marys*. All of these metaphysical texts add insight and confirmation for what I've been receiving and writing.

With ACIM I temporarily shelved my longing for the divine feminine because I initially confused non-dualism and Oneness with all being the same. I felt God had forsaken me until a wise teacher suggested that God and Goddess were One, and if my heart opens by calling God the Divine Mother, then do it. After many years of internal work excavating unconscious guilt and releasing the separated ego mind, I felt the divine feminine once again rising within. It is not to achieve equality with the distorted shadow masculine, but to release both the divine feminine and masculine to rise together and thus reconcile into Oneness.

What triggered the awareness of the rebirth of the sacred feminine occurred while reading ACOL about the "way of (Mother) Mary" in the section The Forty Days and Forty Nights. I felt something inside break open. I stopped reading and went for a hike. Fortunately, I can walk from my house into the expansiveness of northern New Mexico. Two hawks spiraled overhead signaling a message from the Divine. Halfway through my hike, I felt everything in this life, as well as multiple parallel lives, coalesce into a still point of awareness. I knew everything had prepared me for this moment to follow the "way of Mary." I saw that Mother Mary has always been with me as the Mother Goddess light figure who comforted and encouraged my fierce warrior mother role in this dream of separation. The spark of the sacred feminine re-ignited in a new way.

Mother Mary, as an Ascended Master representative of the Universal Mother, also found expression in my deep, deep connection with Mother Earth: my advocacy of the many different ways to learn and process information as many differences among the whole, and my overwhelming feeling of compassion for all those who see themselves as broken, especially children. I knew the voice of the divine feminine had been freed within me, although I did not have clarity of purpose at the time. I felt at one with all life. I was filled with immense grace and gratitude. In ACOL, Yeshua says:

> Those called to the way of Mary are called to be what they want to see reflected in the world and to the realization that this reflection is the new way of creation. In their being they become what they want to create.[15]
>
> The answer lies in the simple statement of as within, so without. By living as who you are in the world, you create change in the world. You create change through relationship. All live and create in relationship. Those called to the way of Mary, however, are called to the creation and anchoring of the new relationship in the new world. Their relationship of union, upon which their contentment is based, is the birthplace, the womb of the new. Their expression is expression of this union.[16]

I heard this message of anchoring the new relationship as returning the divine feminine to the world and joining with the divine masculine in balance. After a few days of contemplation, I allowed confusion to enter my mind, even though I felt this was my purpose in Union with God. I was not sure what Yeshua was actually describing. Understanding came while preparing to write this book. As I re-read the above words from Yeshua, I realize again that in my being, I'm becoming what I'm creating.

In 2016, a series of books I call the Anna books continued the process of healing and breaking open to receive and reclaim the sacred feminine. Two books, *Anna, Grandmother of Jesus* and *Anna the Voice of the Magdalenes*, channeled by Claire Heartsong, expanded my understanding of divine feminine expressed through Mary Magdalene, Anna, Mother Mary and the many women and men disciples as part of Yeshua's ministry. I also became aware of all our incarnations existing simultaneously rather than in the illusion of linear time. I see now that Anna also provides a beautiful example of a Universal Grandmother, a wisdom weaver. These books were preparation for reading *The Sophia Code* channeled by Kaia Ra which shifted my entire being and universe. I felt deep within, the call to be the divine feminine leader I always thought I was supposed to be. The "way of Mary" took on a deeper meaning.

I felt the call to express the indwelling feminine energy called the Shekinah I'd always felt within begin to take form. I thought I was to anchor the new energy coming in as described in the "way of Mary." However, anchoring the new energy is so much more—anchoring the new energy becomes a multidimensional endeavor of co-creating Nova Earth and bringing what we think of as past and future into the eternal now. I could not ignore the messages coming through that I was to do much more than anchor the new energy while staying safely on top of my mesa. Then I received guidance from my inner child to write this book.

## Mystical Truths in a Time of Reason and Scientific Proof

For most of my life I considered a mystic as someone from our past who had experiences which could not possibly be repeated in contemporary times. As I started writing this book, it was a revelation that the multitude of modern-day lightworkers or loveholders can be considered mystics, and that I could actually call myself one. Claiming this opens my heart to receive more and more from my God Self and my spiritual guides. However, it also led to difficult conversations with friends and family who only believe in logic and scientific proof and dismiss spiritual knowing. Everyone has beliefs; who's to say my spiritual knowing of God is the truth? I realize I'm treading on quick sand by even starting this conversation. However, I know deep within my heart that every person is a spiritual being. A mystic is someone who realizes this and pursues returning to our Christ state with unswerving devotion.

As I contemplated writing this part of the chapter, I received Franciscan Priest and Mystic Richard Rohr's daily meditation which was on the subject of *Disciples, Prophets and Mystics*. In fact, I had just signed up to receive his weekly posts and this was the first one I received. Coincidence—I don't think so. When I follow my intuition, synchronicities or holy instants always occur. In this meditation Father Rohr writes:

> Both Catholics and Protestants have failed our people by mystifying the very notion of mysticism. The word itself has become relegated to a "misty" and distant realm that implies it is only available to very few and something not to be trusted, much less attractive or desirable. For me, the word "mysticism" simply means experiential knowledge of spiritual things, as opposed to book knowledge, secondhand knowledge, or even church knowledge.

Our experiential knowledge can come in many forms, and while there is a universality to how we receive, it nevertheless is unique to each person's spiritual journey to remembering our Truth as One with God. This is where the spiritual ego finds ways to make us believe our experience is better and more holy than your experience. The spiritual ego is the part of the separated self that finds ways to influence our spiritual practice in an effort to sabotage our process of becoming divinely human. Rohr continues by noting that we see everything spiritual:

> ...through the lens of our own temperament, early conditioning, brain function, role and place in society, education, our personal needs, and cultural biases and assumptions. Admittedly, personal experiences are easy to misinterpret, and we shouldn't universalize from our "moment" to an expectation that everybody must have the same kind of "moment." We also can't assume that any experience is 100 percent from God. We must develop filters to clear away our own agenda and ego.[17]

When we use what we feel are our spiritual truths to force people to believe what we believe, we are using the spiritual ego. When we learn to trust our inner wisdom, we open to receive the all-encompassing love of the Universal Mother. No one can do this for us and we can't do it for anyone else. When we try to convince them, we can slip into subtle forms of I'm right and you're wrong. When I first became a student of ACIM, I tried to convince my friends that ACIM was something they should read. It led to many uncomfortable conversations. I've learned this lesson over and over again, to love and forgive myself enough to trust that each person is on their own unique spiritual path. Eventually we all awaken to our divine Truth held within Oneness.

So where does this leave us, how do we know what we are receiving from the Divine Mother Father God has not been sabotaged by the spiritual ego? Distinguishing the spiritual ego from a mystical truth comes from the heart. Whenever attack, blame, shame, guilt, accusations, I'm right and you're wrong, I'm special and finger pointing come into play, it is the spiritual ego. Whenever my button is pushed and I feel the need to defend, I'm in the energy of separation.

I remember times when I was convinced of a spiritual truth, only to realize later that it was not. I open my heart to forgive myself and all of us who stumble at times. It allows detachment from another person's story, allowing that their experience is perfectly orchestrated for their awakening. I align with my God Self and witness from a place of unconditional love. Each time I do this, I feel the peace and love of God residing more and more in my heart, and I'm triggered less and less by what is happening in the world.

## Chapter Three

# Women as Mystics, the Old and the New

Why would we want to study and know about the ancient and medieval women mystics? Are they relevant today? When I read about them, I feel deep gratitude for their courage, for keeping the seeds of the sacred feminine alive to rise again. As I write, we are in the great pause and reset of the worldwide COVID-19 pandemic. We are entering a time when all the patriarchal governmental, financial, big business and religious structures are crumbling. They have to disintegrate. They can't be fixed, because anything created within separation consciousness is untenable for the co-creation of the New Earth. Therefore, we are entering a time of polarity, disease, destruction and suffering for many people. Many are dying to their physical bodies. This can be heartbreakingly difficult; however, if we reside in our elevated Self of form, our Mystical Selves, we can lovingly bear witness without being drawn into the drama. We know this is the transition time for creating Nova Earth. The earthly form may die; however, our true spiritual selves do not die. We are limitless divine daughters and sons of God. Death is a creation of the separated ego. We are being called to stand in our truth as divine sovereign beings, to resonate at the highest vibration possible.

Both men and women are being called as lightworkers to be a beacon of faith and hope for all of humanity, to be fiercely protective of everyone's divinity till they can know it for themselves. Like the women mystics of long ago who kept the sacred feminine flame alive, we are being called to do the same—only this time in greater and greater numbers. This powerful collective of all-encompassing unconditional Love of God is creating a grid of Christ consciousness all over the world that is lifting everyone to their highest good. We are being called to save ourselves because no one else can do it for us. We will not be nailed on a cross or burned as a witch—those times are over. Yet we need great courage to let go of all the ties that bind us to our separated self in order to embrace our elevated Self of form. The writings, poetry and songs of these ancient and medieval women mystics may speak to you in ways you could not imagine, and they give us courage during this time of the Great Tuning to Love.

As I've said before, I'm not a religious scholar so I've not studied the women mystics of old, although I knew a little of their stories from a college course on women mystics. I re-connected with Julian of Norwich, Hildegard of Bingen and Teresa de Avila and discovered others, such as Thecla. I am moved by all these women's revolutionary wisdom, their longing for Oneness with God, and their devotion to the Truth that only Love is real and that God speaks directly within us.

The language of these women mystics is highly passionate, drawing on romantic love language to describe their joining with their Beloved Father aspect of God. They were filled with the burning sacred fire to express what they felt was the feminine aspect of God. Because of the times, these women mystics had to be very careful about describing the feminine essence of God; however, she is there through the words they used. I can feel this from their description of falling in love with their sacred Self, with the divine existing within. These women mystics found voice during times of extreme suffering and suppression of women.

I feel as if I have gone full circle from my earlier reading of Goddess-centered books to again read and love more recent sacred feminine books written by and for women. I feel how perfectly it all came together. I believe Yeshua with his channeled texts revealing his True teachings prepared us for the rebirth of the sacred feminine and the return of the Holy Mother, the feminine expression of God.

I've always been a bridge between old and new paradigms. My ministry for atypical children is an example of this—teaching parents, caregivers, professionals, teachers, ministers to see past the labels children are given to the whole divine child. It feels as if this book is also asking me to be a bridge, realizing all that has guided my heroine's journey to see past all the boxes and labels we've placed on our mystical spiritual texts and teachings, and to understand the wholeness and truths uniting all in Oneness.

## Women Mystics Who Fill My Heart with Gratitude

What resonates the most about the women mystics of long ago is their personal relationship with God. Such is the song of a mystic. These were women living in times of extreme subjugation of women when the vast majority could not read or write. Therefore, most of these women came from wealthier families, some of whom were lenient about their daughters being educated despite the cultural prohibitions. Ironically, a way of some independence for women of the Christian tradition was to become a Catholic nun and live in a convent, which provided a safe place away from men to have time for contemplation and inner spiritual work. Yet to be vocal and write about their personal experience with the feminine expression of God in union with the masculine expression of God was profoundly courageous. If they had not done this, we would not know about them today. It feels to me as if they created a foundation for the divine feminine to survive in Christianity and help fuel her re-emergence in the contemporary world.

Teresa de Ávila during the 1500s writes about our relationship with God as an inner journey. This was revolutionary for times in which the teachings of the Catholic Church insisted people needed priests as intermediaries to access God. Mirabai Starr wrote that Teresa saw every person's soul as an interior luminous center filled with love and accessible to everyone. Teresa also believed heaven on earth awaits the new human.[18]

These divine insights are expressed again in contemporary non-dual mystical channelings. The way of Mary in ACOL emphasizes the inner spiritual journey affecting what happens outside of us—as within so without. And ACOL speaks of the creation of Terra Nova as we become divinely human, the new human.

### *Hildegard of Bingen*

Hildegard of Bingen, born in 1098, is a remarkable woman of the Middle Ages who accomplished much in her long life. She had mystical experiences as a child between 8 and 12 years of age and was given to live with an anchoress named Jutta. They lived in Jutta's small cell in a Benedictine Monastery. It is speculated that Jutta taught Hildegard how to speak and write Latin. Eventually so many girls and women were attracted to Jutta's teachings that the cell expanded into a convent. Teri Degler wrote in *Divine Feminine Fire*:

> Between her forty-third year and her death at the age of eighty-one, Hildegard produced what can only be called a monumental amount of literary, poetical, musical, medical, and scientific material. In total, she wrote three lengthy books on her visions, two books on medicine, a cosmology of the world, two biographies of saints, liturgical poetry, and the words and music to a cycle of over seventy songs.[19]

I have a friend who has studied and sings Hildegard's music, which has led to profound spiritual insights. Hildegard was also an artist who illustrated many of the elements of her visions. One that especially appeals to me is the cosmic egg depicting the womb of the Holy Mother. She accomplished all of this while an abbess managing a convent.

One of her biographers, Barbara Newman, says that Hildegard was the first Christian to develop a theology focused on the divine feminine aspect of God depicted as Mother Earth. According to Mirabai Starr she got away with this heretical worship of Mother Earth by describing this feminine face of God through the lens of Mother Mary and Mother Sophia. Hildegard wrote:

> I saw three ways to look at the Motherhood of God. The first is that she created our human nature. The second is that she took our human nature upon herself, which is where the motherhood of grace begins. And the third is motherhood in action, in which she spreads herself throughout all that is, penetrating everything with grace, extending to the fullest length and breadth, height and depth. All One Love.[20]

There are two additional women mystics who spoke directly to my heart for their compassion and understanding of women as spiritual beings: Julian of Norwich wrote about the Mother expression of God, and Thecla, who lived during the time of the early Christian church, saved herself over and over again.

### *Julian of Norwich*

Julian of Norwich lived during the socially turbulent times of the plague. We do not know her real name nor do we know much about her life before she started writing her spiritual visions and truths at age 31. She wrote her *Showings* inside the Church of St Julian in the town of Norwich, England. She never left the safety of its walls, and hence received the name she is known by today. Julian survived three rounds of the plague. The third time, she had a vision of Jesus dying on the cross and he gave her a series of teachings. She was filled with compassion for the suffering of all humanity and a burning desire to be united with God. As soon as she was well enough, she began recording and expanding on the teachings she received. The rest of her life was dedicated to prayer and explaining Jesus's teachings.

What is so remarkable about Julian was her unshakable belief in an all-loving God despite the plague and the continual suffering of humanity. Her *Showings* spoke of a compassionate God, not a wrathful God who would punish sinners with the plague. Her *Showings* are as relevant today as in the thirteenth and fourteenth centuries, especially considering the coronavirus pandemic. Julian taught God is One and his presence is in absolutely everything. Julian's God showed her his vast and unending love for all of humanity.

Julian wrote her *Showings* during a time when the patriarchal Catholic church was a powerful political, governing and cultural institution that preached God the Father; suppressed women and any feminine expression of the divine; warned men to not succumb to women's sexuality unless to impregnate; and saw women as created below men. Nonetheless, Julian wrote about the Mother face of God. I am amazed she got away with it. It is extraordinary even today:

> And so, we have our being in our Father, Almighty God. We have our restoration and our redeeming in our Mother of Mercy, in whom all our attributes are reconciled and transformed into the perfect human being. And we are completed and made whole through the gifts of grace of the Holy Spirit. Our essence lies in our Father, God-All-Power. Our essence lies in our Mother, God-All-Wisdom. Our essence lies in our Master, the Holy Spirit, God-All-Goodness. Our essence dwells in totality within each Person of the Trinity, which is One God.
>
> And so, Christ Jesus, who does good over evil, is our true Mother. He is the source of all motherhood, and we have our being from him, protected by all the sweet love that endlessly accompanies motherhood. As truly as God is our Father, just as truly God is our Mother. She demonstrates this most clearly when she says, It is I.[21]

I was at first confused when reading Julian's reference to Jesus as the Mother. Then I remembered Jesus is the personification of the Divine Mother's love expressed in a masculine body. This is so important for our awakening because Jesus is a glowing example of a man with balanced feminine and masculine energies.

No words can describe the feelings of wonder, thanksgiving, and gratitude I feel as I read these words. I overflow with the grace of the Holy Mother kept alive through Julian who remains a beacon of the all-loving Mother's pure light even today. I like to imagine Julian believing that the love for God aflame within her as she writes these teachings from Jesus will continue to influence generations of people. I believe her eternal soul is watching over earth even now, blessing us and cheering for us as humanity embraces the Holy Mother and awakens to create Nova Earth.

### *Thecla Who Saves Herself Over and Over Again*

A theme of this book is loving and forgiving yourself in order to save yourself. In so doing we expand this love to everyone. Many ancient and medieval women mystics personified this theme; however, the story of Thecla especially resonates in my heart. I knew nothing about Thecla until I read her story in *Mary Magdalene Revealed* by Meggan Watterson, so I did some research. Thecla's story verges into myth holding divine truths.

Thecla is a Saint of the early Christian Church, even though the church fathers tried to discredit her and remove any written mention of her life. Thecla's story is intertwined with the story of Paul the Apostle in *The Acts of Paul and Thecla*. They both lived in the second century during the turbulent times of the early Christian church in which the followers of Jesus' teachings continued to be persecuted. The doctrines of Christianity had yet to be fully formed, therefore women continued to hold positions within the church. A few of these women's names have survived, but we know little about them, as the written information was systematically destroyed. Thecla's success spreading the word of the Gospel demonstrates one woman with a high and powerful position within the Christian faith. Thecla also urged women to withhold sex from their husbands and live chaste lives.

One can easily understand why *The Acts of Paul and Thecla* were ordered destroyed by the church fathers in the fourth century. Tertullian, 155-240 AD, is called the father of Latin Christianity and early church doctrine. To discredit *The Acts of Paul and Thecla,* he was strongly opposed to women preaching and baptizing. In an effort to eliminate women's role, *The Acts of Paul and Thecla* came to be considered an apocryphal story of early Christianity. Nevertheless, Thecla is still venerated in the Oriental and Eastern Orthodox Churches, the Catholic and Episcopalian Churches, and in Coptic Christianity.

Paul the Apostle became a wandering preacher of Christian teachings after Jesus appeared to him in a vision. When Paul visited Thecla's village Konya of Iconium in Turkey she was a young noble woman engaged to be married. For 3 days from her window, she listened to Paul's teachings in the town's square about worshipping only one God and embracing chastity, a condition barely beginning to gain favor with the church fathers. Paul's teachings of chastity were extreme and probably did not consider how this affected women. Claiming her body for herself rather than to serve her husband's sexual needs was a radical idea that caught Thecla's imagination.

Transformed by Paul's teachings, she vowed to leave her fiancé and follow Paul. The appalled fiancé reported Paul to the authorities and he was arrested. Undeterred, Thecla visited Paul in jail to continue listening to his preaching. Her fiancé and the authorities were outraged, and had Paul whipped and thrown out of town. Thecla, as a woman, received more severe punishment. She was stripped and tied to a stake to be burned.

Yet she maintained her strong faith in God, and just as the fire was about to consume her, a heavy rain squelched the flames.

Thecla followed Paul to Antioch, where Alexander the King of Syria desired her to be his wife. When she refused, he tried to rape her. Thecla fought him off, tore his cloak and knocked off his coronet. Brought to court for assaulting Alexander, she was sentenced to death in the stadium. Again stripped and with hands bound, she was led into the arena to be eaten by wild beasts. And again, she was saved when a lioness felt her love and faith, and thus turned on the other beasts to protect Thecla. The women in the crowd, who were initially against Thecla, screamed for her release as they proclaimed her innocence. Thecla jumped into a pit of water in the stadium filled with wild sea lions where she baptized herself in the name of Jesus Christ, and saved herself with the love she felt from her union with God.

Thecla continued to travel with Paul, but eventually left to pursue her own ministry of preaching, teaching, healing and baptizing all—without the oversight of a man—until she died at age 90. Throughout her long life she was persecuted for her faith, especially because it implied that women had the equal spiritual authority with men. In one story, as she was preaching in a cave and is about to be caught by her persecutors, she asks God for help: a new passage in the cave opened, then closed after she escaped, her faith in God saving her. Meggan Watterson wrote:

> I think that the most threatening aspect of Thecla's story is that she frees herself from any illusions that power resides outside of her…She began to go against expectations of a girl, considered the inferior sex in her time. She began to do what her heart was telling her to do. And this was the sacrilege to those in power. That she refused to obey or validate any authority outside of her. Even, and ultimately, Paul's. She

baptized herself because she realized she could. She realized that all along within her she contained the power to save herself. And so, she did.[22]

### *Contemporary Women Mystics*

There are many contemporary women mystics, some known from their extraordinary lives, their art and their universal teachings like Mother Teresa. I've mentioned many in this book. If you are reading this book, you are probably a mystic and have likely encountered many mystics, both men and women, on your heroine's journey of the heart and womb. We continue to grow in number all over the world as we reclaim the sacred feminine and become whole again. There is a reason we chose to be a woman during this pivotal time of spiritual change. It is critical for women to dissolve the shackles of patriarchy, to fall in love with ourselves, and forgive ourselves for feeling victimized. We step into our divine power and radiate the Universal Mother's unconditional love for absolutely every person. We have to lead the way so men can forgive themselves for the suppression, denigration and domination of women. Only then will they welcome the feminine energy residing within and join with us to create Terra Nova. We are becoming the songs of our hearts. We learn truly that life is a song of love.

Surrendering to the Holy Mother Father's love flowing through everyone transforms every living thing and every object into the good, the holy and the beautiful. It unites all in Oneness so the metaphysical texts are no longer needed as we become fully human and fully divine. Surrendering is usually joined with a burning desire for the sacred, dying to the false sense of self that is the separated ego. Women mystics have been tortured, crucified and burned at the stake for their heresy before a patriarchal god. We have deep within our carbon-based DNA a fear of fire, even while holding this yearning to throw all we know as false into the cleansing healing flames of the Divine Mother.

# As Within So Without Meditations

## The Gift of a Question

*She remembers who she is and sets herself free.*

These "as within so without" meditations occur after every movement. If you need to refresh your memory about what is involved in these meditations, please re-read this section in Movement One.

Please start with the two following questions before beginning your inquiry process then read the additional questions. Try to write down whatever arises without judgment or editing what you don't like. Most importantly ask your guides/light family to help with your inquiry work.

For this movement, I offer quotes for contemplation and end with a final question.

Can I love myself enough to forgive myself?
Can I forgive myself enough to love myself?

### *Additional Quotes and Questions*

The thought system of the truth realizes that the external world is but a reflection of the internal world.[23]

Do you believe this idea and if so, why do you believe it? Or, if you don't believe it what do you believe?

All will be well and all will be well and every kind of thing shall be well.
Julian of Norwich

Do you believe "all will be well?" If not, what do you believe?

Do you believe that you are a contemporary mystic on a heroine's journey of the heart and womb?

If yes, what resonates the most about the women mystics described in this movement that can help you on your journey?

If no, what is preventing you from claiming you are a modern-day mystic?

Do you find any inspiration from the women mystics described in this movement?

Return to the first two questions about loving and forgiving yourself.

This is the final surrender.

# Movement Three

# I Am Lilith, Hear My Song

## Chapter One

# Lilith and Sexuality

Our sexuality is just that: ours. It is our own. Our sexuality is the way in which we experience our environment—the heightened sense of awareness that stems from opening to the sensual experience. We have been given so many ways to experience the sensual world around us, our senses each possessing their own unique signature. To smell, to feel, to taste, to touch, to see—so many ways to consume beauty.
Theresa C Dintino, *Welcoming Lilith, Awakening and Welcoming Pure Female Powers*

Literally the last thing I wanted to write about was sexuality! So naturally it has become an integral part of this story. One that I needed to see and write about in order to complete and bring this book to wholeness. This is why Lilith announced herself to me. Not for the first time—however, this time I recognized her. I had plenty of lead up to this. Many signs appeared indicating I needed to pay attention to my acceptance and belief that a woman's sexuality is defined by man—that I'd swallowed his-story completely. I thought denial and rebellion was the answer. However, denial became the shadow Lilith—the myth that women's sexuality is solely reliant on being physically attractive and available to satisfy men's sexual needs. Therefore, I tried to throw out the idea that my sexuality and sensuality could be spiritual because how could it be spiritual if it is defined by patriarchal man? I sanitized it. Spirituality has nothing to do with my sexuality because my God Self is pure, untouched by a physical relationship with a man. While there is some truth in this, it is not the whole story.

Through some deep inquiry work I realized I was holding the following belief: to entertain the idea that sexuality could be sacred means succumbing to man's dominance and control. I became aware how this belief actually perpetuated what I was trying to reject. When I finally realized how convoluted this belief was, I began to see and feel differently. I opened to another possibility of sexual energy being the creative energy of the Universe. It has nothing to do with sexual intercourse. It can be felt during intercourse or not. As all of us know, enforced sexual intercourse is neither sexual nor spiritual.

The his-story myth also affects anyone who is not heterosexual, because everyone acts either in resistance, compliance or independent of the heterosexual man's cultural dominance. Simply stated, we are forced to define ourselves as someone who either is heterosexual or someone who is not. All of us react in accordance to the idea that people's sexuality is defined by how we perform in bed and conform to culturally established gender roles. More so for women than men, it is defined by how beautiful and sexually attractive we can still be, even in our elder years, hence the amount of time and money many women spend trying to look attractive and younger. There is no judgment here—I love beautiful clothes, use the anti-aging creams, and probably spend way too much money on my hair. With all my rebellion in rejecting this idea of women's sexuality as defined by man, I did not know I still held this belief in a very convoluted way. *Resistance does not heal a belief—it just shoves it into the shadow to fester, grow, and show up in unrecognizable ways.*

We accept, we deny, or we reject. We feel guilty or ashamed, we succumb or we rebel. What we are being called to do is re-define, to take back and claim the word sexuality as part of our physical and spiritual selves, to feel ourselves as sensual beings connected to Mother Gaia through our wombs, through the most intimate parts of our body. Seeing all creation as sexual frees women to be their wild sensuous selves connected to the primordial life-giving womb of the Cosmic Mother. *The patriarchal man is afraid of a woman's powerful sexuality that is independent of his presence, for they believe it means the end of their power and dominance.* What it does signal is the end of the false power of violence resulting from masculine energy devoid of feminine energy. It is the end of separation consciousness that for eons has used patriarchy to keep both men and women in the illusion that the sacred feminine needs to be repressed and controlled.

In contemporary times Lilith is considered to be the first feminist because she refused to be dominated by Adam. Embracing Lilith's story allows access to our pure divine feminine power. It frees us to look with clear-eyed determination where we have swallowed the belief that our sexuality is only accessed through relationship with another person, primarily a man. We do not have to submit to this. Lilith's story is our story, she lives within us. We are her in form. I love Lilith, for I am her and she is me. I also see in Lilith's story the entire his-story of humanity, which frees both men and women to return to our divinity. Hear my song of freedom for all.

## Lilith's Story, the Good, the Bad and the Ugly

There are many versions of Lilith's story creating the myth. Myth is more than a story—it sometimes contains a little history; however, it is the symbolism within the myth that points us to spiritual truths. There is her-story and there is his-story. Lilith's story is felt in our cells. We know there was a time when women and men existed equally in divine balance and harmony, when the Universal Mother was seen as the Creatrix of all life. Our connection with Mother Earth was fluid and in harmony with all her relations. We were in a continual state of co-creation with all life. This was when earth was called Eden. The story that survives in written form is the one shaped by his-story, which blames the fall from Eden on Lilith for leaving Adam and on

Eve for eating the apple of dualism. True to any myth, I imagine and give my own interpretation.

Lilith was Adam's first wife. Stop, I say to myself: wife? Wife and husband implies a marriage, which is a patriarchal construct. Already the myth is being formed according to his-story. Lilith was Adam's first female partner. They were created equally by the Divine Mother. They lived happily and peacefully in Eden for a long time. Then Adam started to feel he should be the one to rule—especially that Lilith should lie beneath him during intercourse. Lilith said no, and finally when she could not tolerate his behavior anymore, grew wings and left Adam to live near the Red Sea.

Because Adam complained so loudly about being left alone, God sent angels to Lilith to demand her return to Adam. She said she would not return unless Adam agreed to treat her as an equal. Her words had power because Lilith knew that God was both feminine and masculine, and therefore she was integral to creation. Because Lilith used the secret names of Elohim and Yahweh for the Mother Father God, the angels felt the truth and did not force her return. Adam continued to complain, so God punished Lilith by banning her permanently to the Red Sea. Then the Father God created a woman from Adam's rib called Eve, effectively relegating her to always be second and inferior to Adam. At first they were happy because Eve felt grateful to Adam for giving up one of his ribs. But then Lilith in the form of a snake convinced Eve to eat the apple, releasing dualism, guilt and shame into Eden. Women were blamed for humanity's fall from grace, anchoring the idea that women are naive and can't be trusted. At the same time women are evil and tricky like the snake version of Lilith.

Lilith's story is ancient and complex because it changes depending on the times and on several spiritual traditions. She is mentioned first in the Sumerian Epic of Gilgamesh, where she is called the maid of desolation. Lilith in Sumerian means "of the air." She is mentioned in many different ways and forms, including the ability to fly. Lilith became known for practicing witchcraft and consorting with demons. Some researchers believe she was the Dark Goddess of wind and storms.

It is easy to think the story of Lilith originated with the Sumerians because we have to rely on the written word, but we really don't know. There is evidence of the first woman from the Hittites, Egyptians, Greeks, Romans and then Europeans. With our gradual descent into separation consciousness, Lilith became associated with chaos, sexuality, magic, the occult, and yes, vampires. The purpose of these stories was to discredit Lilith as the first female by demonstrating she was the patriarchal god's massive mistake.

The various faces of Lilith which describe the gradual subjugation of the divine feminine primarily come from the Jewish tradition which influenced the Christian tradition. She is mentioned briefly in the Torah and Talmud as a demon to be feared by men because she could suck their sexual vitality dry. This gave rise to the legend depicting Lilith as a succubus or a vampire. This is an effort to reduce her to a dangerous sexual being, one not deserving to be Adam's wife.

The Jewish Midrash is a collection of commentaries written over time by Rabbis on various subjects to explore Biblical theology. Lilith is described as Adam's first wife, before Eve. Speculation is that the Midrash was trying to explain why there are two creation stories in the book of Genesis. One story drew from the Hebrew tradition describing many faces of God which are both feminine and masculine. The name Elohim is usually considered the feminine side of God and partnered with the male Yahweh. In the English translation of the Bible, Elohim is referred to as He. My feeling is that this was an effort to dismiss Elohim as the Holy Mother aspect of God. Nevertheless, the first Genesis story said Elohim created male and female in the image of God. It is interesting that we can still find instances in ancient texts where the Divine Mother's creative force was known. This story of Lilith contradicts the second story of creation in the Bible that describes God creating Adam first and then creating Eve by removing one of his ribs.

The story of Lilith refusing to be dominated by Adam and banned to the Red Sea is told in the Midrash. The Red Sea is significant because it is shaped like a vulva and is red, which is associated with blood, birth and creation. Through much of his-story, women were banned while menstruating and giving birth because our blood was seen as impure. This was a blessing in disguise, as banning created the opportunity for young women and new mothers to be enfolded within the wisdom of older more experienced women. *The Red Tent* by Anita Diamant is a beautiful story imagining the strength of Jewish women gathered in the red tent of menstruation and birth. Because of this, they were able to hold onto the worship and mysteries of the Goddess. We lost this support in contemporary times as our wombs in the birthing process came under the control of men and modern medicine. Our wombs are still being fought over, with the focus on birth control and abortion, in an attempt to control what men can never do.

The story continues in the Midrash that says Lilith was so enraged by being replaced by Eve, she birthed demon babies. She also vowed to kill any children of Adam and Eve. God again sent the three angels to Lilith and they start killing her babies while she killed Adam and Eve's babies. Eventually there was a truce allowing some of Lilith's children to live when she agreed to only kill the children of Adam and Eve who do not accept the Father God. With their story, the male rabbis have successfully made Lilith into a rage-filled, demon-making, sexual monster. And their Lilith becomes complicit in repressing and destroying the feminine expression of God. This becomes an effective cautionary tale to shackle women's independence and feelings of equality with men to becoming sexual slaves.

At some point in all the stories, Lilith returns to God and takes her rightful place as Shekinah, the indwelling presence of the divine feminine. Because she has been exiled during the week, at every Shabbat ceremony, she is called to return home. This kindles the remembrance of the Holy Mother's all-encompassing unconditional love. Yet I wonder why she keeps being exiled and for what purpose. Are the weekdays so filled with the business of man that we can't afford to reside in unconditional love's compassion except for one day a week? Is one day all men can handle before being consumed by the sacred feminine that unleashes women's spiritual independence which dissolves their control? What would this world look like if the Holy Mother aspect of God returned permanently?

## Lilith's Story Symbolizes Her-Story Within the His-Story of Humanity

The Universal Mother births all beings from her primordial dark womb as equal divine sovereign beings endowed with her creative abilities. The Universal Father gifts them with clarity, discernment, purpose and the ability to manifest creations. There was a time on earth, which we now call the Garden of Eden, when the two-legged, four-legged, winged, the finned, those that skitter and glide, the green and the flowing all lived in harmony. We can describe the communities or tribes of people as matrifocal with women and men existing as equals worshipping the Holy Mother and honoring both the sacred feminine and masculine that resides within. Women were leaders and healers. Their power came from their connection to Mother Earth, from birth and creation. There was no hierarchal government, for the interconnectedness of all life was embraced and known within. All decisions were made in accordance to one's divine knowing of abundance and well-being for everyone. Women's essence was the primordial Mother's creative power, and men's essence was her heart.

Gradually there were signs of disharmony. The fall from grace into separation consciousness did not happen all at once. Perhaps women began to misuse their power by seeing men as inferior because only women had a direct connection to the Holy Mother through the birthing process. Perhaps this became a time of matriarchal rule. After years of this abuse, men started to rebel and destroy the symbols, icons and images of the Holy Mother. Archaeologists have found these shards and broken pieces and interpreted them in many ways, but primarily from the perspective of his-story. With violence men learned they could dominate women and demand submission to their authority and to their sexual needs.

In *The Sophia Code,* Sophia the Divine Mother Creatrix of all life explains that over the past 30,000 years she has been worshipped and held in secret through many mystical lineages. After the fall of Atlantis these lineages preserving the Holy Mother radiated out from Egypt to Tibet eventually stretching from India to France and from Avalon in Britain to the Americas. She says that humanity chose in our free will to explore patriarchal spiritual oppression for thousands of years which resulted in the suppression of the Divine Feminine.[24]

In the book *Unplugging the Patriarchy, a Mystical Journey into the Heart of a New Age,* Lucia René writes that women agreed to give away their feminine power. This agreement was made between men and women at the soul level. But why would we agree to this? Mary Magdalene, in *The Forbidden Female Speaks,* a text channeled by Pamela Kribbe, describes the cosmic womb of wholeness and oneness from which each of us emerged as a soul. Essentially, we broke free from the cocoon of the womb, which caused primordial trauma.

> Your male aspect was the adventurous, progressive aspect of you that initiated your birth. It wanted to experience and discover individuality. Your female aspect was the aspect of

> you that held back and wanted to remain connected to the One Source; it resisted letting go...
>
> Within the totality of the soul's journey, both aspects provide an equally important contribution: the male desire for freedom and individuality and the female longing for transcendence and unity. These are the two essential poles that make the creation of the universe possible; both are necessary...
>
> But the female energy was wounded by the cosmic birth trauma and the male energy went too far in its self-directed separateness, losing touch with Source. The male and female energies became estranged from each other. This estrangement ultimately resulted in the battle of the sexes.[25]

It feels as if this is creation gone wrong. It feels as if it went monumentally astray. Yet the Beloved Infinite Intelligence knows and embraces all potentialities. We are in a time of massive transformation which is propelling both men and women to embrace and balance our heart-centered feminine and masculine energies. Women are dissolving our womb wound and men are dissolving their heart wound as all of us ascend into our hearts. This ignites our sovereign divine power in ways never before experienced.

When I read about our agreement at the soul level to give away our power, it resonated in my place of truth. However, at first it felt contradictory to my knowing the abuse men endured when matrifocal times fell into matriarchy. As I dug deeper, I realized of course there was a gradual descent into patriarchy which women played a role in instigating in order for all of us to plumb the depths of the abuse of power-over in order to experience and learn how energy works. This created the opportunity for men to choose ascension into the heart, learning how to lead with the power of love. Women experienced what happens when playing the victim. This also created an opportunity for understanding our sovereign-based power in a new way. This is the gift of patriarchy: learning to become a pure channel of the Cosmic Mother's loving energy in service to all of humanity in ways never expressed before.

Lilith and Eve are female prototypes for birthing the new humans. As we slipped into separation and patriarchy their story turned into his-story to justify the subjugation of women. The his-story of Lilith and Eve effectively consigned women to three roles: rebel, whore and obedient woman. Lilith plays the role of rebel and then whore, while Eve plays the role of obedient woman. In her weakness she allows the serpent as Lilith to convince her to betray Adam and thus orchestrates our fall from grace. This distorted version of the myth effectively puts the blame for all life's problems on women.

The Rabbis in the Midrash, in an attempt to re-create the Lilith myth for their own political religious gains, spread the story that the truce between Lilith and God included Lilith agreeing to kill any offspring of Adam who did not worship the Father God. In return, God would let some of her children live. We can guess most of the children killed were female. Lilith is often seen as the savior of stillborn babies because she understands what it means to lose her children. This appears to set the stage for continual religious holy wars which again can all be blamed on Lilith—God's mistake for creating a woman equal to man and Eve for destroying the garden of Eden.

Women's sexual energy is seen as destructive, to be feared and contained. At the same time if women obey and deny their sexual nature, we can be seen as pure and worthy of a man's love. What a stranglehold this puts on both men and women. The patriarchal church believes the only way for man to ascend is to deny the body and their sexual urges. Therefore, Lilith had to become a sexual temptress, allowing men to blame women for their own sexual desires. This plays out with the early Christian Church fathers' story of Mother Mary as a virgin birthing

Yeshua. She could remain pure without the taint of being sexually active with a man. This is why Mary Magdalene had to become a whore and Yeshua had to remain unmarried. Those touched by God have to be pure, free of sexual urges caused by women's temptress bodies. The Catholic Church eventually required celibacy for their priests and monks to reinforce the sinfulness of women as a barrier to ascension.

Women cannot go to heaven; we are the vessel of sinful sexuality. When women try to remain pure in a man's eyes, once she has sex with a man, she loses this purity and once again is seen as a temptress and damned. If women stay true to their wild independent nature, we are called witches, the devil's spawn, dirty, unclean—hunted down to be killed or punished. Patriarchal religion can't kill all women for we are needed for procreation. However, we can be damned for eternity.

Women over time became buttoned down, virtuous, denying their sexuality, their sensuousness and their connection to mother earth. The pinnacle of this was the Victorian era when we were corseted, caged and covered entirely in voluminous dresses to conceal our dangerous sexual bodies lest some man become unhinged and succumb to his baser sexual desires. In some cultures, women still remain veiled and hidden. We are still struggling with the prevalent view that men are not responsible for any sexual interaction with a woman—including rape, that it is always the woman's fault.

As the world succumbed to patriarchal structure and values, women retained their knowledge of the Universal Mother even as religions and governments tried to obliterate this knowledge. The worship of the Goddess did not die easily or quickly nor was it ever fully extinguished. Eventually humanity has been left with Lilith's story of women's spiritual equality. We can't pin point the origins of Lilith. As noted, she shows up in many cultures, religions and lands. Lilith calls us to remember a time when the Holy Mother was acknowledged as the Creatrix of all life containing the Holy Father aspect of God. The sacred feminine has been repressed but not forgotten because there is no way to extinguish the Universal Mother's love.

We hold this ancestral and karmic memory in our cells. The sacred feminine has risen out of the shadows, out of the depths of our souls, to return to her rightful place as the Creatrix of all. But like Lilith, part of this healing process is to feel the rage of having our sexuality defined by man. The patriarchal god, devoid of the Divine Mother's balance, exiled Lilith because of the physical reminder of the Holy Mother. Lilith feels betrayed by a god that is not hers and misunderstood. What she knows to be true is being systematically degraded and repressed. We grieve, forgive and rise like the phoenix, reborn as divine sovereign beings. Embodying the rage so it can be released is understandable and necessary to let go of victimhood

There have always been women throughout his-story who retained Lilith's strong, independent, powerful sexual nature with a knowingness of the sacred feminine in balance with the sacred masculine. They pop up occasionally, and many remain unknown and forgotten having existed in the shadows and thus remain hidden. The majority were hunted down, persecuted and killed. There have also been some men who understood the loving creative power of the divine feminine but were despised, ridiculed and killed for their awareness. I imagine these are Lilith's children and her offspring. We are her legacy. And somehow through all the stories and attempts to discredit Lilith she emerges as the Shekinah, repressed and in exile most of the time, but not forgotten entirely.

## Chapter Two

# Lessons from Lilith

As first woman, there are many aspects of Lilith reflected in all women. Lilith knows her truth as a divine sovereign being, then is tested as she experiences all of what it means to be a woman in a patriarchal world. Lilith is an equal partner with Adam then separated and conceived parthenogenetically. She is a black woman, a sexual woman, a raging woman, a shadow woman, a witch who uses magic, a woman of power out of exile and a Goddess of the air and night.

### Lilith as First Woman Is the Black Goddess of Air and Night

When Lilith's presence was felt by me, I loved the idea of the first woman being a rebel, strong and independent, filled with the grace of the Universal Mother. So I researched Lilith online and read some books about her. I got lost in all the interpretations, especially sifting through the black goddess stories linked to the dark demon stories. This is what I know: all human beings are birthed from the primordial black womb of the Cosmic Mother. This is a place of safety, unconditional love, warmth and nurturing. Most human babies are safe in the darkness of their mother's nurturing womb. Black is the color of woman's power. Menses is linked to the cycles of the moon and, as noted, black is a maternal color. So, black is the color of creation.

The genomics studies and research into the origin of man has revealed through DNA analysis that human beings first appeared in Africa. Therefore, it seems to me that Lilith as the first woman had dark skin. Science has proven that we are a mixture of genes no matter our skin color. The wide diversity of human beings is shown through our DNA.

This is important on so many levels because in his-story, women learned to fear the night and the color black. We were taught the dark of night was dangerous, full of predators such as demons or violent men. Men learned to fear the night and the color black associated with women's temptress sexual power-over men. The stories started with Lilith as a demon, a person of the dark, which is to be feared. The Dark Goddess became evil. I feel within my bones that the systematic repression of the sacred feminine is related to patriarchal man's fear of the power of women's sexual strength in the dark.

There are many people from many nations that have dark skin. There is no way to know whether or not the color of Lilith's skin had anything to do with his-story's attempts to discredit her as first woman. However, I do believe every attempt has been made by patriarchal Christian church fathers in relatively recent times to white-wash Adam, Lilith, Eve, Yeshua, Mary Magdalene and Mother Mary into people with white skin, even though they came from the Middle East where people had darker skin.

It is vitally important for me as a white woman to acknowledge and honor Lilith as a woman from Africa. People of color have been and are still being victimized by the systemic propaganda to make the color black and all its variations into something less than human and to be feared. There have always been wise and strong women of color, and more and more women of color are coming forward in their power, strength and abiding fierce love for all of humanity. Their sovereign power is being heard and it uplifts women of all colors.

Realizing all people started in Africa and that everyone's DNA is a diverse mixture of ethnicities means there is no meaning to the idea that one can be categorized as either better than or purer than another person, based on skin color. Everyone is a mixture of genes, there is no pure person, whatever that means. Race is not real. Yet, with all our attempts to colonize women and black, indigenous, people of color (BIPOC), racism became part of separation consciousness.

## Lilith's Spirit Animals

There are two spirit animals associated with Lilith—the Owl and the Snake. When owl and snake are used to paint Lilith as a demon goddess, we can feel his-story's attempt to discredit Lilith's power and the power of all Mother Gaia's living creatures. When we free Lilith from the fog of separation consciousness, we feel the power of the spiritual medicine of Owl and Snake. Both are well-known symbols of the divine feminine. Sometimes Lilith is depicted as an owl, because she grew wings to fly away from Adam. The negative stories depict her as a screech owl—wild, untamed and harmful. Sometimes Lilith is depicted as a snake, devious and evil.

Lilith as a snake comes to Eve and convinces her to bite into the forbidden apple. During matrifocal times, fruit from the Divine Mother's tree of life was encouraged to expand consciousness. Patriarchy's continued existence depended on capping spiritual consciousness, thus the apple from the tree of life became the forbidden fruit. Many use the symbol of the tree of life being buried upside down to illustrate the burying of the feminine divine. Our roots, without the moist, enriching soil of earth, shrivel and die and our branches of growth are smothered and can't breathe.

Lilith with the spirit medicine of the Owl becomes the Goddess of the Air and the Night. Owl sees clearly in the dark of night. Mother Owl with her penetrating gaze sees through the veil of separation. Owl is at home with the darkness of night. She is a silent and effective hunter. Lilith has the power to fly and be free, to take care of herself, to save herself and her children, and to survive. In many cultures Owl is the symbol for wisdom. She can see what others cannot see. Lilith as the first wise woman is not deceived by the patriarchal god and Adam's need to be in control. Her keen vision and insights reveal the ulterior motives of Adam and his patriarchal god. Lilith holds clearly the truth of the sacred feminine and women's sexual energy to create. She knows and holds in her heart the Holy Mother face of God, for she was created in her image.

Snake spirit medicine is extremely powerful because it is the power of creation, sexuality, reproduction, ascension and immortality. Lilith is an embodiment of snake medicine. Lilith is strong with kundalini energy, which is symbolized by the snake emerging from the root chakra and wrapping around the spine to strengthen our energy. Under patriarchy we came to fear snakes because they were associated with the Mother Goddess. They came to be seen as evil, treacherous, slimy and harmful. At times we fear with good reason, for the poison from some snakes can be deadly. However, snakes' poison is the medicine of transmutation. We are in the process of shedding our skins and transmuting the false poison of separation consciousness into rebirth as divine human beings.

The power of Owl and Snake medicine within Lilith explains why Lilith speaks to me and other contemporary women so strongly. Even when I did not know her story, I knew her. I felt her within the depths of my heart womb. And now that I know her story, I feel her embodiment within me.

## Lilith as a Sexual Woman and the First Mom

Sexuality or sexual energy is the powerful life force of creation. It is innocent, and it is divine. Nevertheless, the words erotic, penetration, orgasm, bliss, joining and sensuous have been tainted by their association with sexual intercourse. When used to describe the act of joining with all Mother Gaia's creatures, these words can feel demeaning. We need to free the words and our wombs from the patriarchal definition of woman's sexuality. We receive the cosmic sexual energy of the universe through our wombs. We receive our life force from the womb of Mother Earth through the cervical gateway to our wombs. We experience this spiritual creativity as blissful, orgasmic and sensuous. Let go off the distorted meaning of sexuality influenced by our old patriarchal paradigm. Own your creative life force and allow yourself to feel the bliss that results. Reclaim your womb of creation. No longer do we have to bow to the cutting and slashing of our vulvas, whether literally or through words. When we free ourselves, we also free men from this limited destructive perspective.

Lilith as first woman is sexual. Her strength comes from embodiment of Mother Earth. She feels this union in every cell of her body. All of the Divine Mother's creations are felt deeply within her body: the seasons, the planting of seeds and emerging life, the majestic mountains, flowing rivers, vast oceans, the miracle of desert life and the waning and waxing of the moon in her own cyclical menses. This traditional chant from women's earth-centered Goddess circles says it beautifully:

*Earth my body*
*Water my blood*
*Air my breath*
*Fire my spirit.*

His-story has attempted to sever our physical connection to the earth which has led to denial and often disgust with our own bodies. Contemporary women are beginning to return to this sacred connection with Mother Earth—to rise up and claim our sexuality with words that used to only refer to sexual intercourse. Lilith reminds us of our Oneness with Mother Gaia. She asks us to embody our sexual energy in order to reclaim our power. Reducing sexuality to a single physical act of male penetration has harmed both men and women, no matter our sexual orientation, to dependency on another to fill our sexual desires for wholeness.

It is vitally important to remember that God the Beloved is genderless, embodying both masculine and feminine resonance. The Source Light of Love has no attributes. When we created this dream of separation, we split God in two, the Holy Mother and the Holy Father and we split ourselves in two, male and female. Gender identity was born with this attempt to separate the feminine creative, nurturing, compassionate life source from God. Simply explained, women were given the heart and men were given the mind, effectively creating a situation in which no one remained whole. All our incarnations on earth are the process of returning to wholeness and Oneness with God—who does not recognize gender differences.

I continue to use the words Divine Mother and the sacred feminine in writing about God in order to remind us of the imbalance we created and still create when only the Father face of God is worshipped. *Language has power to shape perceptions and beliefs.* All language is of the past, and reflects the patriarchal social, religious and governing systems. All the names used to describe the feminine person are constant reminders of our second-class relationship with man. It is wo-man, wo-men, fe-male, hu-man-ity and hu-man-kind. Sometimes a word's definition has to be freed in order to free ourselves. This is true for Father God as well as sexuality.

We are in a pivotal time when the sacred feminine has risen to return us to balance by freeing both the fractured masculine and feminine energies. We are creating Terra Nova in which the current damaging definitions of masculine and feminine will have no meaning and will thus disappear. With thoughtful and loving inner questioning, we can see how the words we use create our perceptions and beliefs, especially when it comes to sexuality. When sexual energy is only felt through the body, it reinforces the separated ego's use of the body to maintain its existence. When we free sexuality from the body we return it to its divine innocence and thus free consciousness to express the powerful creative impulses of the soul. *Paradoxically, with sexual energy returned to its divine innocence, we can then re-embody this innocence into balanced heart-based feminine and masculine power.*

Women in their embodied power of sexual innocence will no longer feel compelled to use their sexuality to seek co-dependent relationships with men in order to feel whole and safe. This frees men to also release their dependency on women to fulfill their sexual cravings to possess women's womb of creative power. Reclaiming their own sacred feminine energy and creative power can never be accomplished through sexual intercourse and possessiveness nor can be satisfied through control of another. We've been victims of many men's sexual cravings turning into force and violence. What can't be possessed must be destroyed.

Lilith as first woman knows her divinity and the innocence of her sexuality. She left Adam so as to not fall under the spell of the separated ego's specialness. Her body was hers, not Adam's. As first woman Lilith knew her divine innocence and thus the power of her creative energy. She never fell into forgetfulness as the stories imply. She is still the strong first woman owning her divine sovereign power. Lilith reminds us of our truth. Her story untarnished by his-story reminds us who we are.

Lilith as first Mom was able to birth children parthenogenically. She reminds us that the sexual life force of creation does not occur outside of us. There was an ancient time when women could birth children directly with the light force of their own creative energy. It is ironic that the early Christian Church Fathers supported this possibility with needing Mother Mary to remain pure of the taint of sexuality. However, they were certainly very clear that this was a one-time event to birth the one and only Christ child, Jesus. The myth that Lilith could birth children without the presence of man had to be destroyed or it would undermine the patriarchal church's power-over women and the masses.

With this time of dissolution of patriarchal conditioning we are transitioning into the creation of Terra Nova within the fifth dimension. Many of the children that have already arrived or are incarnating now, not only are free of past karma but some are also free of gender conditioning. They are exploring and calling themselves by many different labels: nonbinary, gender fluid, bi-sexual, pan-sexual, omnisexual, polysexual, transsexual, asexual, transgender and gender neutral. It is helpful to think of identity labels on a continuum rather than an either-or situation: sex, gender identity, gender expression and sexual orientation.

I listened to many videos of young people and talked to people who define themselves outside of the traditional heterosexual and homosexual gender expressions. I feel grateful for these pioneers sent to free us from the box of gender and sexuality defined by two gender identities. What I hear over and over again is the desire to be free, to be whoever they want to be without the confines of gender identity or sexual orientation. This allows for individual expression without needing to categorize themselves or other people. More and more they are demonstrating that personal relationships can happen through emotional connection first, without the constant pressure to perform physically. There is also this intuitive knowing of having both masculine and feminine qualities. We are all Lilith's children.

Young people with their different expressions of self are feeling their way, having to endure a tremendous amount of misunderstanding and prejudice. They are trying to explain and describe who they are, hence the myriad of different labels. Many of us in traditional gender roles are being challenged to free our perceptions and fear of the unknown. As a heterosexual woman who has felt confined by my sexuality being defined by sexual relations with a man, I feel a tremendous amount of my own freedom to see myself whole. I believe these young people are part of the transition into Terra Nova when gender and physical sexuality, as currently defined, will have no meaning. There will no longer be a need for labels. People will become fully human and fully divine, with no defined gender roles as we become one with our Beloved Source that knows no gender. Sexuality will be felt by all as the creative life force of the universe. Everyone will have the ability to give birth, create and manifest with the life force of their own divine energy.

Lilith as first woman and Adam as first man was the beginning of two separate gender roles. We entered a time when we wanted to experience what this would be like. We existed in harmony for a while, until the gradual fall into separation consciousness. Lilith's story as first Mom reminds us always of the birthing power of the sacred feminine. Without this reminder, we would not be where we are today with many young people embodying both the masculine and feminine energies in wonderful ways of expression.

## Lilith as Shadow Woman of Grief and Anger

Grief and anger often go hand in hand. Given how Lilith was treated by the patriarchal father god, it is easy to imagine her anger. She is grieving because the Holy Mother expression of God which is her very Self is being dismantled, repressed, defiled, abused and erased. I can imagine the depths of her grieving as she feels herself being torn into little pieces. She is being called into the depths of her being to let die all which no longer serves her. And in these depths, she rebirths herself. In this cauldron of grief and anger, Lilith begins to remember she also has the pure masculine expression of God within her. She learns to harness the penetrating clarity and allegiance to the truth of her masculine energy as she's reborn into an unstoppable loving force of the Universe. She forgives and saves herself. Lilith is being reborn in women all over the world.

The his-story of Lilith describes a raging Lilith killing babies. This justifies making her into an insane demon woman needing to be controlled and eliminated. How could a loving mother ever kill children? She would not! But the powerful feminine mother aspect of God had to be discredited and suppressed to justify men's treatment of women. This is an outrage I can feel deep within the shadow place where I was taught to shove my anger. I feel this outrage every time any child is harmed.

Most of us have been taught to never show anger because it's unladylike. We are expected to swallow and remain silent if abused or raped, or taken advantage of by men in all the ways they can. When I was in high school, I remember my cousin's boyfriend asking why women get so upset about being raped—they should just lie back and enjoy it. I felt outrage, yet kept silent. I had learned protesting too much meant being dismissed. All the subtle aggressive ways men retain their superiority and control start to multiply over time, until we have a dense ball of unresolved and often unrecognized anger buried deep within us. It often erupts in unhealthy and toxic ways. Unrecognized anger can eventually turn into rage, self-hatred and disease.

Besides the fear of violent angry men, not being able to feel or express our own grief and anger can lead to fearing other people's anger, including: women, friends and family. Not being able to grieve the loss of our wild feminine life force can leave us powerless. Using the metaphor of the labyrinth as our spiritual journey, we remain stuck in one of the folds unable to move forward as if we've stopped living. We feel unable to access our soul's divine spark. This is a barren place of no endings and no beginnings, until some crisis happens to jolt us into awareness.

Recognizing how we've suppressed our anger is usually the first step toward reclaiming our feminine soul and continuing our labyrinth's walk into the womb. As we fold in and out of our walk into the Divine Mother's womb, we grieve and cry healing, nourishing tears to wash ourselves clean and water the seeds of rebirth. Anger and grief when recognized, felt and accepted can then move us out of the dark recesses of our being into the light to be transmuted into the fierce love of the divine feminine. From this place of fierce love, we have the power to dissolve separation consciousness permanently. This is why patriarchal man does not want women to feel our anger: unconsciously they know the power we possess within. Paradoxically it is our anger transmuted into fierce love for all God's creations which will free men to heal their own anger, embrace their feminine energy, and access their own divine power free of patriarchal conditioning.

## Lilith as a Witch Who Burns and Uses Magic

Throughout her-story, "witches" have been wise women, midwives, shamans, medicine women and healers connected to the healing divine magic of Mother Earth. His-story turns them into beings to be feared, seen as instruments of the devil to be hunted and killed. We can see this happening with how words once used to describe powerful wise women over time became distorted. Crone, hag and witch have derogatory connotations. Crone originally meant the crowned one, hag meant the holy one and witch meant the wise one. Women who embrace pagan earth-centered spirituality have reclaimed these names for wise women. It is time for all of us to do so.

The magic associated with witches came to be feared because wise women as healers and midwives retained a direct connection to their own sacred healing powers in union with Mother Earth. With the repression of the feminine energy, people came to fear these powers as sinful, not sanctioned by the church. They forgot they also had the power to connect with the earth, so witches appeared to have powers no one else had. And these powers of the dark women's mysteries had to be erased because they threatened patriarchal systems of governance and control. Therefore, witches became women who worship the devil.

Many of us have read about the European witchcraft trials associated with the inquisition occurring during the Middle

Ages. These trials are described in the 1990 film *The Burning Times* directed by Donna Read and written by Erna Buffie. The number of women killed during these trials is unverified by his-story; however, it is believed to be around 9 million. It is a sign of the success of colonization that few people know about these horrific burning times, known as the woman's holocaust. If it is mentioned, it is dismissed as the imaginings of hysterical women who have no proof.

When I first saw the film at a midlife retreat for women at Ghost Ranch, I knew I'd been burned at the stake in one of my incarnations. It took all my effort to stay and watch. Some women were so physically upset, they left. Many women hold within our cells these karmic memories of being hunted, tortured and brutally killed through crucifixion, hanging or burning. Women started to distrust each other by turning in friends to the authorities lest they also be labeled a witch and burned. Patriarchal authorities feared groups of women because they knew the power of women together. Therefore, women's gatherings and friendships had to be destroyed.

How do we heal these memories and the intense trauma in our hearts and wombs? We let the memories rise, we feel, we rage, we love ourselves free and then we transmute into fierce love by embracing our burning power. In the book *Burning Woman*, Lucy Pearce explains this process through exploration of the Burning Woman archetype. She goes deep into the shadow fear and rage held by women about the systemic burning of wise women and how it symbolically continues even today. Pearce in her book transmutes the fear of burning into the burning passion of the divine feminine. Pearce says, "Burning Woman is she who is inflamed by her own direct connection to the Feminine life force. She who dares to follow her own vision, who speaks up and tells her own stories."[26] This describes Lilith, the first Burning Woman.

As we claim our burning wild passion for our divine sovereignty, we embody our Lilith within. We step out of the shackles of patriarchal repression and we stop playing the role of victim. We save ourselves by falling in love with our wild feminine energy as well as our protective masculine energy. We no longer have to fear our own feminine power. We burn with the unquenchable light within that is brighter than the brightest star. This is not the burn that hurts, but a sacred burning for our Beloved Mother which gently heals and can't be broken. This is also the powerful fierce love that burns and dissolves all of separation consciousness. We are our own sun.

## Lilith Is a Woman of Power Out of Exile

Lilith, as the Shekinah, is exiled during the week and is only welcomed back for one day. Now Lilith is permanently out of exile. The sacred feminine has risen. Compassion returns. The Holy Mother once again is in her rightful place as the Creatrix of all life containing the Holy Father. Lilith has risen to lead, to join and to teach. May both women and men welcome her, embrace her and become her in union with the Universal Mother God.

Even though I had a loving family, for most of my childhood I felt as if I did not belong here. As a child I could not articulate the wrongness. My way out of this uneasiness was a strange mixture of being the good girl, the one who is always kind and follows the rules, and by being silent because—nothing made sense. I can remember in grade school announcing to my horrified friends I was never going to get married and have children. It was my way of expressing that all was not right in this world with being a woman. This feeling faded as I became more and more acclimated to this world where women are considered less than men. My mother fed me books about independent, successful women. This seemed to be the answer to women's inequality with men. Go to college and graduate school. Have a career and strive to make a difference in the world and it would all eventually change. Only it didn't. Not until I answered the longing in my soul for the sacred feminine.

Now in my elder years I definitely feel as if I'm no longer in exile. The Lilith in me is no longer in exile. I no longer feel like a stranger in a strange land. I chose to be here. I chose to be a bright light in this world, to be here at this pivotal time in humanity's awakening. It has taken into my elder years to understand. However, as I look back on my life, I see how every experience was perfectly orchestrated for my awakening to bring me to this place, where I could write this book. All exists within divine timing.

## Chapter Three

# The Song of Lilith's Expression in Me

### Snake Medicine Within Me

While Lilith's story was always within me, I did not recognize her name or her voice. My spiritual sister Sajit Greene, who is a gifted astrologer, wrote in one of her newsletters how Lilith was currently strong astrologically, and she included her own Lilith story. I was so intrigued that I researched the story of Lilith which led to this chapter. This felt important at the soul level. That night I had a dream.

As often happens in my dreams, I'm wandering around in a huge enclosed space with lots of people, lost and confused. Rick is with me, but keeps morphing between himself and an unknown woman. I am searching for a healer or a doctor. When this feels fruitless, I feel an urgency to return to my car. I start running to it with the unknown woman and a large dog I've picked up along the way. We throw ourselves into the car with the dog going first, then the woman and then me. Too late I realize the dog has landed on a large snake, which turns its head and bites me in the left leg. I black out. The next I remember is waking up in a doctor's office and my leg has been treated. Protruding from the snake bite wound are several pencils of various sizes and colors pointing in many different directions. I admire it as I would an art object. I wake from the dream clueless to what it all means except for the transformational power of snake medicine.

Whenever I am unclear about a dream, I ask my God Self to help with interpretation. I am always reminded that every character in a dream is an aspect of self. I've had so many dreams start with being lost, confused and wandering around with lots of people in cavernous structures that I've come to recognize this is the separated state. Usually in each dream, something happens to dispel the confusion. Now instead of feeling panicked, I trust my inner guidance.

Once again, I'm wandering around confused and trying to figure out what I'm doing. With Spirit's help I realize that Rick morphing between himself and an unknown woman shows my masculine and feminine energies merging and balancing. This is encouraging. The dog's appearance in the dream felt unusual. I looked up dog's spirit medicine in my medicine cards and, while I already knew dog's medicine is about loyalty, I was able to understand at a deeper level. Dog is the medicine of allegiance to Self. Spirit showed that dog is an aspect of my divine masculine energy. Dog is a loyal friend, a gentle guardian and protector of the divine feminine energy. Dog going into the car first was the masculine energy protecting, supporting and grounding the feminine energy. When I pushed the unknown woman into the car before me, I was protecting the fledgling masculine and feminine reconciliation.

The snake in this dream was Lilith telling me to pay attention to strong rebirthing medicine. Snake appeared within the safety of my car, which is my inner temple. She was not there to harm, but to transmute the poison of patriarchy into rebirth. Dog went first as my loving friend who knew the snake had to bite me for my transformation. As a loving friend, my masculine energy knows all experiences are part of the plan of awakening. The unknown woman/Rick, as the blossoming marriage of masculine and feminine energies, represented one of the elements necessary for transfiguration. The car or my inner sanctum in this dream became the cauldron of divine alchemy transmuting into my sovereign divine power.

The snake bite was in my left leg, the physical feminine side which is becoming stronger. The pencils pointing in many different directions demonstrated I was to write about Lilith as a way to explore many different paths on my mystical path of transformation. The colored pencils reminded me of the rainbow bridge we are walking to Terra Nova in the fifth dimension showing me that there are many unique paths to Oneness. And because Lilith's story is about sexual energy, I knew writing about sexuality would be the medicine of transmutation. It was the part of me I least wanted to look at, so it was critical to bring this book, as me, into wholeness. I began to realize even more clearly that this book is writing me, rather than me writing the book.

Seeing every character of the dream as an aspect of self, I realized I was able to accept the car as my inner sanctum, the genderless woman, my personal self and the snake as parts of me, but not the dog. Why not, I finally asked my God Self. It was because the dog represented my masculine side. I've been accepting my feminine energy as naturally a part of me because I'm a woman. And because I felt I had no experience of heart-centered masculine energy, I just assumed all the wonderful positive energy was feminine. Though I finally was able to put descriptors to the divine masculine, I did not own it as part of me. How can reconciliation or union occur between the masculine and feminine if I still did not own it within? That question allowed me to see the fierce fiery energy of my masculine dragon as another symbol of snake medicine with the loyal, guardian energy of dog. Embodying my inner Lilith means embodying my divine masculine, claiming the masculine's penetrating light force of awareness and protection with the divine feminine primordial creative impulses of the womb.

Writing about Lilith has changed me in ways I could not have envisioned. This movement is being written during the great pause of the corona virus quarantine. I know within my heart that the Cosmic Mother is flooding earth with her loving energy. Humanity is in the cauldron of transformation with the virus-like snake poison as the alchemical catalyst of transmutation.

By writing this book I agreed to vibrate at the highest octave possible. My song of love is an important facet of humanity's transfiguration into our Christ Selves. This is not the time to play small, but a time to embrace my pure, innocent, balanced female power. It is time to own the Lilith within and allow her free rein.

I am feeling a freedom from the familiar worry of the past. Recently in the time between waking and sleep I received an image of myself on a barge loaded with boxes. The barge is tethered to a small yet valiant dove of love and peace, tirelessly flapping her wings to slowly pull the barge forward. No, I say—and I cut the rope restraining the dove's flight of freedom. I feel so much lighter, feeling the strength of Love's freedom from the woes of the world. All my financial worries for my family triggered by the COVID-19 quarantine dissipate. All the boxes of expectations and attachments I've been carrying around float away. All the stuff which had felt so important dissolves to the point that it is all neutral and has always been neutral. I see clearly how my thoughts create burdens. While the intensity of this awareness slips somewhat, I'm still left with this sense of freedom to own my divine sovereignty.

## The Owl as My First Spirit Guide

When I started working for the UU Urban Ministry I was introduced to guided meditation while on a work-related retreat. In meditation we were asked to visualize our ministry. This was the first time Mother Owl appeared to me.

Later when I was struggling with mothering an atypical child, I often used guided meditations to connect to my inner knowing. In a very powerful meditation, I visualized myself tethered to my son Tyler, aged seven. A very large Great Horned Mother Owl appeared and told Tyler he can ride on her back and they can fly together wherever he wants to go. Tyler is so excited, but cannot move because he is tied to me. I try so hard to untie the rope between us. He is too young; he needs me, I sob. I struggle until I finally find a knife and cut the rope. Tyler gleefully climbs on Mother Owl's back. I ask the owl if I may go with them, and she says No you are not ready yet to fly. Then the vision in the meditation ended. Releasing all my attachments and worries about Tyler took years, until I began to understand that I could not fly until I released Tyler to follow his own guidance.

In 2011 Rick and I moved to northern New Mexico. Tyler had just graduated from art college and was interning to be a tattoo artist. While I was on Facebook, I saw Tyler's post with a picture showing he'd shaved his head and tattooed it with a coiled snake. I thought I had let go of all my prejudices and misgivings about all of Tyler's tattoos, but when I saw a picture of Tyler with his head tattooed, I came unglued. How often will I do this? How often will I have to cut the ties that bind and narrow perceptions? Eventually I knew I had to meditate to calm and center myself.

During this meditation Mother Owl once again appeared, showing I still had a very small rope tied to him. This time it was much easier to cut the rope and free Tyler to follow his own path. Owl then said I was now ready, and I climbed on Owl's back and flew with abandonment and joy. A few days after this meditation, a great horned owl landed on our casita's roof in the middle of the night and hooted till Rick and I managed to come outside to see her. I was awed by her beauty and presence. We briefly gazed at each other and I silently thanked her, then she flew away. This was the first time I had ever seen a living owl. She has appeared several times over the years, always waking me with hooting in the middle of the night. Each time it coincides with needing to be reminded of my ability to see clearly through the dark veil of the separated ego. (I also appreciate the symbolism of the snake tattoo on Tyler's head. To him it means the power of protection and rebirth.)

The female owl is bigger than the male, so I knew my owl was a female. A few years ago, she showed up with her mate. We could hear them calling to each other, and then they both perched on the spiral staircase to the roof deck. I felt so incredibly blessed to receive the power of their combined feminine and masculine spirit medicine. When I started to write this part of Lilith's story, I realized it had been several years since I'd seen owl. That night she appeared, hooting till I woke and listened. I did not get up to go look for her. I was content to just listen to her song. Thank you for being with me all these years, I murmured. And she flew away.

Owl and snake are very much associated with the Goddess and the Shekinah that so strongly resides within me. After all these years, I see more clearly how I've been guided always to awaken and express the energy of Shekinah. The appearance of Lilith feels like an affirmation and acknowledgment of coming into my balanced feminine power expressed as the yang feminine, the burning woman and the Universal Grandmother. Lilith has become an essential part of my heart song. I hope Lilith also resonates and sings within you.

## Chapter Four

# Lilith's Legacy

### The Tantric Path

I am not a student of the way of Tantra. Although as I read *Kali Rising, Foundational Principles of Tantra for a Transforming Planet* by Rudolph Ballentine, I felt my writing was very much in flow with the metaphysical insights of Tantric philosophy. Tantra has existed over a thousand years and received influence from Buddhism, Hinduism, Sufism, Judaism and Christianity. It is about the relationship of humans with the ineffable, infinite and unknowable. It is about balance of opposites and personal transformation which directly affects humanity's evolution of consciousness.

In Western culture, it is Tantra's unique emphasis on the relationship between the masculine and feminine that has attracted the most attention. When I researched Tantra on the web, what predominantly came up was tantric sex. For this reason, I initially resisted the idea that Tantra needed to be included in this book. I came to realize the emphasis on tantric sex has most often missed the richness, complexity and integrating wholeness of the way of Tantra.

Tantra has the power to enlighten our understanding of sexuality as the interplay and dance of the masculine and feminine energies within us. It is a transformative way to understand the dynamics of this dance. It is much more than a method for having better sex with your partner. Liberating Tantra from this limited understanding is part of my liberation of sexuality from the distorted masculine's definition of physical relations with a woman.

Tantra involves the interplay and dialogue between Shiva and Shakti. It is a course of spiritual practices designed to attain

Unity with the Source Light of Creation. Shakti is the Hindu Goddess representing the energy, power and creative feminine life force of the universe. Shakti from Hinduism, Shekinah from Judaism and Sophia as the Holy Spirit from Christianity are all related to the primal creative, indwelling energy and wisdom of the divine feminine.

Shiva is the Hindu God representing the masculine principle of pure thought consciousness. Shiva as stillness is the static masculine yang principle and Shakti is the dynamic feminine yin principle within every person. Shiva is the logical thinking left side of the brain. Shakti is the creative inspirational right side of the brain. When expressed in bodies, the feminine is usually felt on the left side and the masculine is felt on the right side. (This changes if one is left-handed.) Infinite creation is the result of the joining of these two energies as shown in the yin yang symbol. Without Shakti, Shiva is powerless to create. Without Shiva, Shakti can become uncontrollably chaotic. Shakti as the primordial all-encompassing creative life force when joined with Shiva's directive pure light of consciousness brings creation into being and into form. Together they birth galaxies in multiple dimensions.

Men and women have both these energies within us. But separation has cut men off from their heart and feminine power—the creative force to manifest and give birth. And this has created a world in which violence and control are synonymous with power. We've become so used to the denial and suppression of our Shakti energy, that violence as power seems normal. But we all know deep within our souls the primal creative feminine force of Shakti is true power which does not harm. For women this creative untamed power is easier to access because we hold the intuitive nurturing yin feminine within us. When we access and reconcile with our masculine energies, we can transform to express our powerful yang feminine. Both are needed. This is why there are many Hindu Goddesses to reflect the many faces of the divine feminine.

The yang feminine is burning woman, the Universal Grandmother, the power of the feminine life force in action. The Goddess Kali Ma is the yang feminine. She has the power to cut down all the separated ego's structures and systems of governance that glorify violence as power. Patriarchal man has raped Mother Gaia and women's wombs in an effort to destroy what they believe they don't have, the energetic life-giving power to create from love. This is true power, for it is life-giving not life-destroying. Unfortunately, with the persistent devaluing of women, we've boxed men into believing accessing their shakti sacred feminine power of creation is not manly. It is for sissies. Hence big oil violently rapes the earth. Western medicine and big pharmaceutical companies pollute our bodies with toxic medicine. Food is grown by farming conglomerates with little care about polluting pesticides and toxic fertilizer. Our economic systems are based on lack and debt financing—all are forms of violent power-over which is accepted as inevitable.

It all feels way too big to heal. We are afraid of the yang feminine—the burning woman, the Goddess Lilith, the Goddess Kali Ma—that will tear it all down. This is especially true for patriarchal man because he's too afraid to look inside for his own yin masculine, the Shakti creative power in union with the masculine. This is what is happening now. The old separated ego's patriarchal paradigm is dissolving as the Shakti energy rises in joyful and playful dance with Shiva energy. Play and pleasure is another aspect of Tantra. Shakti energy is playful and pleasurable. Pleasure was turned into sin because it became associated with men's sexual needs. Let us reclaim the word pleasure as spontaneous joy of creation and transformation—for both men and women, for everyone on the continuum.

## Can We Forgive Adam?

As women, can we forgive Adam, our personification of damaging masculine energy? Can we forgive the constant violence: rape of mother earth, women and children; the persecution of Jews, and the annihilation of indigenous and tribal cultures and all people of color? Can we forgive the men holding the distorted, wounded, shadow masculine energy? As women can we forgive the wounded masculine energy inside ourselves? Can we forgive and love ourselves?

Through many incarnations men and women have been both perpetrator and abuser, as well as victim. We've all committed atrocities to stay alive. I remind myself that women agreed at the soul level to turn over the reins of power to men in order for both men and women to experience an evolution of understanding of the abuse of power-over. Embracing Lilith occurs with a deep soul-level heart-wrenching forgiveness of ourselves for playing the roles of perpetrator, savior, and victim in many incarnations. When I go even deeper, it means forgiving the perception of separation from God, for our fall from grace. This process is immensely challenging. Once I realized the true intent of forgiving the unforgivable and loving the unlovable, my resistance and misunderstanding started to unravel.

We are not being asked to forgive unloving acts. We are being asked to forgive ourselves for believing a child of God can act outside of God's Love. To use Trump as the current bad guy, I can't love the personal Trump. I can't love the cops killing people of color. I can't forgive those who take children from their mothers and put them in cages. What I can forgive is our loss of innocence. I can forgive myself for wanting to play a martyr and hold onto my rage. I remind myself that many people do not understand what they are doing because they do not remember they are children of an all-loving God, because at times I forget this. When we find we can't forgive, it is because we are trying to do this within separation consciousness rather than with our God Self.

I'm reminded of a dream occurring many years ago when I first started my quest to heal anger at men for seemingly perpetuating patriarchy. The first step was forgiving Yeshua and allowing him to return to my life. I thought my trip to Israel in 2014 with the Take Me to Truth Community would heal this anger. It did not. Once again I was very angry with Yeshua for not healing my anger. I had yet to fully understand healing as an inside job.

In this dream I am standing in line at a gate in what feels like an entrance to heaven. There is a grinning man standing at the gate that people walk through. As I wait my turn, I realize other people are going around me and walking through the gate. I become furious with this man for allowing everybody but me through the gate. The more I yell, the more he grins. Eventually I understand: he is only standing at the gate, pleased to watch the people as they walk through. He is not the gatekeeper, and people are welcome to pass through the gate anytime they want. It is my own fury and beliefs about men which prevents me from walking through. My thoughts fueling the anger stop me from entering heaven, not men. The process of healing anger continued for many years. It is being resolved and cleared as I write this book. I recognize this dream as a turning point for realizing anger at men is of my own making. Nothing outside of me is causing the anger. No one is preventing my entrance into heaven. I am.

## The Cosmic Egg

Once again as I write, what I need to include appears in my life. The symbol of the Orphic egg or cosmic egg was mentioned to me by a spiritual sister and is shown on the book cover. It shows a snake wrapped around an egg, representing the womb of the Cosmic Mother—the cosmos held within every one of us. The snake represents the creative kundalini life force of the masculine and feminine joined in Oneness. The cosmic egg wrapped with snake is attributed to the Greek God Orpheus. It symbolizes a religion focused on the teachings of the origins of life, procreation, immortality, mortality, creativity and wisdom. According to Greek myth, the deity Planes was born from this egg as both male and female of light and goodness. It became a symbol of Gnostic Christians who are reborn again into the immortal light of their own gnosis or knowledge of spiritual truths.

The cosmic womb egg is a symbol of the sacred feminine. There is a wonderful icon painted by Robert Lenz of Mary Magdalene looking straight at the viewer holding an egg in one hand and pointing at it with the other hand as if she's reminding us that all creation comes from the womb of the Cosmic Mother held within each person. There is nothing outside of us, only a reflection of what we hold within. If we are holding fear, then the world we create is of suffering. When we listen to our God Self, the world we create reflects only love, abundance, grace, peace, purity, balance, health, harmony, happiness and perfection.

This ancient symbol feels appropriate for Lilith who could birth parthenogenetically and is associated with the wisdom of both Owl and Snake. It also feels like a wonderful symbol for the creation of Nova Gaia. We are birthing ourselves and mother earth as both masculine and feminine joined in Oneness. We are being reborn from the wisdom held within into our divine sovereign selves into Christ consciousness. This is what the egg and the snake represent—the alchemical process for transmuting the poison of fear and separation into the birth of divine human beings, so Lilith, Eve and Adam are reborn anew within us.

Lilith as the first woman created equally with Adam as the first man harkens back to the time when all lived in harmony with the Star Nations who walked freely on earth. Many of us have karmic memories of living in Atlantis or Lemuria with Star Nations. The ancient star mounds in the Ohio Valley provide physical evidence of this time of harmony. Ross Hamilton in *Star Mounds, Legacy of a Native American Mystery* writes that the remains of Star Nations are places which are supposed to be seen from the sky. Indigenous wisdom informs us that people gathered in these places to communicate with their star ancestors who lived on earth eons ago. Hamilton believes that one hub and power center of this great cosmological network and organization was the Serpent Mound.[27]

When I first learned of the Serpent Mound in Ohio, I was in the midst of the energy of snake medicine infusing the writing of this chapter on Lilith. Snake spirit medicine is very high for humanity right now. The poison released from the snake bite symbolizes this age of transformation. The boil of racism and genocide of indigenous and tribal communities has been pierced. The boil of violence, rape and suppression of women has been pierced. The boil of patriarchy's power-over has been pierced releasing the poison to be transmuted into divine love. As snakes shed their old skin for new skin, so humanity is shedding the old separation paradigm of fear to co-create the New Earth based on love. The Snake of the Serpent Mound is holding an egg in its mouth. The symbol of the snake and egg comes to us from the Star Nations which feels prophetic. The Star Nations have known from the beginning about the Cosmic Mother's grand plan to birth divine humans to create Terra Nova.

The Order of the Magdalenes originated with the reigns of Hathor and Isis who received their knowledge from the women leaders of Atlantis. Hathor, Isis, Mother Mary, Mary Magdalene, Anna (grandmother of Yeshua) and Joan of Arc are all members of the Order of the Magdalenes. They knew about this prophetic mission and the significance of the Cosmic Egg. I feel the women from the Order of the Magdalenes are Lilith's daughters. Women mystics are Lilith's daughters. With the rebirth of the divine feminine essence, it is all coming into the light. Our Star Nations left us a reminder in the form of the Serpent Mound that can only truly be appreciated from above. I find this immensely comforting knowing the prophecy of Terra Nova is coming to fruition.

Do I, do we have the courage to embrace what the Cosmic Egg symbolizes to birth the new earth, to express and manifest only love and the Mother's miraculous grace throughout the world? May we fall into presence and into God over and over again till that is all we know.

# As Within So Without Meditations

## The Gift of a Question

*She remembers who she is and births a new humanity.*

If you need to refresh your memory about what is involved in these meditations, please re-read this section in Movement One. Please start with the two following questions before beginning your inquiry process then read the additional questions. Try to write down whatever arises without judgment or editing what you don't like. Most importantly ask your guides/light family to help with your inquiry work.

Can I love myself enough to forgive myself?
Can I forgive myself enough to love myself?

### *Additional Questions*

What about Lilith's story resonates with you and/or disturbs you? How does it inspire your heroine's mystical journey? If it does not inspire you, why not?

As you read about all the ways women and our feminine power have been repressed, demeaned, demonized and violently suppressed, what emotions arise? How can you accept and harness these feeling to love yourself and forgive yourself?

What do you feel about the idea that sexual energy is the spiritual life force of the Universal Mother Father, and not narrowly defined by physical intercourse?

What information in this chapter helps you the most on your spiritual journey?

Return to the first two questions about loving and forgiving yourself.

This is the final surrender.

# Movement Four

# Healing the Mother Daughter Patriarchal Wound

## Chapter One

# The Wound of Separation

*My Heart weeps with love*
*Compassion seeps through the cracks*
*Welcome home, She sings*

I woke this morning awash in tears of grief and shame. It is time to feel into what my body is telling me. I need to grieve, let go, let down, acknowledge the deep wound I've been ignoring. I need to stand on the ground in the rain of my tears to magnify the Holy Mother Holy Father Sophia God within, until all that does not serve me slowly dissolves and dies. I realize I am not only grieving my own mother daughter wound passed down to my daughter, but also the mother daughter wound in my mother and her mother and all the mothers that came before me.

It feels as if my heart is being broken over and over again—and I feel it in my womb. I also feel the compassion and loving arms of Universal Divine Mother sharing my tears for all the children separated from her arms. I am hearing: let your heart break open so the compassion can pour in, so it will never close again. I feel I am weeping millions of tears for thousands of years for all mothers who couldn't be and can't be what their children need. I weep for mothers who watched their children go hungry and suffer; for mothers who've had their children taken from them, sold into slavery, or died through genocide; for mothers whose children were raped and tortured; for mothers who believed that being severe and critical of their daughters helped them survive in a man's world; for mothers who smothered and controlled their children, mistaking possessiveness for love; and for mothers who thought acting like a man, including violent behavior, was the path to safety and equality. How can we heal this wound within our wombs with the loss of our Divine Mother? I remain for days in the holy water of my tears. This is the separation that resulted when we tried to sever the feminine expression of God from the masculine expression of God thousands of years ago. All humanity lost our Universal Mother, and we've been grieving and lashing out ever since.

The Cosmic Mother Creatrix is the feminine energy birthing all that is. The Cosmic Father's masculine energy of penetrating source light is contained within the Mother Creatrix. The Divine Mother is the womb of life. Women are this feminine energy which gives birth. Science reveals that each human being and all mammals are biologically female first before an added hormonal development turns the embryo into a male. Women are the source of life and thus in order for the power-over paradigm to succeed, men had to gain control of our bodies.

Separation begins in the womb and is amplified when the infant leaves the womb. This wound of separation, enhanced by patriarchal conditioning passed down through the mother's line, affects us and all our children, both sons and daughters. Therefore, our spiritual journey becomes the process of returning to our womb to heal this wound of separation. Within our abdomen we connect to the primordial essence of the Universal Mother fueling inspiration that ignites and grows into new creations. By feeling into the belly, which carries our hidden emotions and feelings, we heal and become empowered. Our womb or abdomen, when connected to our heart becomes the heart womb of love.

Connection with our ancestors and all life is carried within our wombs. In *When the Women Were Drummers*, Layne Redmond writes, "All the eggs a woman will ever carry form in her ovaries when she's a four-month-old fetus in the womb of her mother. This means our cellular life as an egg begins in the womb of our grandmother. Each of us spent 5 months in our grandmother's womb."[28] This blew me away. Both grandmother wisdom and trauma are passed down through the female line connecting us to all our ancestral grandmothers. We are therefore a bridge between our ancestral grandmothers and the primordial womb of the Divine Mother. As we heal the trauma held in our wounds, we heal our ancestral wounds, as well as the karmic trauma from thousands of parallel lives.

The mother daughter wound was created when masculine and feminine energies were separated and associated with male and female bodies. With separation, we denied and suppressed the divine feminine. While the Divine Mother's all-encompassing love can never be extinguished, her origin sound, resonances and energy were reduced to a glimmer, a distant muted tone. In this illusion of separation, it left the world greatly imbalanced and damaged as all humanity lost their heart center, especially men. Women profoundly felt this loss in their womb and women who tried to speak their spiritual truth were demeaned, ostracized, blamed, beaten, crucified, burned at the stake, raped and murdered. Before current times, women had two choices: to either remain the property of their father or wed and become the property of another man. There have been moments in recorded history when women found a way to be independent, but they were few and far between and did not last long. We hold in our wombs the ancestral cellular and karmic memory of this violent persecution of the feminine spirit.

Throughout his-story the role of women was primarily to give birth and take care of the children so men could be the providers and sometimes the protectors. Women's job was to make sure enough children were born and lived to ensure the survival of humankind. This meant our bodies were not our own, and more often than not became vessels for men's sexual appetites and need to produce mostly sons to fight the wars. Constant pregnancy and birth took its toll on most women's bodies and we died in great numbers—even during times of peace—while men were dying in battles and wars. Women and children were huge casualties of war, with the conquering men raping and killing women and children. For women this created ancestral and karmic anger that our only purpose was to breed children to perpetuate the power-over paradigm.

Women feel this trauma in our wombs. Menstruation and childbirth can be painful. Painful cramps and painful childbirth are mostly expected and accepted. I had very painful cramps until I conceived a child. There is a huge unconscious belief that women must suffer. This has it seeds in the his-story of Lilith and Eve's betrayal justifying the suppression of women's innate wisdom and power. As we heal these deep wounds in our wombs, painful menstrual cramps and painful childbirth is disappearing

With repeated trauma to our wombs, we lost our innate connection to Mother Earth, the rhythm of the seasons, and the ability to communicate with all her relations. This womb wisdom fuels the wisdom of the heart to expand love through intuition and connection with all that is. With eons of trauma, our wombs become a void where we shove all our painful and unwanted feelings and fears. We shift our energy away from the belly which houses emotion, connection and intimacy. When we disconnect from our womb, we lose the ability to feel our emotions and access our intuition thus leading to denial and the loss of our feminine power. With nothing to ground and restore us, we deplete our loving energy and with it our core feminine strength. Conditioned to rely on men for survival we become possessive of their love which often transfers to being possessive of our children's love.

We feel the disconnection from the feminine divine individually and collectively. Even women who have not experienced severe trauma in this lifetime have experienced it in other incarnations and will carry any unhealed patterns into this lifetime. The abuse women have endured for eons lives in the collective female consciousness which affects every human being.

While women have much more freedom and independence today, we still struggle to remember our true feminine power within the negative power-over values and structure of patriarchy that separates, demeans, dismisses and annihilates. Over eons women's wombs have constantly received the systematic destructive programming to destroy our wild untamable love of the Holy Mother and Her daughter Mother Gaia. It has been burned into our cells and our karmic template. Trauma and patriarchal conditioning are passed down the female line as the mother daughter wound.

Several days before Christmas, I woke in immense pain. I felt I was being dismembered and then put back together again. As I prayed to the Holy Mother for clarity and relief, I received the insight that I was embodying the wounding and severing of the female aspect of God. I received a knowing about the mother daughter wound and all the core sacred wounds carried by both men and women through all our parallel lives. A friend emailed a picture of a clay image of a dismembered Great Mother Goddess and this visual image helped verify, and thus integrate and dissolve some of the grief I was feeling from the systematic dismantling of the Divine Mother.

While the overall pain lessened throughout the day, my lower back and hip pain intensified as if all by myself I was birthing the sacred feminine and masculine. Through the separated ego I can never be enough of a mother to heal the entire world, thus the birthing pains. By opening my heart completely in surrender to the Divine Mother, the pain in the womb dissolves because separation from the Holy Mother is impossible. This is my mission, my calling to return the Cosmic Mother's resonance, to heal this wound of separation and to reconcile the masculine and feminine energy returning balance to the world.

I received another insight from the Universal Mother that men and women patriarchal leaders and their supporters are like angry toddlers acting out the loss of their mother. They feel abandoned, hurt and confused about finding their Divine Mother within. Like any small child, they do not have the resources to understand what happened. In a continuous tantrum they take it out on women and any group or culture which honors Mother Earth, blaming them for a loss they can't comprehend. All women's wombs are colonized and traumatized. It was and is brutal. This is essentially what patriarchy is about, a misguided soul-destroying attempt to control the power of love not realizing that it perpetuates their never-ending pain of seemingly being abandoned by the Holy Mother's all-encompassing compassionate love.

## Healing Our Own Core Wound of Separation

*Sometimes I feel like a motherless child*
*A long way from home.*
African American Spiritual, 1920s

This song is about the heartbreak of black children torn from their mothers' arms and sold into slavery. It cries out from the aching, broken heart of all women of color and indigenous mothers whose children died or were beaten and enslaved by the onward march of white men's greed to colonize and dominate. Women of the four colors, black; yellow; red and white, have all lost children to the power-over paradigm that exists through conflict, violence and war. It is time all women come together to support and share our grief, to stand together and say, "no more, we will no longer sacrifice our children to the outdated power and control structure." We all swallowed the delusion that colonization brought progress to the ignorant. Lauren

Walsh and Shaina Connors, founders of the Global Sisterhood, wrote in one of their monthly newsletters:

> Capitalistic, colonialist and patriarchal societies don't value emotional fulfillment. They don't value deep and meaningful connection, spiritual growth, communion with nature, or the simple pleasure of being alive unless it enhances that system's power. The first nation people, our indigenous brothers and sisters held something much more lifesaving than what colonial powers considered as progress. They embraced interconnectedness with Mother Earth and all living beings. This reverence for all life had to be eliminated for the values and structure of power-over to gain dominance.

All of us during our current and parallel lives have experienced this soul-wrenching violence. This continues today with the suffering of women and children still being subject to human trafficking, rape, abuse, hunger and neglect. Within this lifetime's still point of awareness we can go deep within to understand and forgive our own pain of being both victim, perpetrator and savior presently and in other lifetimes. Loving ourselves is the only answer to become a holy vessel only vibrating love to end all present-day abuse. For when we completely love ourselves with balanced masculine and feminine energies, we return to our natural state of Oneness forgiving all with compassion. The illusion of separation consciousness dissolves.

This song is universal because sometimes we feel like a motherless child, abandoned, punished and neglected. Everyone has felt the loss of the Universal Mother and we feel a long way from our true divine home. With this wound of separation, our biological, adopted or absent mothers never seem able to soothe or love us enough to heal the aching in our soul for our own internal Divine Mother. We are being guided to mother ourselves, to dissolve our anger, our pain, our grief of not feeling worthy or never good enough. We have within the ability to heal our wound of separation and when we do, we do it for all of humanity.

Each of us experiences the wound of separation in different ways resulting in what many call a core wound—the wound that stays with us for lifetimes. Recognizing our core wound that bleeds from the universal wound of separation helps our awakening process. It is a sacred wound because we are being asked to dissolve the wound in order to create the new, to become divinely human. My core wound is feeling second best, never being perfect enough, or smart enough or good enough. Some people have a core wound of abandonment, or never feeling wanted, or being powerless or being left behind. All core wounds originate with the false perception we could separate from Sophia God. Thus, we all feel unworthy of the Holy Mother Father's love.

After the night of feeling dismembered, the next night the Divine Mother sent the following dream. I have birthed twins, a boy and a girl. For some reason I feel compelled to take my babies on a trip, safely bundled up and tucked away in car seats. My husband Rick and I drive to a public place, somewhat like a shopping mall, where he stays with the babies and I wander around lost and confused. What I am doing here, no one seems to know. I receive polite but sad smiles, people shaking their heads because they cannot help me. I start to panic as I don't remember where Rick parked the car. I need to get back to my babies. I remember I can call him on my cell phone. Some man I do not know answers the phone. He tells me Rick is not available to talk. I am furious and yell at him to put Rick on the phone immediately. I ask Rick where he is and he says that he brought the babies home. I am upset he left and ask him to come get me. He says no and to walk home. When I hang up and look outside, it is pouring with rain.

I woke overwhelmed with a sense of sadness and grief, unable to make sense of the dream. I knew it was important, but no amount of centering, taking a bath or walking the labyrinth helped. It felt obvious I had birthed the divine masculine and feminine, but otherwise I remained clueless. Part of the difficulty was knowing that Rick would never leave me somewhere and tell me to walk home in the rain. I opened to receive guidance from my God Self.

The collective unconscious does not have the wisdom to understand the rebirth of the joined divine masculine and feminine and therefore the general public cannot help. This indicates that I'm feeling unsupported and alone in my quest to balance the masculine and feminine energies. I felt lost and panicked because I needed to get back to balance, represented by my babies. I tried to find Rick, the masculine support in my life, to help. I am at first furious that I can't talk with him directly. I've been furious most of my life at Yeshua and the Father God for seemingly leaving all women to cope alone while favoring men. In the dream I learn Rick has left me, the babies are safe at home, and he tells me to walk home in the rain.

Rick, as a representative of the healed masculine, gave me a gift. There is no one preventing me from talking to him, only my anger. The babies are safe, the masculine presence can love and protect. Mother energy does not have to do it alone. The Father is equally important. I am to walk home in the rain of my tears washing clean the anger, sadness, helplessness, confusion and grief. Through my tears I feel the Holy Mother's compassion and love. I have within both the feminine and masculine resonance necessary to birth, nurture, grow into maturity, and balance the masculine and feminine within. There is nothing or no one outside of me that can help. The divine sovereign power of a reconciled feminine and masculine resides within. Therefore, I am never alone.

## Loving Our Inner Child to Forgive Ourselves and Other Women

The process of falling in love with ourselves is a willingness to look with clear loving eyes at the shadow place where we've hidden: our deepest fears, uncertainties and doubts; painful experiences we wish to forget; and emotions and feelings we've been taught to ignore. This shadow place is hidden within our inner child, the wounded child feeling cut off from our God Self and the knowledge of Oneness. We hold our inner child within the womb which is directly connected to the heart. This is why when we are upset, we often feel queasy, nauseous and crampy. Because the womb is connected to the heart it can physically hurt and choke us in the throat. We literally feel our throats are closed to speaking our truth and sometimes ache from unshed tears. All the area surrounding our abdomen including our lower back and hips has been weakened by our loss of faith in our inner wisdom. My wounded inner child has been shouting at me for years through migraines, neck, back and hip pain.

The child within can easily feel confused and lonely, overwhelmed with sadness, shame and bitterness. If we ignore our inner child long enough it can turn into dis-ease within the body. The body is our last-ditch effort to get us to listen to our hearts and heal the wounds in our wombs. If we ignore what our body is telling us, dis-ease can kill us. *We are being called to heal the division between our inner child and our inner angel that knows Oneness*. We visually or physically walk the labyrinth into the Holy of Holies of our heart womb to remember our spiritual path connects our wounded inner child to our God Self. How we do this is unique to our path of awakening. It is a spiritual journey of the heart and womb. All spiritual journeys reveal truths which intersect and speak to everyone.

Visualize a time when you were most happy as a child. I can see myself as a 4 to 6-year-old girl who has yet to lose faith in a loving world. I see myself learning to ride a bike for the first time, filled with love, freedom and power. I see myself singing loudly with abandonment in love with the harmony of sound. I see myself going to the library with my father so excited to explore new books. I see myself, arms and hands intertwined with my best friend. I feel my mother's loving arms around me when I can't sleep. I discovered that even for those whose early childhoods were filled with suffering and abuse, they can usually find at least one moment when they felt joy. I had one woman say it was when she slept in freshly washed sheets dried in the sun's warmth.

## *Visualization*

> *Visualize a moment of joy. Hold on to this moment and magnify the feelings of connectedness, peace, freedom and love. Next visualize your inner child who feels lost, hurt, angry and confused. Tell her she is a beautiful innocent child filled with joy and laughter. Tell her you are sorry you've not always been there for her, however now you are present to guide and protect her. Smile lovingly, take her hand, then gently draw her into your embrace. Feel your heart overflowing with love for this child who is part of you. This courageous child who willingly holds all you do not want to see until you are ready to love yourself enough to forgive all that no longer serves you. Through this visualization you have the opportunity to mother your inner child the way you wished your mother had loved you. This allows you to regain your innocent divine authority that truly never left.*

Periodically I have been angry with three neighbors for their hateful and hurtful behavior. During a time when I was holding on to this anger, I visualized hugging my inner child tenderly and lovingly. I tearfully thanked her for pointing to where I still needed to grieve, accept my feelings and heal. I said I was sorry for still judging some people, and she replied, "but that's not what you are doing, you are judging me." I felt the truth of these words in my heart. When we judge another, we are also judging ourselves. I can feel the heaviness of this judgment inside of me. My inner innocent child has been neglected, judged, bruised and battered by me. I am still doing it. The only person I'm hurting is myself. Where is the forgiveness? As I truly felt this within my heart, the tears stopped, the anger started to dissipate and I began to feel more peaceful.

Along life's path we continue our walk into the labyrinth of our womb of creation and feel Mother Earth's love. This is a process and sometimes we stop for a while at the path's turning until we feel strong enough to continue. This may be a long pause while we visualize loving our inner child over and over again until only love remains. Loving our inner child completely allows the phoenix child to be reborn, burning the radiant sacred fire of our divine sovereignty.

Sometimes after a system upgrade, we return to loving ourselves at a higher vibration. Sometimes as we fold back out, the confusion and pain returns. Our journey's path calls for infinite patience and complete trust in our Higher Holy Self to continuously guide and send messages of love. Always remember the labyrinth of our heart and soul leads to our center, our Holy of Holies. No matter what is going on around us, no matter any confusion or doubts that periodically surface, our path is assured. We cannot become lost permanently. If the path folds once more into darkness it is there for us to find more treasurers of the heart, those glimpses of light shining through even in the darkness. We can dance with the darkness in joy. Our inner child embraced in love knows the way out is simply walking the unicursal path of our heart.

### The Perpetrator, Victim, Savior Triad

The Universal Mother births infinite wondrous variety continuously. In separation consciousness we chose to use this variety to divide and conquer. This wound of separation is a universal wound that connects all of us no matter our race, culture, religion, gender identity or nonbinary. The majority of us have lost our connection to our indigenous roots no matter what color we are. The ongoing attempt to obliterate indigenous cultures in the name of progress, profit, resources and religion hollowed out people's natural connection to spirit and their divine essence. Apathy, rage and a feeling of victimhood is left.

The masculine and feminine has been in conflict for thousands of years which has led to the disintegration of both. This created the perpetrator/victim/savior dynamic in which women of every color get victimized more and more, leading to denial, fear and the idea that men are our savior. The distorted masculine energy gets lost in aggression and ruthless violence, as demonstrated by constant wars and violence against mother earth and all her relations.

When the victim decides they've had enough and refuses to play victim any more, change occurs. She saves herself. Revolution occurs. This is the dynamic for anyone who has been victimized. We have to do the internal work first to say I've had enough, no more, I'll save myself like Thecla, and Jane befriending the dragon thus saving herself and the prince. Saving ourselves through social justice revolutions requires embracing both our heart-centered masculine and feminine energies in balance. Examples of these types of revolutions are: the civil rights movement for black people leading to "Black Lives Matter"; the movement to legalize gay marriage leading to freedom of sexual expression; the parental movement to achieve free and appropriate education for children with disability labels leading to freedom from patriarchal indoctrinated education; and the women's rights movement including: legalizing the right to vote, the feminist movement, and the "Me Too" movement leading to the rise of the divine feminine.

All of these social justice revolutions required many people to look inward to imagine what they wanted this world to look like. Often it ignited the need to get in touch with buried anger and trauma. The process results in lots of anger being felt and expressed, hopefully in non-violent ways. There is a massive amount of societal anger with those expressing their rage. It is a necessary part of the practice of owning our feelings and then moving through them to claim, "I am not a victim."

We gain practice following our hearts. We gain a knowing in our inner temples which results in men, women, nonbinary, cis and trans acknowledging and feeling the divine feminine within themselves and every person on earth. When we honor the feminine essence, we see change in the outer world. We regain balance between the feminine and the masculine. We allow ourselves to accept our feelings. Today, we are being called to the revolution of love. This is an inner revolution of acceptance, trust and surrender to unity consciousness. We are being called to dissolve the core wounds that have kept us enslaved to suffering. We dissolve all that does not serve us in order to embrace our magnificent divine human self. This is the final revolution to co-create Terra Nova. And everyone does it together. No one is left out of the Divine Mother's plan.

The movement to free ourselves from victimhood is a process of remembering our divine nature. We acknowledge how much we have been programmed to uphold the doctrine of power-over. This is a process of forgiveness first for ourselves and then for the perpetrators. The Mother's plan is love and always is and will be. Even during these destructive polarizing times, we can trust our return to Unity consciousness. We are learning to trust by loving ourselves free of victimhood. *Understanding the victim, perpetrator, savior dynamic directly affects our ability to accept and heal the mother daughter wound.*

### *We Are Not Victims*

While all these revolutions are still ongoing, they initially started when the affected people stopped seeing themselves as victims. This is an essential part of the process to heal the shadow masculine and feminine. One of the most powerful lessons from ACIM is, "I am not a victim of the world I see."[29] When we chose to forget our true divine inheritance, we created the illusion of victimhood. Each of the perpetrator, victim and savior triad exists on a continuum from extreme abuse to ordinary daily judgment. Whether you see yourself as perpetrator, victim or savior these roles originate with our choice to perceive ourselves separate from our Beloved Source.

In choosing the separated false self to guide us, we all believe we are victims, even those who are culturally seen as perpetrators or saviors. This is true both collectively and individually. In order to stop feeling victimized we often take on the role of perpetrator or savior. We do this to ourselves and others. We initiate acts of cruelty on those we see as inferior or try to save the people being harmed often seeing them as less than. The separated ego is devious and slippery.

There are many examples of the victim, perpetrator and savior triad in all individuals, races and cultures. This imbalance fuels how separation consciousness maintains control. Throughout history many white people have either ignored or treated cruelly men, women and children of other colors, or tried to save them by conversion to their religious and cultural beliefs. *The answer always lies within. Doing our inner work frees us from the past which we believe dictates our future.* We forgive ourselves for choosing the separated ego as our guide for thousands of years. We love ourselves until we remember our truth as divine sovereign beings. We see through this dense confusing dream of suffering to know everyone is of the whole; everyone is divinely equal. Choosing love over fear frees us from enacting the perpetrator, savior and victim triad.

## Freedom from Suppression of the Feminine

Since the nineteenth century feminine energy has been gaining strength, with the movement to acquire the vote being a turning point. The feminist revolution to achieve equality with men is part of the process of leaving the victim role. While it is a two-edged sword leading women to try and be more like men, it is necessary in order for women to feel strong enough to reclaim our inner wisdom. The "Me Too" movement has brought to light all the rape, torture and abuse women have experienced and are still experiencing. Thousands of women are coming forward to say, "No more, I will not be a victim anymore! I have much to teach this world about compassion, spirituality and universal love." A tremendous amount of collective anger is being felt, grieved and cleared into fierce love for ourselves first and then for everyone. With this energy, the distorted wounded masculine has breathing room to heal.

The indwelling spirit of the divine feminine—the Shekinah, Holy Spirit, Shakti—has never been extinguished. It exists in all of us within our hearts and womb when we feel compassion for a hurt child or animal, a suffering adult and our family and friends no matter what they are experiencing. It exists in our moments of joy and communion with others. While loving kindness and compassion are still seen by many as weak emotions, they are our strength and connection to our divine truth which has flickered but never gone out. The divine feminine has been on the rise for several decades. Women in their divine strength no longer fear leading from love and being themselves within patriarchy.

The knowledge of the Shekinah within our wombs is the power to bring balance again to earth. As in the stories of *The Paper Bag Princess* and *Jane and the Dragon*, women embracing their power can tame the monster or dragon of patriarchy into the divine masculine's supportive protective energy. Women's intuition, mystical wisdom and connection to the earth has always existed. *We have been persecuted, seen as less than, because the separated ego knows that women in their full balanced power will dissolve separation consciousness permanently*. The wise women, mystics, healers, shamans and medicine women have always existed. We've been repeatedly killed, dismissed, labeled crazy, wild, ugly and uncontrollable. However, the Shekinah never disappears entirely. Lady Ragnell was spelled by the distorted masculine in the form of her stepbrother to be seen as ugly and loathsome for staying true to her inner knowing. The spell is released when Sir Gawain, the supportive masculine energy, honors Lady Ragnell's own sovereignty.

During the Victorian age, Western medicine fueled by increased research, was becoming much more sophisticated about treating wounds and diseases. This created interest in the psychology of erratic, delusional behavior with the purview of the Western medical model of treatment. There was much abuse sanctioned in the name of progress. Women who refused to obey their fathers, brothers and husbands by tapping into their suppressed wisdom were labeled with the women's disease "hysteria." While that diagnostic label no longer exists, we often are called hysterical whenever we threaten patriarchal values. Women have been sent to insane asylums for trying to be true to their sacred selves. Not being understood or supported can break one's spirit, and sometimes we've felt no choice but to take on the role of insane, mentally ill women. *The world of separation consciousness is insane—not our sacred inner wisdom that knows the truth of Oneness.*

At a retreat I attended in 2002, there was a woman participant who had been committed to a mental institution because she was not always a compliant wife. Her husband convinced her she was unstable and needing help because she behaved in crazy ways. During the retreat she was in turmoil because at times she saw him as her savior from craziness, and then she'd break down because the experience had been terrifying. She was not ready to let go of victimhood, to feel her anger, to grieve and trust her inner strength and knowing as sacred, rather than crazy. This would mean releasing her husband's role as savior to saving herself. She was at a retreat to question beliefs she was holding which were not serving her. We all felt she had taken a courageous first step to trusting her inner wisdom.

With over twelve thousand years of women being convinced we are the inferior sex; we became very afraid and secretive. We began to not trust ourselves or acknowledge our anger—and very often to not trust other women, especially women of a different color, religion or culture. This distrust of ourselves and other women is passed down the female line through the mother daughter wound. Women helping other women, gathering in circles and groups is powerful spiritual medicine for what ails us. This is why women's friendships and women's groups have historically been highly discouraged and often violently suppressed. We brutally learned this during the burning times of the inquisition when women were so scared, they turned on other women to save themselves and their families. Healing the mother daughter wound means joining wholeheartedly not only with our daughters but also with other women. Sharing our stories and learning from each other helps in regaining our inner wisdom and power. I'm not crazy, other women have similar experiences. The love and support of my woman's Co-Creators group provides insight, clarity and care during times when I cannot find these inside myself.

Sometimes we are harder on other women because we think they should know better. We've lived by the patriarchal values of success at any cost in order to succeed like a man. Thinking the only solution to power is to become more like a man than a man, we can become just as dismissive and controlling of other women as the men we emulate.

The patriarchal values of conquest, domination, control and division are dissolving as more and more women gather together to share our heroine's journeys. We hold an ancient memory of being in circles of women to honor and embrace the Universal Mother. We remember when we came together to pass our wisdom to other women while we gave birth or to explore and strengthen our connection to the Divine Mother and to earth. We long for this support and nurturance. We hold the heart womb space for each other to share and learn about ourselves without being judged and dismissed. We learn to listen unconditionally, realizing that each one of us has our own unique experience to contribute without co-opting another's story and voice with our own voice.

Women of all colors are gathering together and learning to be gentle with ourselves. We are bonding and joining to heal thousands of years of enforced division and suspicion among women fostered by our programmed obedience to the patriarchal values of power-over. Within these circles we remember the strength of our feminine power in community. The world can no longer survive in the separation that destroys those who give life.

Within these circles we restore the strength of our womb to heal the wound in our belly to literally birth Terra Nova. It requires a lot of inner courage to be in these circles and learn to listen unconditionally, to create trust with each other. But it is worth it, as it saves our sanity and our souls. As we connect to our inner wisdom, the universe opens and we meet other spiritual sisters who listen unconditionally and offer their own inner wisdom and mystical truths. We also open to our spiritual brothers who are learning to trust their inner sanctum and feminine energy. We gather allies. The connection is worldwide. We come to know our feminine energy is flowing and receptive. It shapes our inner landscape.

To heal the mother daughter wound in our heart and womb, we embrace this truth in order to become spiritual mothers to ourselves. By mothering ourselves we learn to embrace our intuition and inspiration. We bless our nurturing and compassionate wisdom to fiercely follow our heart to birth a new paradigm of power within.

## Chapter Two

# Healing Our Sacred Core Wound

At a Way of Mastery 10-day retreat I attended, the teachers used the symbol of a piano note we play over and over again to describe the sacred core wound. In other words, it is a tone or resonance we continually play until our inner ear opens to hear another higher vibration. Eventually our one note becomes many notes as we join in harmony with the symphony of love.

There is a spiritual metaphor that has been around for many years that I find helpful in understanding our process in healing the sacred wound. I am walking down the street and do not notice a huge hole. I fall in. I am stunned, disoriented and upset, so it takes a while to figure out how to get out of the hole. Eventually I do. I may fall into this same hole a few more times and struggle to climb out. One time I walk down the street and catch a glimpse of the hole—but it's too late and I fall in. This time I remember quickly how to climb out. Next time I am walking down the street, I notice the hole before I fall in. I may walk down the street often avoiding and walking around the hole. One day, I walk down the street and the hole has completely disappeared as if it never existed.

When we fall into a hole of our own making, it is probably a situation we've experienced before. There may be different actors and a different setting, but the essence of the problem is the same. A prime example is having a relationship with the same type of person over and over again and it always ending in anger and separation. This happens often with our romantic relationships in the search for the one with whom we want to spend our life. If these types of relationships continue to end in anger and pain, then it is time to go inward. This also happens with long-term relationships when they've been sustained with co-dependent behaviors. There is no reason to judge, all relationships within separation are co-dependent. I have certainly spent many years of my marriage dissolving the ties of co-dependency that bind me to outdated expectations. Until we do the inner work to understand the feelings and beliefs that guide our actions, we will bring the unhealed part of ourselves into any relationship, potentially giving us another opportunity to do our inner work.

The hole we fall in can either be a place we remain stuck or it can become a portal to healing and transformation. We always have a choice. Some people remain stuck in the same hole for their entire life, which generates another lifetime to heal this stuck place. Of course, sometimes it takes us awhile to understand, which is why we often fall into the same hole many times before we can walk around the hole. Once we see the hole as a portal to a higher vibration, we walk through, and it dissolves as if it was never there.

I have fallen into many holes associated with my sacred wound during my life. Many have been variations on the theme of being a perfect loving mother. This is a mother who protects and loves unconditionally; who creates space for her children to grow and follow their own hearts; who listens without criticizing; and who provides appropriate structure. Of course, this ideal of being a perfect mother was created with the separated ego that wants me to fail in order to keep me believing in separation from the Beloved Source. Thus, I fall short of my ideal over and over again. I'd fall into the hole of worry about my children never quite trusting they are always safe within God's loving embrace. The inner work I've done with my daughter Sarah while writing this chapter shows me that I've never been an ideal mom and that ultimately is a blessing.

I often fell into the hole of self-doubt, self-judgment and anger at God for how women have been treated. I brought this anger into this incarnation from many other lifetimes. There were periods in my life when I lived in this hole for a long time. And while I've cleared an immense amount of anger, it still visits at times.

Unraveling the ties that bind us to co-dependent behaviors, letting go of expectations, trusting, and releasing the need for certain outcomes allows the higher vibration deep within my inner temple that knows all is perfectly orchestrated for my awakening. There are no exceptions, every person is waking according to their own divine timing, even those who seem deeply buried in the denseness of separation consciousnesses. These are the lessons we learn after falling over and over again into the same hole until it is healed permanently and the sacred wound exists no more. Healing the mother daughter wound passed down through generations of women dissolves the cycle of victim, perpetrator and savior for all of humanity.

## Recognizing Divine Masculine Energy as Our Spiritual Foundation

I equate masculine energy with the mind and feminine energy with the heart. As a result, I've judged the mind—thus masculine energy—because our thoughts can create suffering. In separation consciousness we've tried to create a world dominated by reason and logic, dismissing our heart as muddying the waters of scientific truth. Even those who consider themselves religious or spiritual often let their mind and thoughts lead without input from their heart.

ACIM was channeled in the late 1970s and began to gather a following that is now worldwide. It greatly influences my spiritual journey. In ACIM, Yeshua introduces the idea that our thoughts create the belief we are separate from God, but because separation is an impossibility, this is an illusion. ACIM introduces us to Christ awareness. In the Western world, other channeled metaphysical books and texts prior to ACIM helped prepare the way for ACIM and some still have a huge following, such as Christian Science and Unity Churches. While the idea of non-dualism or separation from our Source was not new to the metaphysical texts of Eastern religions, it was a revolutionary idea in Western cultures that became centers for science and reason as our guiding light.

While I do not believe the teachings of Yeshua in ACIM intend for students to make an enemy of the separated ego, that is what happens for many devoted students. The idea of embracing the ego to dissolve it may be seen as blasphemous by some ACIM students as well as students of other metaphysical texts. When we spend so much time seeing the ego as something to eliminate, our resistance reinforces its presence. When we embrace the ego or separated self as part of our personal self, we can transform it from an unrelenting task master into a supportive helpful assistant, or what ACOL calls the differentiated Self.

When ACIM was channeled, Yeshua had to use the intellectual language people would understand at that time. Yeshua also used masculine pronouns and nouns—God the Father, the sonship, brothers, the kingdom of heaven. Gender neutral language and/or feminine language of the Holy Mother would have been immediately rejected by most men and women during the 1970s, and still is by many even today. They confuse mind with left-brain thinking.

Unfortunately, many devoted long-term students of ACIM stay stuck in the left-brain, unwilling to allow the divine feminine resonance of the right brain to balance and lead from the heart. Yeshua's channelings to other receivers over the years changed to include more gender inclusive language and information on the divine feminine, as people were more willing to accept the idea that God is the Universal Mother encompassing the Universal Father.

One of the most profound facets of my heroine's spiritual journey has been to heal my misconceptions of masculine energy. This was influenced by living within the separated ego's patriarchal system and thus equating all masculine energy as harmful. Many teachers and students' interpretation of ACIM did not help with my confusion nor heal anger toward dominating, controlling and often violent masculine energy.

For the purpose of healing the mother daughter wound, it is important to understand positive masculine energy. It is helpful to feel into the difference between the separated self and the differentiated self of the divine masculine. The separated ego is a construct of our thoughts that supports the belief in separation from our beloved Divine Mother Father of All That Is. Because we can't separate from an all-loving, all-encompassing God, this world is an illusion or a dream of separation. Even though I know deep within that this is a dream, I look at myself in the mirror every day and I appear to be real. We are powerful creators and there is a purpose to this dream of separation.

Within dualism, differences among people are used to separate, divide, possess, control or conquer. In the process of returning to Oneness as fully human and fully divine, difference becomes unique differentiation—the one in the many and the many in the one. Many harmonious notes resounding within the symphony of life. For some, using the image of being a unique facet of God's diamond light helps with understanding Oneness. As does life as a giant jigsaw puzzle, each piece unique and necessary to complete the whole. Each being has a unique shape, color, design and purpose in Union with God that is part of the whole. This uniqueness adds to the infinite ways God's love is expressed and extended throughout the multiverse.

The differentiated self is the masculine energy of individuation, discernment, focus, clarity and direction. While writing the chapter about Lilith, I discovered that masculine energy is also a loyal friend and guardian of our creative energy. Its energy makes each one of us uniquely ourselves within the whole. Male energy is outward focused, it is what enables the manifestation of spirit into form. Female energy is focused inward. It is the energy of home, embodiment and the Primal Source Light of Pure Love. The sacred feminine is all-encompassing and does not differentiate. Masculine energy wants to be of service to feminine energy in order to manifest her longing to continuously birth and create. This sacred union of the masculine and feminine essence is needed to manifest the divinity of humanity. New realities of creation can be joyfully explored and experienced in ever changing forms of manifestation. The separated self seeks to destroy this joyful creation, to separate and divide.

The differentiated self can be understood in the mystical mantra "I Am that I Am." The I of this mantra is the differentiating masculine energy that gives supportive focus, will, clarity and direction. The Am is the sacred all-encompassing, flowing, inexhaustible feminine energy of creation. When the two energies are joined in blissful union, creation happens. Therefore, masculine energy is the foundation on which creation can occur, providing the support, protection, focus, clarity and direction for the chaotic, untamed, inexhaustible feminine energy of birth and creation.

Without the differentiated self of masculine energy, feminine energy loses its purpose. Without the feminine energy of birth and creation, masculine energy becomes stagnant and creates in distorted, often harmful, ways. The two energies were never supposed to be separate from each other. They are whole in Oneness with the Mother Father. Separation has no meaning to God. During this earthly human experience, we attempted to separate the two energies into genders thus creating a perception of this imbalance, both individually and collectively.

Losing our connection to both masculine discernment and feminine wisdom created a hole in our womb. Women lost our center and our foundation. We no longer had access to the lower power chakras: the root, the sacral and the solar plexus. We lost the ability to access our feminine power. The masculinity of patriarchy was damaging as we lost faith in our innate ability to create from love. We forgot how to follow our hearts and save ourselves. We passed this wound to our daughters and sons. The hole in our womb is healed when we regain the foundation of the masculine energy, when we become grounded again in mother earth. The released feminine joyful wildness and inexhaustible resonance gains focus and direction as we become invincible in our fierce love. This creative feminine luminescent life force fuels the mystic's spontaneous insights and knowing of Oneness with the Beloved, thus manifesting into form the harmonious joining with the sacred masculine. A reverence for all creation is birthed into being.

As we awaken to the One within the many and the many within the One, gender becomes irrelevant or at least neutral. All the qualities listed as feminine energy or masculine energy remain in union without the gender classification. Most of humanity is not there yet. Therefore, it is part of the process of dissolving the separated ego to recognize and understand our feminine and masculine essence.

## Symbols of Sacred Union

There are several ways of visualizing this sacred joining. The yin yang symbol is a visual demonstration of the balanced masculine and feminine energies. They exist together in a circle representing the womb of existence, symbolizing the infinite Oneness of the Mother Father God. The black side represents the dark primordial heart womb of the Holy Mother, and within it exists a core of masculine energy symbolized by the white dot of individuality, clarity and vision. The white side represents the penetrating light of discerning wisdom, clarity and focus of the divine masculine. Within it exists a black dot symbolizing the core of feminine energy of birth, creation and renewal. Therefore, even when we separated genders, we retained a piece of the opposite gender's essence. All is contained within the circle of the Cosmic Mother's all-encompassing love.

Women have a yin feminine and a yang feminine. Relying only on the nurturing caring qualities of our yin nature without input from the yang energy renders women powerless to manifest our inspirational desires. If we are totally in our yang without input from the nurturing yin, we can become enraged, toxic and controlling. The yang feminine is our power supported by our yin feminine. As shown by the yin yang symbol, the yin energy is the dark nurturing primordial womb of creation. The pure light consciousness of the yang within the primordial womb is what manifests creation into form.

Men have a yin masculine and a yang masculine. The feminine yin qualities have been severed or severely repressed and denied. Because this yin energy has been so thoroughly demeaned by patriarchy, men have focused almost solely on their yang masculine energy. The penetrating light force of clarity and vision without the support of their nurturing yin masculine creates empty power that turns into aggression and violence. This is the false power-over paradigm which is devoid of love and is soul destroying.

When my back kept freezing, I spent a lot of time crawling around on the floor in pain. I finally decided I needed some help. Lori, a mystical soul sister from our Co-Creator's group, suggested an unusual chiropractor. She said he was very connected to his spiritual guides while working with the energy of the back. Out of desperation I made an appointment. As I look back on the experience, I realize how perfect it was for providing an example of a very kind and supportive man who was doing his own inner work. He considered himself a mystic. In many ways, our conversations and sharing helped the most. After one of my heart-opening sessions while I was driving home, Spirit took over driving the car. I was aware my hands were on the steering wheel; however, my attention was completely absorbed with the vision's message coming through my God Self. I had been re-reading *The Sophia Code* and experiencing the initiations of the seven Divine Feminine Christ Ascended Masters that are part of the Sophia Code cosmology. White Buffalo Woman appeared suggesting that I embody the spirit medicine of the Chanupa, the sacred pipe she gave to the Lakota people.

She reminded me that the bowl of the Chanupa is a symbol of the Holy Mother's heart womb lit with her sacred fire of love. The stem of the pipe is the symbol of the Holy Father's clarity of purpose to enable the holy smoke of the Holy Mother's sacred fire to be carried through the body into the world. White Buffalo Woman asked that I visualize the Chanupa with the bowl resting within my womb and the pipe stem along my spine carrying and releasing the smoke of divine fire or kundalini energy. She said by embodying the Chanupa, my womb and my spine would strengthen to balance the feminine and masculine energies, which would lead to healing the back pain. After the vision, I returned to my body and driving the car. I wish I could say after the vision, I instantly healed but I did not. There was much more to be revealed about the anger I'd been ignoring and stuffing away. The embodiment of the Chanupa is a process.

## Repressed Anger

Repressed anger is one of the most toxic emotions passed down through the mother daughter wound. This chapter at times has been difficult to write because I did not want to acknowledge how I'd passed on my buried fear of anger to Sarah. Discussion of the sources of women's anger weaves in and out of this book and in turn affects my awareness as I gain wisdom as I write. Women pass down through the mother daughter wound an inability to express anger in healthy and, eventually, freeing ways. Women's needs have been silenced within patriarchy because we are supposed to be the caretakers and caregivers, but never the care-receiver. Unable to express our needs, we become angry—and then bury it as we were taught by our mothers. All women are angry until they do the inner work to acknowledge and free their anger from the shadow.

Both my brothers and I received the clear message from our parents that expressing anger was not allowed. This came verbally from my father and subtly from my mother. This meant there was very little outlet for anger. We either stuffed it away, learned to control it with an iron will or let it burst out in unhealthy ways. I stuffed it, one of my brothers controlled it, and the other brother let it out in fits of rage, usually while watching sports. My father tried, mostly successfully, to never show his anger at another human being. This is the stoic velvet hammer approach of a gentleman, and while it feels safer than uncontrollable rage or aggression, it still is scary. The difficulty with the tight control is that it leaks out in conversations through hurtful comments. While I loved my father, especially during those many times when he was playfully loving, I was secretly afraid of his contained anger. I never wanted to experience what would happen if his self-control snapped—the small eruptions were frightening enough. I did not fully understand it and I certainly could not articulate it, especially while I was young. However, what I did learn is that anger is bad.

A few years before my father died in 2004, I was visiting my parents in Tulsa, Oklahoma and we went to a restaurant for dinner. We were joined by Daddy's sister, my brother and his wife. The conversation turned to the impending war with Iran and whether or not President George W Bush should send in troops. My father and brother were in favor of war, and I was not. They relentlessly attacked my opinions to prove I was misguided. Mother stayed silent while Aunt Happy tried unsuccessfully to point out that I had the right to my own opinion. For the first time ever, I felt overtly bullied by my father. I had learned to never discuss politics with him, but when my brother asked for my opinion, I gave it. I felt attacked for expressing my feminine voice. Daddy got so angry he started shouting, and everyone in the restaurant heard. I was embarrassed, emotionally upset and angry. I told my father he was treating me like dirt, everyone but my aunt was horrified. I left the table and went to the bathroom to cry and calm myself. Mother appeared and said nothing. I know she was checking if I was okay, but she said nothing—she never did. Only Aunt Happy expressed sympathy and support.

The next day I hugged my father and apologized for yelling. He never did apologize, although I could feel his embarrassment. My brother did apologize for asking the question and then berating me for my answer. All the following was reinforced: never invoke a man's anger; never speak up for your beliefs; never support another woman lest you get included in the anger; women's support does nothing; a woman has no right to feel upset; and definitely no matter what words you use, never tell a man you are being unfairly treated. I then stuffed my feelings away so I could continue to be the loving daughter responsible for caretaking men's egos.

The message I absorbed from my mother was: girls take care of the family, especially men, so their anger does not get out of control. This meant repressing my angry feelings, locking them away so deep they never fully emerge. Of course, my anger would leak out or erupt at times, although not very often. When anger did erupt, it left me feeling out of control, helpless and guilty as if I'd failed, so I'd bury it again. When anger would emerge occasionally from my brothers or father, my response was to go silent and do everything possible to keep my fear and emotions in check and make sure nothing I did would ignite the fire of uncontrollable anger. But once it happened I was terrified it would happen again. I was never afraid they would hurt me—actually the opposite. I was secure in knowing they'd always protect me, and I was grateful. It is a strange convoluted feeling, one I only understood once I'd acknowledged my buried anger and then allowed myself to feel the anger in my body. Owning my feelings of anger created the opportunity to dissolve it.

I know my father loved me in the only way he knew how. He could be very caring and lighthearted. I also know my brothers are basically kind and caring people. Patriarchal values of power-over have been absorbed over lifetimes for men also. Unless they learn to go inward to own and accept their feelings, they'll not be aware of the subtle forms of dominance, aggression and gaslighting they exhibit toward women almost all the time.

I believe this fear of men's anger is part of the mother daughter wound passed down from mother to daughter. We teach our daughters to bury anger as we were taught to bury our anger. I remember a time when Sarah was in high school and she was very angry about how she was being treated by friends. I was trying to help her see past the anger, when she cried, "So I can't even be angry?" It stopped me, and fortunately I said of course she could be angry, but I did not own it. I realize in retrospect how I modeled it was okay to feel the positive emotions, but not anger. I was afraid of anger no matter who was expressing it. We hold deep within our cells and karmic memories the fear of men's anger. Patriarchy taught women to be obedient and compliant or we'd be institutionalized, punished or killed. We also learned to fear the anger of women needing us to conform to the rules of behavior for all women, lest we wake men's harmful anger of suppression, control and sometimes violence.

I have friends whose mothers looked the other way or did not believe when a family member raped or abused them. And if we go deeper into our mothers' lives, we often find they themselves were abused or raped by fathers, brothers, uncles, teachers, strangers and boyfriends. Their answer is to teach their daughters compliance and obedience as the only way to survive. In doing this they can be overly critical, unsupportive and sometimes abusive of their daughters.

When I allowed myself to feel all the anger I'd buried for decades, the opportunity was created to dissolve it. I stopped the thoughts of anger being bad and realized it is only unresolved energy. My thoughts created a monster, a dragon that I thought would consume me if I let it out. Now most of the time when I become angry, I allow it some space and allow myself to feel it so I can transmute it into the fierce love of the divine feminine. The dragon I was afraid of turned into my fiercely protective masculine energy.

## The Soul's Pre-Planning Process

As I begin describing my relationship with grandmothers, mother and daughter it is helpful to remember we choose our family and close friends during the pre-incarnation planning process. We choose the experiences that we believe will help with our awakening and sometimes they are abusive. We choose from our soul family that has incarnated together on earth for many lifetimes. We choose our earth family based on who can help us dissolve the sacred wound we've been carrying lifetime after lifetime. We choose the pivotal players who can help each other in healing and dissolving our sacred wounds. Sometimes the actors in our play act in agreed upon harmful ways in order to quicken our awakening process. We've had lifetimes as a man and as a woman. We've had lifetimes of being predominantly a perpetrator, or victim or savior. We have plumbed the depths of duality and suffering. Yet because of free will, nothing planned is set in stone. The desired awareness and healing may not happen within one lifetime. However, the Holy Mother's plan for awakening is guaranteed because love is real and fear is an illusion.

Our Soul Self or what some call the Over Soul, which is a matrix of all that we are, is much larger than our God Self and our earth-based personal self. Our Soul Self is multidimensional and expresses itself through many dimensions, incarnations and timelines simultaneously. Our God Self or I Am Presence is aware of all these incarnations and ways of being, and therefore acts as a bridge between our earthly personal self and our Soul Self or Interdimensional Self. The awakening or ascension process on earth is perfectly orchestrated with the infinite co-creation and expansion of our Soul Self with the One Source Light's indescribable all-encompassing love for all that is.

I acknowledge that when we look outside ourselves, the world still appears to be in the grip of immense trauma, suffering and pain. When I start feeling trapped or in despair of never waking from this earthly dream of separation, I remind myself that this life is a small part of my Soul Self, and soon I'll return to Oneness. I am also aware during this pivotal time of humanity's awakening that this is my and everyone's last lifetime to incarnate on earth in forgetfulness. All karmic debt has been healed and released. The human-based separated ego is gone. Patriarchy is over. Love is all there is. This dream of separation and fear is a holy experience, one I chose in order to express God's love in ways not previously manifested. I unite with my Over Soul and my soul family to greatly expand the experience of unconditional love. As I write this, I'm aware of how inadequate these earth-bound words are for describing the indescribable. Yet I feel the expansiveness and love within.

These words do not create complacency. They ignite hope and a commitment to continue my inner work to heal the trauma by removing the destructive programming that has kept me enslaved for eons. I remember and embrace the times when I was in seamless, fluid, joyful, co-creation with all organic life, so I can return to co-creation with the Cosmic Mother during this planetary awakening.

## Chapter Three

# The Mother Daughter Relationship

This movement about the mother daughter relationship describes the patriarchal programming that is passed down through the mother line. It affects our relationships with children, siblings, partners, and other women and men. Therefore, even if you do not have children, I believe it is necessary to explore and understand the relationship with our primary mother figure in order to recognize and heal patriarchal programming which affects all relationships. The primary mother figure can be a birth mother, stepmother, adopted mother, godmother, or another woman such as: an aunt, a grandmother or a special friend. Some women were raised primarily by their father. An absent mother has its own set of concerns about what we learn about mothering and relationships.

Whether or not you have a daughter, what Sarah and I learned about the mother daughter relationship helps with understanding my relationship with my mother as well as my son. And if you have no daughters, it can help in understanding how the relationship with your mother affects how you raise and care for your sons. If you never had children it still affects all your relationships.

The late 1800s and early 1900s was a time when the patriarchal strictures governing women's lives was loosening. In the USA, it was a time of women's suffrage, the abolition of slavery and the spiritualist movement. More and more women wanted to be educated and were actively involved in trying to make the world a better place. While most education within separation is a form of indoctrination to the power-over paradigm, it is part of the process women needed to experience in order to eventually be in a place to say No to victimhood.

This education movement included women of all colors. For example, in 1847 Elizabeth Blackwell became the first white woman to receive a medical degree in the USA. In 1864 Rebecca Lee Crumpler became the first Black American in the USA to receive a medical degree. Susan La Flesche became the first Native American woman to receive a medical degree in 1889. This trend continued with more and more women attending colleges and graduate schools in all professions.

I clearly see how the efforts of many women paved the way for who I am today. I am grateful to have grown up with the freedom to vote, the freedom to go to college and graduate school, the freedom to choose any career I wanted, and the freedom to get married or not. Women who came before me prepared a path that helped me follow my heart's spiritual journey. The spiral from one generation to the next is always upward and inward into the heart, like the labyrinth. Both my grandmothers in their own way were pioneers for women's freedom from victimhood.

## Relationship with My Grandmothers

### *My Maternal Grandmother*

I never met my maternal grandmother. She died when Mother was 18 years old and a freshman in college. Sarah Edith was her name and Sarah is my name, although most people call me Sally. Even though women were breaking down barriers to education, teachers' colleges were about all there were for women's higher education. Edith attended teacher's college and evidently was a talented mathematician. However, as was expected of women, when Edith married, she stopped teaching in order to raise a family. Mother's stories of Edith were full of love for my mother and her brother. Edith was constantly volunteering which was mostly the only outlet for married women's intelligence and ambition. This must have influenced my mother's desire to volunteer for what she felt were worthy causes. Edith expected her daughter to go to college and I can imagine was delighted that there was a wider variety of colleges from which mother could choose. I am glad she was able to watch her daughter leave for college before she died.

### *My Fraternal Grandmother*

My fraternal grandmother was a remarkable woman. All of her grandchildren called her Mommu, though her given name was Neal. I learned a lot about Mommu's life as I interviewed and recorded her and my grandfather, Daddy Pat, about their lives. She went to the Emporia Teacher's College in Pittsburgh, Kansas, and was teaching second grade in Coffeyville, Kansas when she met my grandfather. Mommu then left to teach in Nowata, Oklahoma followed by teaching 3 years in Laramie, Wyoming. Teaching in the west was unusual for women, so this seems very courageous and independent of her. When she came home for Christmas in 1915, she became engaged. As to be expected, she gave up teaching when she married.

I adored my grandfather, but Mommu was more problematic. She was a very determined and independent woman within the confines of family life. She managed the household and ruled the family and could be quite controlling. I imagine Mommu in present times might be a very successful business woman. While I loved and respected her, I was always somewhat wary of her. Though she could seem aloof, with her grandchildren she was always considerate and conscientious. Mother told me when I was an adult that I was very much like Mommu, only with more compassion. As I have mostly dissolved my need to control my life and the people within my orbit, it feels what's left is the compassion.

Mommu was a Christian Scientist, so I got an early introduction to the metaphysical teachings of Mary Baker Eddy. I now consider Christian Science to be a precursor to *A Course in Miracles*. Mommu's deep devotion and faith made an impression on me, although I dismissed it as not having any relevance in my life. Nevertheless, when I became a student of ACIM, I recognized the similarities immediately, and I'm grateful for the early exposure. The following story illustrates how I was influenced by Mommu's faith.

I started getting migraines when I was 12 years old and continued to get them until a few years ago. Sometimes they would disappear for a few years, only to return. It usually took about 2 days in bed to recover. Sometime in my twenties while I was home for the summer, my cousin was getting married. The day of the wedding I got a migraine, but I was still determined to attend. While at the church, Mommu approached, placed her white-gloved hands on either side of my face and gently told me the migraine was created by my thoughts, and therefore I was not sick. Immediately I felt a wave of peace wash through me and as I sat in the church, the migraine disappeared. This had never occurred before. It took many, many years until I understood what she was teaching.

I feel grandmother Edith's influence passed down through my mother, and I feel Mommu's influence passed directly to me. They each had a hand in shaping my life: the love, independence, the belief in education, and the strength of women to the home and family. Nevertheless, the frustration of being confined to the home and raising children leaks through in mother's stories of her mother and my witnessing Mommu's need to rule and control her home and family. After Mommu died at age 94, my father told me that she was a remarkable woman, but not very loving. I know mother often struggled to balance Mommu's opinions on how she should manage her family with her own desires and beliefs. Fortunately for my brothers and me, our mother's love for us was always foremost in her interactions. Within these stories is the sacred wound of being the "second sex" and the expectation to always serve men's needs. The patriarchal wound passed down through the female line is usually variations of this theme of being second best, not good enough and abandonment of our wild feminine selves to obedience in order to be protected by a man.

## Relationship with My Mother

Mother was born in 1920 at the end of WWI and the year the 19th amendment was passed in the US giving women the right to vote. It always boggles my mind that mother's generation was the first to grow up knowing they could vote. It was the start of the Roaring Twenties, a time of prosperity, the jazz age and a loosening of the mores designating women's appropriate behavior. This was reflected in freer clothing (like trousers or shorter skirts), shorter hair and more women in the workforce.

Mother was born to an economically comfortable family. The expectation that white women should be educated in order to be better wives for their husbands and raise intelligent children was becoming the norm. This created a situation in which mostly women with financial means went to college and sometimes even graduate school but were still expected to marry and stay at home to take care of the children. My mother went to Smith College with Betty Freidan, who wrote the *Feminine Mystique,* considered to be a catalyst for the feminist movement. The seeds were being sown for women within a certain socioeconomic class to be educated and work outside of the home.

During WWII, some women once again got a taste of independence by working and making money while men were needed to fight. They were hired into jobs essential to keeping the country functioning. Then of course the men returned from the war and women were expected to hand over their jobs and return to raising children. The 1950s were all about the patriarchal family, women being dutiful wives, birthing children and rebuilding after the war. This created a highly frustrating situation for women who felt they had more to offer than only staying at home. Therefore, women like my mother put their education to use by becoming volunteers: running school boards, PTAs and nonprofit organizations while leaving time to take care of the home and children. While all these female volunteers were an enormous benefit for society, their unpaid work was considered secondary to the importance of men's jobs.

Like her mother, my mother was always volunteering, primarily for the Young Women's Christian Association (YWCA), the United Fund and Tulsa, OK museums. While we lived in Houston, mother became the president of the local YWCA and was elected to the National YWCA Board. When my father was abruptly transferred back to Tulsa, she had to give up her dream of serving on the national board. Daddy was in the oil business, and we moved often from Tulsa to four different towns in West Texas, back to Tulsa, then to Houston, and then back again to Tulsa. Mother said she had nightmares about moving. I did not like it either. I found out much later as an adult how bitterly disappointed she was to give up her spot on the national YWCA board. In Tulsa she served as president of the local YWCA, but it did not provide the same opportunities as being on the national board.

Mother was passionate about the visual arts—drawing, oil painting, collage and the fiber arts. She had wanted to major in art in college; however, her father felt she could not make a living with art and encouraged her to major in English. Teaching was an acceptable career for women. One of Mother's professors suggested she do a double major in art and English but she was too scared to try. Later when she told me about passing up this opportunity, she admitted how much she regretted not following her heart. Eventually she was able to attend graduate school in her forties and received a master's degree in art history from the University of Tulsa. This led to volunteering at Tulsa museums, cataloging paintings and working in their stores.

Working in the museum stores gave her an idea to start her own business and sell American folk art.

Mother inherited some money and two Illinois farms from her father, which gave her the financial independence to buy or do things she wanted. Seeing this encouraged me to want to work for a living so I would not have to be dependent on a man for money. When mother went to the bank to get a loan to launch her business, the bank representative refused unless my father would co-sign the loan, even though she was using her own money. My father was quietly furious. In protest he removed his considerable business account from that bank and moved it to another bank more open to working with women. The respect he held for mother's capability made a huge impression on me.

Mother's store opened while I was in college. It lasted for several years and while it received wonderful reviews, it was never financially successful. When she closed the store, it was the first time I saw my mother visibly depressed. Her art work followed the same pattern. She received wonderful reviews but sold very few of her paintings. I know she felt these failures deeply. This wound of never being quite good enough or successful enough is passed down through the female line. I have felt it many times and only now am aware enough to clear it.

Many of my friends' mothers were highly educated but gave up all their hopes and dreams of a career to tend to their husbands' homes and raise children, as expected in the 1950s through the 1980s and even somewhat today. Some of these women channeled all their frustrated ambitions into their sons and daughters—sometimes in controlling and unhealthy ways. This is the distorted feminine energy reacting to the subjugation of women for thousands of years. Equality with men is denied and our wild feminine power is suppressed.

## *My Story as Daughter*

I was born on my mother's birthday in 1950 which created a special bond between us. Mother always said I was the best birthday present she ever received. I believed her. She never gave me any reason not to. When I was 4, she commissioned an artist to paint my portrait. She called me her golden child. As I got older, I began to realize not everyone had a loving mother. As a young adult, having a loving mother started to feel unusual and not the norm. It has only been in the last few years in conversations with my two brothers that I realized how much mother worked behind the scenes to ensure that all her children were safe, cared for and treated properly, especially in school.

Nurturing and caring for children above all else is passed down through the female line. It is an embodied memory of the Holy Mother's love for all her children. Yet with the devaluing of the feminine spirit came the shadow side of this love. Some women became over possessive and demanding of their children, hoping their children would fulfill their mother's unrealized ambition and desire for something more. Women modeled for their daughters this behavior of sole responsibility for caretaking the family. I never talked about this with my mother; I just knew, this was my role. We tend to the men and siblings in the family and in return the men and boys protect and provide for the women and girls. But in so doing, we learned our needs came second. In retrospect I see how my mother sacrificed her needs to take care of her family.

I learned many things from my mother. I learned how to be a loving mother. I learned the art of listening and caring about people. I learned kindness and compassion. I learned what it means to follow your dream and what happens when you don't. I also learned that following your dream can end in failure. I learned about strong women and being myself. I learned that sometimes sacrificing my needs was necessary to maintain the status quo in the family. I learned anger was an inappropriate emotion for girls and to bury it as she did. I learned from my mother that I had value—and I learned sometimes it was not enough. I learned I was special because I was a girl but my brothers were also special and equally loved. I learned it was okay to be unhappy at times and that she was always there for me, a loving presence. I learned women are supposed to stay silent when men get angry.

My mother gifted her children with a childhood that allowed squabbles, mistakes, failures and disappointments all wrapped in many moments of joy. Mother was a visual artist who painted with oils, created gorgeous tapestries with needle point and created wonderful mixed media paintings with fiber arts. She was constantly experimenting and creating. She encouraged my creativity with pottery classes and various art and handcraft projects.

Mother learned early that I was passionate about music, so I started piano lessons when I was 5 and sang in the choir. She gave me a guitar one Christmas much to my delight. Her mother had been an accomplished pianist. So not only did I inherit her name but also her passion for music. It is my children who inherited Mother's visual art talent.

Sometimes she didn't understand me because we did not discuss feelings, but it was okay. We read books, hundreds of books. In many ways this is how we shared our feelings. We were always reading and blocking out the world. I shared children's books I loved the most and she always read them. This continued as I grew older, and eventually we shared spiritual books we were reading. She gave me many biographies of successful women. I also fell in love with the Nancy Drew mysteries and read all the books in the series. Mother explained to me when I was an adult that her intent was to foster the belief that a woman could be anyone she wanted to be. I became a feminist before it was a popular concept. To this day, the written word can speak to my heart in ways nothing else can.

Mother gifted me with the space to be myself, to be introverted and to hide away when I wanted. I could be upset, a stubbornly difficult teenager, or unkind to her and yet I knew there was nothing I could do to stop her loving me. I was angry when she talked too much. I was angry and embarrassed when she fell asleep during a presentation in grade school. I was angry and upset at times when I felt she did not understand. I was angry when she never asked questions about my feelings—yet I never volunteered to tell her. And on a certain level it felt okay. She taught me the power of forgiveness because she always forgave her children for any disagreements or misdeeds.

Mother was deeply spiritual and had a strong Christian faith. Nevertheless, she never imposed her faith and beliefs on her children. We were never forced to attend Sunday school. She said each person needed to find their own spiritual path and faith. Mother lost her family of origin in 8 years. First her mother died, then her younger brother died in WWII and her father died toward the end of the war, just after my oldest brother was born. She told me her faith got her through these years of grief. After Mother died in 2007, I found a book she had read and underlined about *A Course in Miracles*. I wish I had known, so we could have talked about it.

## Sarah and My Stories as Mother and Daughter

This book is dedicated to my daughter and is for all daughters everywhere. Literally this book would not have been written without my daughter Sarah's courage to work together to heal our mother daughter wound. I am of the generation trying to prove women could do it all: be married, work full time, give birth, raise a family, volunteer, and have a social life. This was how we were going to win equality with men: by proving our ability to do it all. The feminist revolution was in full swing when I birthed Sarah.

My first two books tell the story of my relationship with my son Tyler. This book is for Sarah and includes the story of my relationship with my daughter. The spiritual work we are doing together in my elder years is profoundly healing and makes this book possible. By working and sharing with Sarah, I came to understand more fully the mother daughter wound I was carrying and how I passed this wound to my daughter. It is the catalyst for my embrace of the Universal Grandmother archetype. This joining and healing the relationship with my daughter means I relate our story backward, to seeing it with new eyes of understanding.

When my husband Rick and I moved to New Mexico from Massachusetts, Sarah was living and working in Washington, DC, and then rural Virginia. She eventually moved to Santa Fe and received her master's degree in counseling and art therapy. She works as a trauma therapist in Santa Fe. We talk frequently and she is able to visit us regularly which is opportunity for mother daughter healing.

Sarah's therapist education and training provides the language and insights that help us understand the mother daughter dynamic. Her training gives her many techniques for acknowledging and feeling the core sacred wound she's been carrying lifetime after lifetime. During the pre-soul planning process, we chose each other and agreed to do this work to heal the mother daughter wound. Sarah initiated this process. At first, I did not know there was anything to heal.

A few years ago, Sarah called me, extremely upset and crying about an incident in which she felt deliberately excluded from a gathering of friends. It felt like middle school all over again. I suggested she come visit so we could hike and talk about it. When I hung up, I asked myself, where was I during these middle school years when I was unaware of Sarah's experiences? I realized I'd been consumed with Tyler's needs, getting him out of the public school system and ensuring he was able to stay in a private school for children with language-based learning disabilities. I was also working full time.

After Sarah arrived and we were walking, I apologized for being so consumed with Tyler's needs that I was unaware of what she was going through. We held each other and cried. Then she shared what it was like growing up with Tyler. She talked about how she decided the best way to help mommy and daddy was to be the best student possible and to handle problems herself. And she did excel at almost everything she decided to do, especially visual art and academics. She said I was never an absent mother and she knew I loved her, but somewhere deep inside she felt abandoned and unloved. I finally understood I contributed to this feeling of abandonment by writing two books on how Tyler was a catalyst for my spiritual journey, never once considering how Sarah felt.

I became aware of how I passed down from my mother the expectation that Sarah needed to be strong in order to take care of herself and to tend to the men in the family. I relied on her to be okay so I could take care of Tyler, and there was an implicit understanding that she should support my efforts. After all the training and writing I had done about not forgetting the needs of the siblings of atypical children, I was mortified and heartbroken to have missed what was happening with my daughter. I couldn't believe I never asked her how she was doing. After all, I taught about the gift of a question and unconditional listening. I assumed she was okay because that was how she presented herself and, to be truthful, that is what I expected.

There has been a lot of healing over the past few years for both of us. Sarah was the impetus for finally recognizing how much anger I'd buried for decades. The process of clearing this anger is described in greater length in the movement on anger. Sarah was also the catalyst for me to go deeper into understanding the mother daughter wound. This came about when she told me her sacred wound was abandonment. It took great courage. She was concerned that I'd feel hurt. Initially I was dismayed because I could not understand how this was possible. I had wanted her and loved her so much.

I spent a few weeks opening to how I contributed to Sarah's sacred wound of abandonment. I started with reminding myself that each person carries within through all their incarnations, the sacred wound of separation. My sacred wound of feeling second best led me to try to manage and control everything, to make Sarah and Tyler's lives as perfect as possible, believing this showed how much I loved them. This did not fuel Tyler's core wound of feeling left behind as I was constantly advocating for Tyler's educational rights so that he would not be left behind.

Sarah and I had already done a lot of healing work about being emotionally unavailable at times because of my concerns for Tyler. However, I began to look with new eyes at the birthing and nursing experience with Sarah, and acknowledged unprocessed feelings of grief and anger. As a baby and small child, she would not have understood those times that seemed as if she'd been abandoned. So the next time she came to visit, I shared my story, crying periodically as I talked. I had never allowed myself to feel and cry about my experience of giving birth to Sarah. The telling of it was immensely healing, especially for me.

In an effort to control the birthing process, Western medicine successfully convinced women that strangers in the form of doctors and nurses knew what was best for us and our babies. We gave birth on our backs instead of squatting, making the birthing process more painful. Cesarian births increased, and bottle feeding was extolled under the guise of being the best for the baby. Women even went through a period when we were encouraged to let our babies cry when they were hungry so they'd be trained to a strict feeding schedule. Thankfully I did not follow this advice. When Sarah was born in 1985, there was beginning awareness of how detrimental all of this was to new mothers and infants. I know the birthing process within many hospitals has become kinder and gentler for mother and baby. More and more women are using licensed midwives and birthing at home. There is a massive amount of grief to be healed from the wounding in our wombs by men adhering to the power-over paradigm, trying to control the birthing process, because the one thing they cannot physically do is conceive and birth new souls into life.

It is important for women to share their stories of giving birth and nursing. When I review those years, I realize how my friends and I rarely talked about how we felt being pregnant, giving birth and nursing. We shared information and took Lamaze classes to learn about natural child birth, and I was fortunate to deliver at a hospital following these methods. But we did not talk about our feelings. It is only recently I've shared my feelings with a few friends and they shared theirs for the first time. I share my experience of birthing and nursing Sarah because it is another example of the mother daughter patriarchal wound.

When I became pregnant at age 34, all I wanted was a girl. This was very important to me. In a sense, I felt birthing a girl would allow me to relax and not worry about gender if we decided to have another baby. While I wanted a child, I did not enjoy being pregnant. I was constantly nauseous for the first 4 months and also developed gestational diabetes. I was very thin, but for some reason the obstetrician and his nurses were terribly worried I would gain too much weight. This added extra stress.

Sarah was 2 weeks late and the birthing process was long and exhausting. The medical team was worried about Sarah's heart rate because she had eliminated in utero. I had to wear a heavy belt to monitor her heart rate, which contributed to pain in my back during contractions. A representative of the company who built the belt offered $100 if he could film the birth. I was appalled. It was such an intrusive and uncaring offer. Rick and I said No. Thankfully a nurse removed the belt because she felt it was not needed. Once Sarah was born, they whisked her off to be placed in an incubator. I was shaking and crying uncontrollably; when a nurse asked what was wrong, I complained I had spent all this time giving birth and I'd not even seen Sarah or held her. The nurse immediately put me in a wheel chair and took us to see Sarah in the incubator. For a new infant born with the sacred wound of abandonment, I realized this experience contributed to this feeling. Never doubt that infants retain memories within their cells of the birthing experience. The influence of separation consciousness starts immediately.

In the morning they brought Sarah to me to nurse and I held her for the first time. I thought this would be easy; it is natural. But it wasn't. The nurses kept telling me I would be okay. Rick stayed home from work for 2 weeks, but could not assist with breast feeding. And I foolishly followed a friend's advice to tell mother not to show up for 2 weeks so I could figure out this mothering thing by myself. That was a mistake. I so needed my mother's love and support. We learned to do it alone, because asking for help from other women had been systematically programmed out of us.

I was determined to nurse Sarah. There was and still is a lot of controversy over the benefits of using infant formulas instead of breast feeding. The patriarchal propaganda extolled bottle feeding, while implying women should not nurse because that is what poor people and animals do. My mother was told breast feeding was harming my brother Mark, so she did not try to nurse me. I felt outraged for her. I have a friend a few years older than me who said the doctors never gave her the option to nurse. They made her take a pill to dry up the milk and she was too young and inexperienced to protest.

Sarah and I did not immediately bond over breastfeeding. I realize I was so tense that she could not relax. The more she did not relax and nurse, the more tense I got. After a few days I was able to nurse by lying on my side on the floor and placing Sarah next to me. She would only do this from one side, so I'd manually express the milk from my other breast to make sure the milk would not dry up. Our female pediatrician was wonderful, encouraging, and assuring me this was not unusual and that Sarah and I would eventually work it out. We did after about 2 weeks, which felt like forever.

After that all was well until I decided to work part-time when Sarah was 6 months old. Sarah and I had bonded while nursing and she was content. To prepare for going back to work Rick tried to give her my milk from a bottle. She completely refused. Fortunately, she was in family day care with a wonderful woman who loved the small group of children under her care. Mabs became Sarah and Tyler's second mother, and they loved her unconditionally. When Sarah refused to take the bottle, Mabs would have all the other children stand in a circle, sing and clap to distract Sarah long enough for her to nurse from the bottle. I would breast feed Sarah before dropping her off at daycare and then immediately nurse after I retrieved her. It meant Sarah would nurse several times during the night to prepare herself to go without much nourishment during the day. I was exhausted.

Before I became pregnant, I was involved in a year-long project with a group of professionals from all over the US. We met four times in a year and our last meeting occurred soon after I returned to work. I had to fly to Des Moines, Iowa from Boston, Massachusetts. I did not want to go on this trip; however, I felt I had no choice. For days I expressed milk to freeze, and Rick took time off from work to care for Sarah the days I was gone.

For 3 days Sarah refused to drink any milk from the bottle. She fussed and cried and Rick was beside himself with worry. A friend came over and slowly encouraged Sarah to take the milk by dripping it into her mouth with a spoon. Rick said that Sarah was most unhappy with this effort. When I finally arrived home, I was longing to take Sarah in my arms and nurse, but she refused. I was heartbroken by the whole affair. Fortunately, Sarah relented and we nursed that night before bed.

I am sure all this drama over nursing added to Sarah's sacred wound of abandonment. It just was. It was not something I understood at the time. I was doing the best I could with the belief and determination that women could work outside of the home while raising children. It still is a divisive issue.

Like my mother, I fiercely loved my children and felt it was my responsibility to make sure they were always safe and fairly treated in school. I was a product of the feminist movement: do it all and raise strong, independent, well-educated daughters and sons respectful of women. I passed this all to my daughter—who learned early not to ask for what she needed emotionally. She became the best student ever, and sacrificed her emotional needs so she would not be a burden while so much of my energy was focused on caring for Tyler.

### *The Silent Scream*

When I did some research into whether or not there were any therapists focusing on the mother daughter wound, I discovered there are very few. I came across Rosjke Hasseldine who has been a pioneer therapist for healing the mother daughter relationship. One of her books is titled *The Silent Scream*. This resonated deep within—the idea that women have been silently screaming for thousands of years to be heard, to be released from the bondage of unexpressed feelings and needs. I realize it describes me, and I soon learned it describes Sarah.

It has been over a year writing this chapter and Christmas came again with the mother daughter wound once again calling for healing. Both Sarah and Tyler are scheduled to visit. I receive a call from Sarah—she's in crisis, triggered by a feeling she needs to change her relationship with the man she's been with for 6 years. She is depressed and panicky and scared that it means she needs to break up with him. He is her best friend. Because they live together, she told him she needed a break and packed herself and her kitten to come spend at least 4 weeks with us through Christmas and New Year. During the pandemic she's been doing all her therapy sessions with clients via Zoom or phone, so she can work anywhere.

When Sarah arrived, she asked me to listen, and I said I could do that. She told me through many tears that she's always felt divided, not whole. When she decided to take a break from her relationship, she felt the core of herself inside her womb come together for the first time ever. And she grieved. Sarah admitted she was deeply depressed to the point she felt as if she no longer wanted to live. She did assure me she would not follow through with this feeling. I remained calm and trusted in Sarah's ability to heal herself because I've been in that place of despair. I knew there was something other than a potential break up fueling this depression.

### *The Gift of Depression*

Women's depression is often a consequence of suppressing our wild, creative, intuitive feminine wisdom. Eons of patriarchal conditioning passed down the mother line can render us incapable of plumbing the depths of our unconscious yearnings for freedom from the cage we've built around our hearts. We have been programmed to give our allegiance to the traditional patriarchal structures that keep us tied to cultural and family traditions which rarely honor the longing of our soul. We learned to bottle up our feelings and needs—shoving them deep inside and into our shadow. When our inner feelings erupt, we become too scared to look inside because we were taught that it is wrong. We will continue to run away from the truth of who we are until our bodies start to hurt. When we feel dying is preferrable to continuing to function in our stagnant life, depression ushers in the dark night of the soul. It also ushers in the possibility of change. This is the gift of depression. We have to stop all that does not serve us to look deep inside in order to listen to the voice of the Self that's been waiting to get our attention.

What if we have the courage to see depression as a gift, an opportunity to delve into those youthful dreams we set aside in order to appease a patriarchal god that demands the sacrifice of our Soul's yearnings? Does Sarah have the courage to see her depression as a gift to embrace her Soul's yearning? Does she have the courage to stop running from her pain to eventually engage in a compassionate life full of joy? Do I have the courage as a mother to trust Sarah's pain and hold the space for her to understand the gift of depression?

What triggered sharing her deepest hurt occurred when Sarah volunteered to arise at 4am to drive Tyler to the airport in time for an early flight. We live an hour-and-a-half from the Santa Fe airport. Rick and I offered to go instead but she said she felt it was important to have a reason to get up in the morning. I stripped the sheets from Tyler's bed then decided to also strip Sarah's bed so she'd have clean sheets for the remaining week of her visit. I ignored the tiny voice whispering to wait. When Sarah returned from the airport, she was tired, wanted to sleep, and understandably upset that I had removed her sheets. With her help I remade the bed and she went to sleep. She felt this was an example of how I've not understood her needs which was the trigger she needed to tell me her deepest wound.

Later in the day she asked, "Can you help me?" I listened as she shared her deepest wound. This is the wound of the inner child existing in the shadow, unacknowledged and cut off from our God Self until the hurt becomes so overpowering, we are forced to pay attention. Sarah talked about how she thought I never really loved her because I did not hug her as a child when she was upset. All she wanted was for me to hug her and tell her it was okay. She saw other children receiving hugs from their mothers and wondered why I did not love her enough to hug her. She reminded me of a time when she told me about receiving a hug from a mother in nursery school and then the mother realized she was not hugging her son and kindly let Sarah go. Sarah felt so ashamed. I thought at the time how lovely it was that another mother hugged her. I was clueless that her story was a call for love through hugging.

Sarah began to feel that she did not deserve to have her needs met, as if it was her fault; and this turned into denying what she wanted even if it was offered to her. She shared the many times this happened, like when her aunt offered to style her hair for a family celebration of my parents' fiftieth wedding anniversary. I remember her continuing to say No, even after I encouraged her to say Yes. Sarah told me she so wanted her aunt to do this, but something inside told her she did not deserve to have her wants met.

I listened to Sarah, amazed at her courage and was also emotionally devasted. I had a momentary thought that this could not be true, and then I felt the truth deep inside. Who does this, I asked myself? What mother would not hug her small child in affirmation of her love? How could I have missed this when I loved Sarah so much? This brought up my memories as a child about not receiving hugs.

I shared the following with Sarah during a span of 4 days, most of the time holding her hands or with my hand on her knee and hugging her. I realized that a physical presence was necessary for some deep healing for both of us. I began to admit to myself my aversion to hugs. Sometime around third grade I made a semi-conscious decision to be more like my father than my mother. I felt my father was more powerful, and that if I wanted to survive I should emulate him. My father did not hug. I am sure it was me who conveyed to my mother I no longer wanted to be hugged.

One night after Sarah had told me about her unmet need to be hugged, I asked Mother Mary's help in understanding why hugging was so uncomfortable that I'd stopped embracing my young children. I received a dream of being forced to have sex with a man and being held down and pursued with his deep assurance that this was something I wanted. I woke upset. It felt totally unhelpful. Mother Mary said that I carried this terror of being restrained from many lifetimes and it manifested as an aversion to hugging. While this explained my difficulty hugging adults, hugging a child is different. I could not forgive myself. I told Sarah this felt like trying to forgive the unforgivable.

I remembered a friend who had birthed five children asking to come over and hold Tyler when he was a baby. She loved the full-bodied hugs of babies which was one reason she had had so many children. She wanted another baby but was honoring her husband's feeling that five children were enough. I understood her love of hugging babies, and neither one of us thought that maybe these hugs did not have to end when the children got a little older.

In my mind everything I did was for my children—while also working, volunteering, taking care of the house and planning family time together. Rick and I split the household chores fairly equally. We arranged our work schedules around the everyday activities of raising children and their schools and day care. Yet each of us had issues with unrecognized anger, Rick from an emotionally abusive mother and me from burying my anger about living within patriarchy. So yes, we'd argue at times and evidently Sarah felt all of this. As is often typical in families of my generation, the children came to me whenever they were upset. I always listened, responded and supported. I felt I was open minded, fair and flexible. Sarah validated this, yet what she needed most as a child was physical reassurance, a loving hug.

Our move to New Mexico in 2011 started the process of deepening my spiritual journey of awakening. As I learned to let go, trust and receive, I began to hug friends and sometimes even new acquaintances. If I felt unsure about a person's response, I would simply ask if they wanted a hug. The culture of New Mexico is more open to hugging, unlike the white puritan culture of the Northeast. In addition, I started regularly going to spiritual retreats which encouraged opening to receiving God's love, and therefore hugs between participants were freely given. When Sarah moved to Santa Fe, I started hugging her more.

The last day of another visit by Sarah, we hugged each other with a full-bodied hug while we both cried. I kissed her and said how much I loved her and how grateful I was that she had the courage to tell me her deepest wound. We ended with the symbolic affirmation of my brushing her hair and creating an inverted pony tail braid. After she returned to Santa Fe, I received a text saying she believes I have always loved her, and I cried with relief and gratitude.

Maya Luna has written a poem that beautifully expresses the process of healing the mother daughter wound. Maya writes about giving up on healing trauma through all the traditional ways in which the separated state conditions us to fix ourselves. Instead:

*Today*
*I gave up*
*On healing my trauma*
*I gave up*

*On practicing the skills*
*To become whole*
*Today I gave up*
*On evolving*
*Into that ever elusive*
*Better version of myself*
*Today I submitted*
*To the wound of love*
*I stopped pointing at it*
*Looking at it*
*Soothing it*
*Tweaking it*
*Fixing it*
*Finessing it*
*Hiding it*
*Polishing it*
*I stopped this game of separation*
*I crawled inside the wound*
*And spread it open*
*I decided to wear it like a gown*
*I accepted my total and utter*
*Failure*
*To be anything else*
*But me*[30]

Sarah and I crawled inside the mother daughter wound, we spread it open and abided in it without trying to fix anything. We stayed present with each other as we shared our hurts and pain, we cried, we held each other, releasing judgment and blame. I learned hugs are a way to be totally present and loving—a physical demonstration of what it means to listen unconditionally.

Depression is a gift that helped us crawl inside the wound.

## Crawling Inside the Wound Becomes Total Surrender to What Is

For both men and women our first formative experience with feminine power and love is through our mothers. With the feminine essence severally damaged and fractured, the cultural ideal of women being all-loving, nurturing and powerful in our wisdom is a myth pointing to long forgotten ancient times. We keep thinking this ideal mother will show up, yet she never does within separation. Daughters growing up within patriarchy often feel they have to choose between feeling empowered and being loved. Being loved traditionally has meant accepting our place as the second sex. Even with the best intentions from more cognizant loving mothers, this feeling of worthlessness is subtly reinforced by the patriarchal culture. Feeling empowered means shedding the distortions of the feminine that kept our grandmothers and mothers from being fully who they could have been. If mothers are unaware of their own conditioning, it can lead to continuous conflict between mothers and daughters.

The mother wound affects both sons and daughters and this carries over into all of our relationships. Therefore, healing this wound is essential. This wound affects daughters' relationships with other siblings whether male or female. Remember before incarnating we choose our family based on how we can help each other heal our core wounds. The day Sarah took Tyler to the airport and shared her deepest wound, Tyler's flight was canceled and Rick had to return to the airport to bring him home. Sarah admitted to me that she was still resentful of Tyler, which obviously affected her relationship with him. Tyler's return gave her a wonderful opportunity to talk and share with him. I continue to be grateful and inspired by her courage to express her deepest feelings.

Tyler shared with me later that he told Sarah how difficult it was growing up with dyslexia and always being in the shadow of a sister who was such a talented student and gifted artist.

Sarah told me that she was aware of this, and thought making herself small by not fully embracing her gifts would help. I'm guessing this revelation will start to ease Sarah's resentment and allow it to dissolve, so they can have a more honest and loving relationship. Now that Tyler has found his passion in the art of tattooing and watercolor painting, he no longer needs to feel he is in Sarah's shadow. The healing begins for Sarah to dissolve her feelings of resentment of Tyler for seemingly limiting my love for her.

Women must do the work of healing and clearing their core wounds to stop the continual transmission of this destructive feminine energy. Of course, fathers are complicit in upholding the patriarchal structures and distortions contributing to the mother daughter wound. There is also much healing to do with father daughter relationships. *Healing relationships with fathers gains clarity, once the mother daughter wound is understood.* Absorbing patriarchal programming from mothers can feel like betrayal of what our heart knows and desires. This plays out in the relationship dynamic between husbands and wives. Over and over again, daughters witness the conflict arising with their mother's conscious and unconscious support of patriarchal structures and values. We want our mothers to be our guiding light, to be on our side instead of our fathers'. When Daddy yelled at me that time in the restaurant, I wanted my mother to empathize, to help me navigate and to understand what was going on. Instead, she remained silent when I so needed some feminine wisdom. *Forgiving our mothers opens the door to forgiving our fathers.*

After Sarah shared her deepest hurt, I realized I held a very deep fear that maybe I was a failure as a mother. I abided in this pain of failure for a few days until something inside shifted to self-forgiveness. Even though I missed consistently showing my physical love, both my children have always felt comfortable coming to me without fear of judgment or criticism. This creates an environment and expectation that both Sarah and Tyler can talk to me about anything troubling them. While it still took an immense amount of courage to share her deepest hurt, Sarah did have every reason to believe I would be receptive and not angry. I also knew Sarah came into this incarnation with the wound of abandonment, so that no matter how I behaved toward her, it would trigger the feeling of not being loved or wanted. With this understanding I accepted that I've always done the best I could with the awareness I had in each moment, and the pain began to dissipate.

Crawling inside the wound in order to surrender to what is feels counterintuitive. But what happens is that we bring light to our deepest wounds and fears, the ones that have been hidden in the shadow. Crawling inside the wound instead of trying to soothe, polish or fix it is an act of saving ourselves.

It is a pause on one of the many folds or turns of our mystical labyrinth journey into our heart and womb. It may happen more than once. Even in our darkest moments, we can be assured that we won't get lost. We know the folding in and out of our journey is necessary for dissolving all that does not serve us. It is a constant path of surrendering to what is until all that is left is our true divine self, existing within the Cosmic Mother's primordial womb of infinite beginnings and endings, infinite creations, infinite possibilities and infinite love.

## Chapter Four

# Forgiving Mothers, Daughters, Sisters and Ourselves

We have lived so long under patriarchy's programming, passing on the fears of separation is automatic unless we've done the cleansing inner work. The three overarching patriarchal roles of rebel/heretic, whore/temptress, obedient/pure woman, and all the variations of these roles are still in play even though women are much freer to follow their hearts than they ever have been before. In order to keep women from accessing their inherent power sourced from love, we learned: to fear men's anger and our own; to believe men were both our persecutors and saviors, providers and protectors. We learned to bury our anger and our wild beautiful hearts; to not trust and to compete with other women especially for men's approval; to decorate ourselves in sexually attractive ways under the gaze of men; to never be more intelligent than a man; to constantly second guess our innate knowing of our feminine bodies; to be wary of strange men and to never walk alone at night; to believe that following our hearts is selfish; and to believe that our wants and needs are always secondary to men's wants and needs.

I thought I was reinforcing independence from these fears to Sarah, but I taught resistance—which keeps the fears ever present. These fears are in the collective unconscious and are still insidiously and often blatantly present. We learn them from other women and our female friends and they are reinforced by our fathers, brothers and other male family members. We learn them from the media. This is life within separation consciousness.

Sarah shared that when she is upset and cries, she feels guilty because she feels she has no right to cry. No healing occurs because she can't accept how she's feeling, leaving her stuck in a cycle of being upset, overwhelmed and alone. Many women share the belief that unless we experienced some type of overt trauma, we have no right to complain, feel angry or cry about our struggles. I held this belief until I accepted and cleared my anger. I have friends who experienced abuse as a child, or rape, or an abusive marriage and they also feel the same way. Life within separation consciousness is traumatic and we've experienced lifetimes of trauma.

One summer after my junior year in college, I worked as a substitute child care worker in a psychiatric hospital for children. I often worked on the ward for young children. A 4-year-old boy was terrified of being touched. One day I walked into the day room and he was crying. Every part of me wanted to reach out in some way to ease his pain. Yet he was terrified of me coming too close. He eventually told me he was crying because he'd been pushed off the swing by another child. I told him it was okay to cry and he yelled, "No, my father told me never to cry!" He was wound up tight, afraid to cry, judging himself for crying and expecting harsh punishment from me. I felt helpless to provide any comfort to relieve his unrelenting pain.

This may feel like an extreme example of what happens when we teach our children that feelings and physical reassurance are unacceptable. Whether traumatic or subtle, everyone living within separation's power-over paradigm receives this message over and over again: succumbing to our feelings is weak. Many cultures teach that hugging for comfort is also unacceptable, yet acceptance of our feelings is the only way to move through the trauma.

During these challenging talks with Sarah, I realized that while I knew my parents loved me, I was a silent child, never asking for what I needed emotionally. I am not sure why I felt I had no right to ask for emotional support. I certainly knew not to discuss feelings with my father. I would sometimes cry, but not very often. I could tell mother the circumstance that caused my upset; however, we never explored our feelings. I learned to be both strong and silent from my father, reinforced by my mother's model. All this contributed to how I behaved as a mother.

I did not talk about my feelings with my mother and Sarah, although sometimes I shared my feelings with friends. I did not know how to accept feelings to release them so I buried them. I realize that this is part of the sacred wound of separation passed down to our daughters and sons. Acceptance of feelings is a necessary step in dissolving separation consciousness and returning to Oneness. However, we can't accept our feelings if we bury them. And we can't forgive and love ourselves if we refuse to look at our feelings of guilt, shame and blame. We can't move past anger and depression to wholehearted acceptance of love over fear, if we refuse to accept our feelings. Yeshua says in ACOL:

> Realize that your desire for your life to be different, your desire for your unhappiness to be gone, is very unlikely, in truth, to stem from the details of your life. Even so, you are not called to accept what you do not like, but to accept that you don't like whatever it is you don't like. Then and only then—when you have accepted how you feel—can you respond truly. Only when you have accepted how you feel do you quit labeling good or bad; only then can you deal with anything from a place of peace.[31]

Yeshua goes on to say that power to effect change comes from acceptance of who we are now, not how we've been in the past or how we think things will be in the future. He calls this radical acceptance of the present that leads to gradual lessening of things we do not like.

Through our sacred sharing to heal the mother daughter patriarchal wound, Sarah and I are learning through acceptance of our present relationship to unravel the threads of enmeshment to return to holy relationship. I am still learning to listen compassionately, instead of offering suggestions and tools for healing. I am gaining clarity on how caretaking is the result of not trusting Sarah's mystical heroine's journey, not trusting her God Self, not trusting the all-encompassing embrace of the Divine Mother. Caretaking is the response of the earthly mother. Caretaking is literally saying: I know better than God. I am gaining valuable experience through unconditional listening, which holds the container of love for Sarah to support her own knowing and healing. She is very clear that this is the gift she needs from me.

It is time to heal the rape of our wombs and Mother Gaia from lifetimes of suppression and violation—to halt and clear the patriarchal wounding passed down through the mother's line. In order to do this, we must learn to love and forgive ourselves for choosing to experience separation consciousness expressed in the form of patriarchal control. It is helpful to remember that both women and men at the soul level agreed to play this victim/perpetrator/savior conflict. Lucia René wrote in *Unplugging the Patriarchy*:

> Women agreed to give away their feminine power!...At the beginning of the Patriarchal Age, we all signed up for the same task, women and men alike. We all agreed to play out the third-chakra-based society, with its focus on power, for the evolution of the masculine and, therefore, humankind. Females have been repressed for thousands of years, and we have never understood why, but we actually agreed to help men learn about power so that all of us, men and women alike could ascend into the heart.[32]

This agreement at the soul level became our divine sacrifice. It feels as if we did not realize the magnitude of how lost we would be for thousands of years. Or how successful the power-over paradigm's programming would be in enslaving us with episodic continual trauma. It feels as if we agreed to sacrifice so we could suffer.

We inflict pain, suffering and sacrifice all the time within separation consciousness. This is related to our sacred agreement to experience patriarchal control and abuse of power: we agreed to suffer in order to be transfigured, to be remade holy in an expansion of Love as our true power. Our suffering made us stronger in our ability and courage to forgive and love everyone unconditionally, even those who appear to harm us.

For thousands of years women have passed down through the generations the belief we must sacrifice our needs for our family, especially for the males. Some women's sacrifice includes rape from their fathers, brothers, husbands, friends, soldiers and strangers. Many times, we've been called to the ultimate sacrifice of giving our grown male children—and now our daughters —as fodder for war. Sometimes our children die before us through conflict, disease and accidents. We pass on to our daughters the belief that we are vessels of suffering, birth and death. Child birth contains pain, our punishment for being born a woman as Lilith and Eve's daughters. We are always anticipating making the ultimate sacrifice.

*With the rebirth of the divine feminine, we free ourselves from the belief that we have to suffer*. There are some women strong in their spiritual essence who no longer feel pain during child birth. I feel and see women of all ages who are done with sacrificing their needs to caretaking people's egos. We realize and trust that our children are capable of doing their own inner work, dissolving the co-dependent ties that bind, even if death of the body is part of their divine plan. In claiming our divine power, we free men to do their own inner work. This requires complete trust in the sacredness of all life, that absolutely everyone is safe and cared for within the Divine Mother's embrace. We do not die. We are all part of the divine plan for earth's ascension.

Sacrifice does not have to be denial of Self; it can be divine. Our shadow is willing to be sacrificed. Dancing with the darkness of our shadow allows us to discover what is no longer sacred in our life, thus divine truth is revealed. Both sacrifice and sacred descend from the Latin word sacer meaning to consecrate, to make holy. Within separation consciousness, sacrifice feels like the double-edged sword of giving up something dear to us to gain our place in heaven. This diminishes our higher purpose and denies our Truth as divine beings. Under patriarchy this is what sacrifice came to mean: not a sacred act but a denial of the Holy Mother Father, and our God Self for an authoritarian father god. When we use the word sacrifice, we feel as if we have to give up what we love to appease an angry male god. God never asks us to sacrifice in order to continue our suffering. Instead, sacrificing something causing us to suffer is an act of surrender. Surrender occurs when we crawl inside the wound instead of massaging and trying to fix it.

The patriarchal Christian Church wants us to believe that Yeshua suffered and sacrificed himself for our sins. We can do no less—we must continually sacrifice and suffer in order to ascend to heaven. Yeshua's crucifixion occurred within separation consciousness. Therefore, to his disciples and students, his crucifixion felt like a sacrificial death and the end of his living body. Yeshua was divinely human when he agreed to be nailed to the cross. His death was not a sacrifice in the patriarchal sense. His death was an act of surrender to make holy on earth what had been lost to separation. His resurrection showed us that bodies are sacred and cannot die through violence or disease but only through our ability to create, experience, and then let go. *The Holy Mother Father never asks us to suffer. It is a choice we choose over and over again when we use the ego self as our guide.* Our original purpose as children of the Cosmic Mother does not involve suffering, but to experience life as divinely human. Yeshua says in ACOL:

> The death of an only son, then as now, would be seen as a sacrifice of enormous proportions; the greatest sacrifice of all. The point of the story, however, was not one of sacrifice but one of gift giving. The greatest gift of all was given, the gift of redemption. The gift of redemption was the gift of an end to pain and suffering and a beginning of resurrection and new life. It was a gift meant to empty the world of the ego-self and to allow the personal self to live on as the one true Self, the one true offspring of God. The gift of redemption was given once and for all. It is the gift of restoration to original purpose.[33]

It is difficult to let go of our unease when we use the word sacrifice. Let us reclaim the original meaning of the word sacrifice to consecrate all in our lives. I replace the separated ego's idea with the feeling that I am making sacred what does not serve me. Burying feelings of anger, blame, shame, guilt, inadequacy, second best into the shadow does not serve me. When I recognize and embrace these feelings as part of my physical experience, they become sacred and are gently transformed into the holy, into wholeness. Sacrifice becomes a divine gift, not an act of suffering. What is sacrificed or remade holy is my perception of being separate from the Holy Mother Father Sophia God. I surrender to my Truth, my God Self. It is an alchemical process of turning fear into love.

I danced with the darkness of crippling back pain for almost 3 years to learn to accept feelings, forgiveness and love of Self. The shadow side of anger, shame and blame was sacrificed, restoring an awareness of my divine sovereign Self. The embrace and dissolving of the sacred wound leads to the restoration of the heart and womb. As we return our heart and womb to Oneness, mothers pass down to their daughters the remembrance of their innate sovereign power. This is how we raise strong compassionate girls comfortable in their feminine wildness and power of fierce love. This is how we raise compassionate, heart-centered boys respectful of their own divine feminine energy. Our agreement for men to play the perpetrator and women to play the victim is fulfilled and released.

## The Feminine Archetypes

Carl Jung, father of analytical psychology, defined archetypes as universal, archaic symbols and images originating from the collective unconscious. As humans we have used symbols, myths, metaphors, stories and legends to express the dynamic, creative life force of the ineffable, such as: eternal truths, the cosmos and the divine in all its forms and expressions. Myths and symbols can elucidate ancient spiritual beginnings of earth and the evolution of humans in ways we can grasp while residing in duality. Archetypes are derived from myths. We often use archetypes to try and understand what we were before we fell from grace, when we were whole and holy. Knowing ourself through archetypes can be a path to enlightenment, to remembering our God Self. The distortion of the feminine energy resulted in the overarching patriarchal roles of rebel/heretic, whore/temptress and obedient/pure woman. While there are many variations of these three roles, the purpose remains the same: to keep women from thriving.

Many women lightworkers, loveholders and mystics teach through the symbolism of archetypes before patriarchy perverted the divine feminine. On our spiritual journey, we embody these archetypes till they are needed no more. The feminine archetypes that feel universal to me are enfolded within wise woman: mother, healer, leader, teacher, warrior and artist.

There are many Goddesses symbolizing these archetypes that can help in understanding ourselves as a process of returning to wholeness. All these archetypes evolve into the power of the Creatrix, our divine feminine power. They overlap, interact and weave together. Like walking the labyrinth, our lives fold in and out, changing and embracing archetypes depending on where we are in our journey.

The fractured archetypes are all about upholding the distorted values of power-over to control the untamable, wild, intuitive energy of the sacred feminine. I resonate with both the perverted and sacred archetypes, melding them into wholeness. Our spiritual journey is to clear the patriarchal perversion of these archetypes.

Within patriarchy wives, leaders, healers, teachers, artists, mothers are left alone as long as our words and actions support upholding a male-dominated world. We became obedient wives or prostitutes. A variation of this role is temptress. Women dress and act in ways to be sexually attractive to men. As teachers we taught the party line to our children in schools and in our homes. We became healers—so long as we upheld Western medicine as the only way to heal disease in the body. We became leaders by playing the male power game, sometimes becoming more effective purveyors of patriarchal power-over than the men we are emulating. We often lost our wild inner wisdom, which we squelched in an effort to conform, or we were labeled insane. We literally became warriors, joining men fighting in wars. Movies have evolved into women being just as physically tough and violent as men—all in an effort to be seen as equal to men. Women's artistic endeavors were denied or seen as second rate to men's—our only role historically was to marry.

While there has been a loosening of the fractured archetypes, they often remain hidden in our subconscious or shadow place, unknowingly sabotaging our power. The destructive programming runs deep in our wombs. One of the most important perverted archetypes to clear is the mother archetype. The fractured mother archetype is the obedient wife, teaching her children to always uphold the patriarchal system. Girls are expected to massage the male ego and boys are expected to be tough and strong to protect and provide for the girls. Sometimes it is the devouring mother who expects her children to be what she could not, to fulfill her thwarted ambitions, to provide the love she was denied in order to fill the hole in her heart and womb. We pass these expectations and beliefs through the mother daughter wound. For example: you'll be safer if you marry so you'll have a man in your life to provide and protect you and your children. If you rebel too much you will be homeless and alone when you die. I thought I was teaching my daughter to be independent, not realizing how much I was still conveying about the secondary role of women. It is so subtle that even with the best intentions, we miss it.

The true mother archetype evolves from the Divine Mother. When we feel the embrace of the Universal Mother, we return to holy mothering which is nurturing and life affirming. We create an unconditional loving space for our children to grow, trusting in their divinity, creating the atmosphere for them to blossom into their Christ Selves. We nurture and mother ourselves and all God's creations. This is radical self-love. It encompasses the Universal Grandmother archetype that holds the universal container of love for humanity till every person wakes to their divine sovereignty. As we restore our wombs, we create an unshakable foundation upon which we become the Creatrix, birthing and creating from the power of love. This heals the sacred wound of separation permanently.

## Mothers and Daughters Are Constantly Searching and Finding Each Other

Demeter is the Olympian Goddess of the harvest, agriculture and earth's fertility. Persephone is the daughter of Demeter and

Zeus, the father God. Hades in a rare trip out of the underworld sees Persephone and falls in love. When Zeus promises him one of his daughters for a wife, Hades asks Zeus for Persephone. Zeus and Hades kidnap her because Zeus knows Demeter will not give her daughter willingly. Once Persephone is in the underworld, Hades provides everything she wants to make her life there agreeable. He builds her a garden and treats her with respect and love. She loves Hades in return, and helps the spirits of the dead cross over.

Demeter is enraged by the deception and the loss of her daughter. In her misery she neglects her duties to the earth. Plants begin to wither and die, bringing blight upon the earth. Zeus sends Hermes to the underworld to return Persephone to her mother, but Hermes sees that she is content though conflicted, for she loves both Hades and her mother. Zeus therefore decrees that Persephone will live in the underworld for 6 months and with her mother for 6 months, giving us winter and summer.

There is a his-story interpretation of this myth that paints Demeter as wrathful and vengeful. It is necessary for daughters to separate from their mothers in order to find contentment with a man. Zeus, the all-powerful Father God, knows best. He negotiates and placates, but his final word must be followed.

The her-story of Demeter and Persephone describes the deep connection that exists between mothers and daughters. It also describes the wound of separation when a patriarchal god supports men first and women second. It describes the benefits of men who are supportive and respectful of women. Her-story knows that Demeter as a Mother Goddess would never take revenge on humanity and the earth for the loss of her daughter. Winter is not a time of death and sorrow, but a time of needed respite and deep nurturing for both the earth and humans to prepare for rebirth and renewal. It is a time for going inward to cleanse all that does not serve us anymore. Persephone, in balance with Hades, is blessed by her mother to provide the underworld with deep wisdom for endings and beginnings.

Within separation this story leaves us with an awareness that mothers and daughters are constantly searching for, finding and disappointing each other until they heal the wound of separation. The earthly mother is supposed to prepare her daughter to survive within patriarchy. Therefore, mothers and daughters have to separate for the daughter to mature into an obedient woman. With the return of the Holy Mother Creatrix enfolding the Holy Father, the mother daughter relationship returns to one of deep communion and love, for there is no separation within Oneness. Persephone and Demeter are constantly searching and finding each other in the process of healing the patriarchal wound of separation.

This was the most difficult chapter for me to write, as well as the most healing. It involves searching and finding my truth as a mother and as a daughter. Healing my relationship with Sarah took me into the depths of despair and self-incrimination. I felt the last of my ideal image of the perfect mother shattering as I realized that within separation consciousness there is no way to be a perfect mother. Mother Mary is my guide. I am palpably feeling Mother Mary's compassionate embrace radiating from my heart as I finish this movement and start other movements.

I invested many years in the belief that no matter what I was professionally, I would be a loving mother, like my mother. My mother was loving, yet she let me down. I am not saying this as an accusation or to blame. It is a way to connect with feelings I keep shoving away. To see how mother let me down feels disloyal. It is what Sarah is doing, looking at where I let her down and at times feeling guilty because she feels disloyal. She does not want to be hurtful. So yes, as painful as it feels, I acknowledge my mother let me down and I let Sarah down.

Just saying this is a relief. Mothers and daughters have been letting each other down for over 12,000 years: searching, losing and finding ourselves over and over again. We've been conditioned to live within patriarchy. We transmit patriarchal values, sometimes unconsciously and sometimes deliberately. We adopt these values in order to survive. The severity of our mother wound depends on the severity of the wound our mother received from her mother. I am grateful to my lineage of grandmothers who did so much in each of their lifetimes to be as loving a mother as they possibly could be.

I have a friend whose mom never fully admitted her son molested her daughter and then went on to molest his nieces. I felt outrage that a mother would not protect her daughter. When I feel into this, I realize she was so ashamed of what this said about her as a mother, she could not admit it to herself for fear of being judged as much as she judged herself. Plus, as an obedient conveyor of patriarchal power, she did not know how to heal this situation. When my son was cutting, I did not want to talk about it for fear people would judge me as an awful mother. When I did share it in one of my workshops, I received an upwelling of gratitude from other mothers who were going through similar experiences.

I have friends whose mothers remained silent and did not protect their daughters from rape and abuse by their fathers. I have a friend whose mother refused to believe she'd been raped by a trusted teacher. This feels like the ultimate unforgivable betrayal, when the person who is supposed to love and nurture does nothing. These are women who've been so traumatized and paralyzed by fear of violence that they can't protect themselves, much less their daughters.

I have another friend whose mother grew up in an abusive male-dominated family. She transferred the abuse she received to raising her daughter in critical, demeaning, emotionally abusive ways. As mothers we want our daughters to be tough in order to survive in this male-dominated world, and mistakenly, feel that compassionate love will create weakness and an inability to survive.

Another friend dismissed the divine feminine because her mother had been emotionally unstable and abusive toward her. She was very angry that I could even mention feminine energy could be loving. She felt I was creating dualism and separation by saying God is both feminine and masculine resonances in Unity. She was a very loving and engaging person, but did not realize that the loving part of her was her heart, which is the Holy Mother. And does this matter? Yes, it does because there was a hard-core place of anger at the feminine within her shadow she refused to heal, and it eventually killed her with cancer.

Upsetting men can be dangerous. We can lose our home, our children, our way of surviving. It is only recently that women are able to work and make enough money to support ourselves, and sometimes a family, outside of marriage. I have written how we came to absorb the patriarchal energy which limits and represses our divine feminine wildness and creativity. What I am acknowledging is how that is passed down the female line. It means I can't blame men for everything. We are all in this together. We all agreed to experience this together.

Women have absorbed patriarchal values of power-over for so long that, even with the best intentions, we often unconsciously transfer them to our daughters. My mother loved, supported and never intentionally criticized her children. However, she never hugged me when I was upset. She'd let me cry without telling me to stop, but never uttered comforting words. She remained silent when I was verbally attacked by the men in our family. I feel she trusted my ability to work through what I was feeling. With perspective I see it as a gift that she did not vocally join in my pain. However, I learned to not talk about my feelings and bury them because she did not talk about her feelings. Her idea of being a loving supportive mom was always to appear okay. This lessened somewhat as she aged. That is what I learned to mirror back. To this day I'm able to fake being calm when I'm not, often to the point I almost convince myself. Mother could talk endlessly, which always annoyed me. Now I know it was to cover up her feelings of insecurity and an inability to honor her feelings. She told me I was such a silent child, yet we never figured out that I learned this from her.

I learned contemplation, introspection and inner dialogue when I was an adult. I shared spiritual books with mother, yet we never shared our feelings about them. We did not know how to do this with each other. I conveyed to the child Sarah my confusion about feelings. Sarah and I are learning to share our feelings with each other as adults. I still have a tendency to listen to what she is feeling, but not completely share what I'm feeling. This is the residual earthly role of being a mother who is always wise and calm. While I try very hard to not criticize Sarah, I do at times. I wanted her to grow up strong and independent so men could not hurt her, yet I missed her cries for love. Not hugging her when she was hurt and needing the physical demonstration of love led her to believing I did not truly love her. She learned to deny what she wanted by silencing her voice.

My role of mother is changing. I embrace my inner reality of "as within so without" and that giving and receiving are one. I let go allowing Sarah to do this for herself. This is the process of unraveling our enmeshment, so we can enter into holy relationship. Holy relationship embraces compassion for each other's frailties, misunderstandings and misconceptions. It is uncharted ground. Sometimes it feels as if we've made it worse because we changed our comfortable way of interacting. It feels scary to keep going, as if we've lost our way. We can't go back, so we have to trust in our divine selves and our process of surrendering to the God within to lead. We arrive at a place of certitude and clarity in the power of love to create anew.

While we transfer the wounds of patriarchy and separation through the matrilineal line, we also convey forgiveness and love of Self. All incarnations exist in the eternal now of Oneness so healing in the present clears and dissolves all our parallel lives. All mothers within duality have let their daughters down. Within dualism we will never be the daughters our mothers want us to be or the mothers our daughters want us to be. However, our mothers and daughters are exactly what we need to assist our spiritual journey. If we look at our mothers with clarity and compassion, we can forgive them for succumbing to thousands of years of patriarchal domination, and we can see it in ourselves. One of the most effective ways to forgive ourself is to forgive our mothers for doing the best they could with the awareness they had at the time. *Forgiveness stops the search for our mothers as we find ourselves.*

As in the pre-incarnation planning process, we chose our parents and family so we can assist healing each other's core wound in order to complete our soul's mission on earth. Sarah brought in lifetimes of trauma and abandonment, and I fed into this till we could find a way to begin to heal it together. I brought in lifetimes of trauma and feeling never good enough, and with Sarah's help I'm dissolving that core sacred wound. For me only occasional dips into the habits of the separated self are left. We trust our internal mothering—infused by the love of the Divine Mother—to liberate ourselves from the separated ego. We love ourselves free.

Our deep sharing that occurred as adults is divinely perfect timing because we had the needed wisdom and awareness to embrace our hearts and allow the Holy Mother's love to dissolve our mother daughter wound. With this dissolving I gain a deeper awareness that we are always creating in every moment, and therefore it is always perfect timing—whether or not we choose peace or the separated self. Because at some point we become so tired of the suffering, it provides a crack in the barriers we've erected around our heart to let in the light of our God Self.

Once we abide long enough in our heart, our outer reality changes to seeing love everywhere, even in the trauma of life. We realize we no longer need drama to feel alive. We can witness without being drawn into life's battlefield. With our heart leading, we can act from love without succumbing to the beliefs of the separated self. We realize that the words "what if" are unhelpful. We make choices, and no matter what we choose, they always become instrumental in our awakening. Our God Self only has one goal, which is love. The words that everything is always perfectly orchestrated for our awakening is no longer a phrase I repeat. It is rather a deep knowing.

With this deep knowing we realize we are powerful co-creators, whether we are following our heart or the separated ego. I fully realize there are no accidents. There can't be if we are creating in every moment. We can't have it both ways, the bad stuff is created by something or someone outside of us and the good stuff we create. When I know I'm always co-creating, I know I've also created those experiences that caused suffering, though I want to blame others. This can either liberate or keep me stuck in fear. The trick is to not fall into judgment or fatalism when we realize that we create every experience in our lives.

Instead we take responsibility for our lives by doing the inner work of forgiveness. When we do, we begin to appreciate what we have learned and how it leads to falling in love with ourselves with all our human flaws and frailties. I want to laugh and cry all at the same time. I feel blessed, sad and open to love all at once. It has taken 70 years to fully understand I'm always co-creating. I can continue to co-create with the separated ego as my guide or I can surrender to my God Self. I co-create with the inner sacred which then reflects the sacredness in all life.

Walking my prayer, walking in beauty becomes my path into the labyrinth of my heart and womb. I still stumble at times and get stuck on one of the folds. But I don't stay there very long anymore because I've felt the extraordinary mystery of Oneness and felt fully loved. I walk the Holy of Holies within my womb and feel the interconnectedness of all life here on earth and within the cosmos. I'll keep returning to this feeling with shorter and shorter intervals in separation until it is all I know.

My grandmothers and mother did the best they could with the information and awareness they had at the time. I am doing the best I can right now with the awareness I have, which is constantly expanding. As I dissolve my mother daughter wound, I help dissolve Sarah's with my higher resonance, and she helps dissolve mine with her higher resonance. Thus, our wombs are restored and we become the conveyors of spiritual healing with feminine and masculine wisdom in balance. This is the process of forgiving the distorted and wounded masculine energy still being expressed in men and women. This is the process of dismantling the separated ego held within and then forgiving our mothers, our daughters, our sisters and all women everywhere for our part in creating this dream of separation. Women are searching and finding each other. We open to receive the Divine Mother's merciful compassion for all her creations.

# As Within So Without Meditations

## The Gift of a Question

*She remembers who she is and dissolves the sacred wound.*

If you need to refresh your memory about what is involved in these meditations, please re-read this section in Movement One. Please start with the two following questions before beginning your inquiry process then read the additional questions. Try to write down whatever arises without judgment or editing what you don't like. Most importantly ask your guides/light family to help with your inquiry work.

Can I love myself enough to forgive myself?
Can I forgive myself enough to love myself?

### *Additional Questions*

The following questions not only focus on our mother relationship but also on relationships with our children, primarily with a daughter. If you have no children but have an ongoing committed relationship with a child, it may be helpful to consider some of these questions. If you do not have a daughter, the questions can be asked about a son, a nonbinary or trans child.

Calling God the Holy Father has been the norm for thousands of years. How does this make you feel?

How do you feel when calling God, the Holy Mother? Does it make you uncomfortable or does it free you?

Can you name your sacred wound of separation?

- How does your sacred wound manifest in your life?

- How has your sacred wound been affected by patriarchal conditioning?

The perpetrator/victim/savior dynamic affects everyone within separation consciousness. The perpetrator and the savior play these roles to avoid feeling victimized. Women have predominately played the victim role which ensures that we continue to be the primary purveyors of patriarchal programming to our daughters and other girls.

- If you feel you are a victim, what have you learned to free yourself from this role?
- How have you also played the roles of perpetrator and savior to yourself and others?
- How have you perpetuated these roles with yourself, children, grandchildren and other young relatives or friends?
- Do you see the perpetrator/victim/savior dynamic in your relationship with your mother?
- Do you see the perpetrator/victim/savior dynamic in your relationship with your daughter(s) or sons(s)?

How have you enacted the three traditional patriarchal roles of rebel/heretic, whore/temptress and obedient/pure woman?

How can you transform these roles into freeing your feminine untamed, passionate, intuitive and creative pure essence?

What happens when you follow your heart that knows no boundaries?

What sings in your heart and sets you free?

The following questions can be asked about biological mothers, stepmothers, adopted mothers, absent mothers or a primary mother relationship with another woman. You can talk to your mother anytime whether she is in a physical body or not.

Is there anything that needs to be forgiven in your relationship with your mother?

What small step can you take right now to improve your relationship with your mother?

How does the relationship with your mother affect your relationship with your daughter(s)?

How does the relationship with your mother affect the relationship with your son(s)?

Is there anything that needs to be forgiven in your relationship with your daughter(s) and/or son(s)?

Do you feel the only problem you have with your daughter or son is a result of their relationship with their father?

If so, are you being honest with yourself? How does this affect your relationship with them?

What small step can you take right now to improve your relationship with your daughter(s) and son(s)?

If you have sons but no daughters, how does the relationship with your mother affect your relationship with your son?

If you had a daughter, do you think your relationship with her would be different than with your son or the same?

What small step can you take right now to improve your relationship with your son?

If you have a child who does not fit into the traditional gender roles, how does the relationship with your mother affect your relationship with this child?

What small step can you take to improve your relationship with them?

How does your relationship with your mother and/or daughter(s) affect your relationships with other women?

Return to the first two questions about loving and forgiving yourself.

This is the final surrender.

# Movement Five

# The Siren Song of Anger

## Chapter One

# Transmuting Anger into Fierce Love

*Burning and Weeping*
*There is no escape from love, She says*
*I step into the flames of the Mother's compassionate gaze*
*Welcome back, She says*
*The light shines on all those deep dark places I couldn't love*
*Let your ship burn, let it all burn down*
*You are safe, I'm holding you*
*You are floating on the vast ocean of my Love*
*I let my ship burn into ashes*
*And out of it emerges the fire-breathing dragon in my belly*
*How he rages and rages*
*How he longs to be free*
*I'm afraid to let it loose, it will consume me.*
*Make the dragon your friend, She says*
*He won't harm you, he's been waiting for you*
*I don't know how*
*Chop of some heads, She says*
*Really, I can do that?*
*Why not, it's all in your mind anyway*
*So, to pulsing, heart-pounding music*
*I chop off patriarchal heads.*
*Leaving my swords on the bloody battlefield,*
*I stand before Kali Ma*
*Bowed under the weight of wearing*
*all the illusory cloaks of my personal self*
*Into her sacred cleansing fire, I throw the cloaks of:*
*Specialness and privilege*
*The good girl and the nice girl*

*The pretty girl and the polite girl*
*The perfect mother and the imperfect mother*
*The imperfect wife and the judging wife*
*The shamed woman and the blaming woman*
*The controlling woman and the fix it woman*
*The one who holds it together and the scared woman*
*The singer and the failure*
*The perfect woman and the aging woman.*
*Till I stand naked before*
*the Holy Mother's penetrating gaze of love*
*Naked in my purity and innocence*
*I walk into the flames of my fire-breathing dragon*
*Claiming my body as my own*
*Claiming wild audacity and youthful intensity*
*Claiming my elder self's wisdom and vision*
*Claiming my divine sovereignty*
*Claiming my burning love for the Beloved*
*Welcoming my dragon's masculine energy*
*of protection, clarity, and purpose*
*Freeing my wild feminine energy of birth and creation*
*Embracing fierce love and compassion for myself*
*Live your life as a prayer, She says*
*You've always been on a heroine's spiritual journey*
*to remember that your life is a song of love*
*You are a wisdom weaver, so let's begin writing*
*For I Am always there within you.*

Much of the content of this book is possible because I could no longer ignore the back pain resulting from life times and decades of buried repressed anger. I did not think I was an angry person, not Sally, she is always nice and considerate. I'm not one of those scary angry people who hurt those around them. As my father taught me, I kept a lid on those thoughts and feelings which sparked anger. Of course I did get angry, but I always turned it inward, chastising myself for being angry then repressing it. My story is not much different from many women's stories.

Dr Harriet Lerner, in *The Dance of Anger, A Woman's Guide to Changing the Patterns of Intimate Relationships,* wrote that women must listen to what their anger is trying to tell them. It can point to some difficult truths. As women we learn to silence or deny our anger, or to vent it inappropriately, often in toxic ways. Sometimes it is a combination of both. We pass this down through the mother daughter wound. Anger can leave us feeling powerless and helpless because we've been taught anger is destructive, unbefitting a woman's true nurturing and self-sacrificing nature. We witness every day the destructiveness of men's anger and come to fear our own anger. Many women adopt this destructive anger out of self-preservation. My father thought anger could be controlled if it was never felt or expressed. I thought I was a nice person because I never felt or expressed my anger. I learned this from my mother.

Many of us think anger is bad. Any emotion not felt and expressed blocks our ability to love and forgive ourselves. It stunts our spiritual growth and delays our return to Oneness. I have already described the many ways women's divine feminine essence has been repressed and almost obliterated under patriarchy. We've begun to understand how we've bought into the role of victim. With this victim role, we unconsciously agreed to play the patriarchal overarching roles of rebel/heretic, whore/temptress and pure/obedient woman. In retrospect I see how I unconsciously fell into these personas which fueled the anger I constantly suppressed. It is too dangerous to allow the anger out because as a rebel (witch, healer, wise woman, shaman) we were hunted down and killed.

If we pay attention to our anger, it usually points to injustice. Once we feel ourselves as being unfairly treated, we slip into the old habits of the separated ego. We spend our time blaming and judging the person who has treated us unfairly. We project onto others what we dislike about ourselves in an effort to avoid going inward to heal the deep anger and shame we carry in our shadow. We can stay stuck in a fold of our labyrinth for quite a while. We are not being asked to forgive the unfair treatment, only to feel our anger. If we allow ourselves to accept and express our anger in healthy non-destructive ways, it leads to complete awareness that we are not victims. Through recognizing our anger, we can feel it and then transmute it into fierce divine love. This is the yang feminine, which is our feminine power. We will increasingly feel how anger is neutral energy, and that it is our thoughts creating conflict. Yeshua in ACOL says:

> If anger arises in you now, it does not mean that you will react in whatever way anger once called you to react and it does not mean something is wrong with you or that you are not spiritual enough! It simply means that you are involved in a situation or relationship that has called forth that feeling. It is in the expression of that feeling who you are is revealed, not in the feeling itself. The feeling is provided by the body, a helpmate now in your service as a route to true expression.[34]

## My Story of Anger

I incarnated into this body in 1950. It was a time of prosperity. WWII was over and men reigned supreme in the work environment. More and more women were in the workforce in lesser paying jobs, usually in support of men. More and more women were going to college and many were acquiring advanced degrees. We were being raised to believe we could be anyone we wanted to be, which led to demanding entrance into the predominately male professions. The feminist movement took hold. By the time I went to college and then graduate school, women's rights were being reported by the media and being discussed or argued in families and in courts. Of course, it was constantly being demeaned, for example calling those women "feminazi," bra burners and ball busters. In an effort to discredit feminist arguments, propaganda fostered the idea that feminists want to destroy families, are dogmatic, hate men and want to have as many abortions as possible.

With the feminist revolution came the sexual revolution. Birth control became much more available for single women and we experimented freely with sex outside of marriage. While we were free to explore our sexuality while single, what did not change was men's attitudes about women's sexuality being under the control and gaze of men. The sexual revolution freed men to be even more aggressive about demanding sex from women. There were constant assumptions that a date meant sexual intercourse, and for some women it meant abuse and rape. It would be a rare woman my age who had not experienced: unwanted groping, subtle and aggressive sexual language including innuendos and gaslighting, all designed to make women feel inferior, the second sex. I was one of those angry women. Even though I had kind and considerate brothers, male friends and eventually a considerate husband, I blamed men as a group for creating and perpetuating patriarchy. I realize that I incarnated with this anger.

I attended a woman's college and sang in an a cappella group. We often sang in concerts at men's colleges, and sometimes someone would hear me sing and ask me out on a date. I was fairly naive in the beginning. I was also introverted and shy, unsure of myself in social situations. Twice in college I barely escaped being raped. One of the men sent a nasty demeaning letter as a result. I spent way too much time refusing to have sex with men, only to be called frigid or told I'd led them on. Once I arrived at a small party where I knew most of the people and was aware that everyone was looking at me oddly. My friend told me a man I'd turned down had spread the word I was easy and would sleep with anyone. There were kind and decent men I liked and dated. Yet inevitably the question of sexual intercourse always occurred. So, I finally had intercourse with a man I never saw again just to get it over with and say I was no longer a virgin.

After visiting me in collage, my brother Mark said I looked like an unapproachable angel while I was singing. He said some men find this intimidating and others find it challenging. He thought this was why I received so many unwanted sexual advances. Within patriarchal separation, both men and women have been conditioned to play certain roles. There is not much wiggle room to change our roles because of these conditioned expectations. Men expect women to adhere to the roles of the three overarching fractured archetypes and their variations. The pure woman is what men saw when I sang. In graduate school I decided to dispense with the angel image and slept with several men I did not care about and immediately forgot. This did not last long because there was no pleasure and I disliked myself. Unconsciously I was playing out the role of whore. After graduate school my boyfriend at the time left me in the car for 2 hours while he had a drink with a friend in a men's only club. I could not hide my rage, but eventually buried it. Unwanted sexual interactions continued into the work force. I lost a job because I refused to sleep with the boss. At one job my boss told me he'd had a vasectomy if I wanted to indulge. The silent rebel surfaced in my continual refusals.

I did not complain. I accepted this was life, the price for being blond and pretty. I buried it all, my anger and shame. I did not talk about it with my mother and rarely mentioned it to my friends. Unless I'd been raped, I felt I had no right to feel anything. I shared in the chapter on the mother daughter wound how women learn they have no right to feelings unless it is a catastrophic trauma. In truth, many women remain silent and swallow even catastrophic trauma. While this is not as prevalent as it once was, these attitudes still persist.

A few years ago, when I was in the worse of back pain, I kept having thoughts of Marilyn Monroe. It confused me: why Marilyn Monroe seemingly out of nowhere? I was 12 when she died and I didn't like what she represented, nor her movies. She became famous playing a dumb blond with a big heart and men seemed to be idiots for liking this over-sexualized woman. I asked my God Self: what about Marilyn is so important? The answer was, "you know why she killed herself." And, I do know why.

The stereotypical blond woman image is someone who is attractive but her lights are out. While I've never been treated that way by my family and friends, nevertheless I felt the pervasive stereotype. Men were always telling dumb blond jokes and expecting me to laugh. When I didn't laugh, they told me I had no sense of humor.

To men, Marilyn was a sex object, not a person. She died her hair blond and acted dumb in the movies to become a successful actress. Evidently, she was an astute business woman. Marilyn started her own film production company so she could choose her roles in order to be paid as much as men. Nevertheless, she was still cast in roles for the benefit of men wanting women to be sexy and available. Marilyn was married three times and had many liaisons with famous men, President Kennedy being the most famous. All wanted to be seen with men's ideal of a desirable sexy woman with no brains to challenge them. Increasingly she became addicted to drugs. I believe she committed suicide because she despised herself for never being able to rise above the trap of being loved as sex object rather than for who she really was. She had made so many compromises, she did not know how to love herself.

While Marilyn's story may or may not feel extreme, it shines a light on the many subtle and not so subtle ways women have compromised their power to appease and please men. She was the personification of all the women's overarching patriarchal roles designed to keep us feeling second class and a victim. Marilyn was both temptress and pure in her seeming naïveté as shown in the movies *Gentlemen Prefer Blondes* and *The Seven Year Itch*. This was how men could have both the sexual temptress and the pure woman at the same time: make her dumb but kind at heart. Marilyn's rebel side subtly surfaced as an astute business woman and her insistence on playing more demanding dramatic roles. However, she never entirely escaped the image of being a naive sexual temptress, a sex object.

Marilyn's body was not her own—it belonged to men's sexual appetites. Even today our bodies are not ours with the renewed fight over birth control and abortion, and the continued prevalence of molestation and rape. Reviewing Marilyn's story allowed me to understand, drop my judgments and forgive her for catering to men's needs. It helped me forgive myself for all those times I've done the same.

I was a walking contradiction: I liked being blond and pretty, yet I hated what it implied and often what it attracted. I wanted to prove I was not dumb just because I was blond and that my body was my own. But I felt like Sisyphus trying to push that boulder up a hill, constantly getting rolled over, and never reaching the top. I brought my buried, unfelt anger into marriage with a kind, considerate, loving man who also has issues with unhealed anger from an emotionally abusive mother. We managed, had many good times, raised two wonderful children, and are still married. Nevertheless, both of us have had times of conflict, anger and sniping at each other throughout our marriage. I blamed Rick for being an angry person many times, yet never understood how much repressed anger I was holding. I shoved decades of anger back there until my lower back started screaming at me to pay attention. The many years of sometimes crippling back pain and my daughter were the impetus to finally realize how many decades and lifetimes of anger I was tightly holding within my body.

## *My Journey of Dissolving Anger*

My lower back froze a few years before we moved to New Mexico. When I say froze it means my back spasmed, so I was unable to move without intense pain to the point that I fainted once. Each time my back froze, I did the spiritual work to uncover what I thought would heal the pain, and some relief occurred. By May 2018, my back was constantly freezing, so I was spending a lot of time not moving and then crawling around on the floor. My response was to push through hoping some type of exercise or physical therapy would work. I finally admitted I needed some different help and contacted a recommended chiropractor. The energy work was helpful; however, it was talking with a kind spiritual man to uncover the emotional cause of the back pain which finally started the process of exposing how much anger I had buried. This was a pivotal step for me. From a few uncomfortable experiences, I made it a practice to always see women medical doctors and healing practitioners.

I cannot remember the sequence of all that occurred in the 2 years of intense healing and clearing buried anger. I received many visions, divine messages, insights from my God Self—all with the divine purpose of acknowledging the totality of anger I held, in order to let it into the light of transformation. Through it all, my spiritual sisters in the co-creators group bore witness and held the container of love for healing to occur.

Once I had made the decision to see a chiropractor, I thought I'd get relief after a few visits. When that did not happen, I was such an emotional mess that I cried during my next appointment, much to my embarrassment. This was the start of more spiritual discussions than energy work. My back continued to freeze especially when getting in and out of bed. Crawling was the only option. By lying on my back on the floor with my knees up rolling side to side, I'd be able to pull myself up and eventually stand.

One night while in bed I had to go to the bathroom. All I could do was cry because I did not think I could move. As I lay there trying to calm myself through breathing, I heard very clearly the words, "pick up your bed and walk." I knew it was Yeshua and these words were from the Bible. I took a deep breath, got out of bed and walked to the bathroom and then back to bed with no pain. I wish I could say the instant healing lasted. It did not. But I realized this experience showed that back pain was my body's desperate cry for me to go deeper than I'd ever gone to shine the light on all the past unhealed painful and hurtful experiences. Until I did this, absence of pain would be temporary. I also learned that it is my thoughts creating the suffering. With one thought of belief in Yeshua's message, I got out of bed and walked.

All my buried memories of uncomfortable and hurtful experiences with men began to surface. My spiritual guides very clearly told me I needed to share these experiences with two men. I felt safe telling these stories to Rick. The only other man I felt safe with was my chiropractor. I see how divinely perfect my chiropractic sessions had been arranged. Relating these experiences to Rick was difficult enough, however telling them to my chiropractor took every ounce of my courage. As a woman in my late sixties, I felt silly, embarrassed and ashamed confessing these youthful experiences. He lovingly held the space with zero judgment.

What I didn't expect was how much anger started to surface. I didn't know what to do with it. Letting it all come to the surface was necessary, but now what? When Christmas 2018 arrived, I compartmentalized the anger, temporarily shoving it away. The back had stopped freezing, and I was managing the residual pain. Tyler and Sarah came for a week-long visit. Before they arrived, the toilets backed up and Rick and I spent several hours outside with a plumber's snake unclogging the pipes to the septic tank. Next the well sprang a leak the day they arrived, so we had no water. We switched to our rain tank backup system and implemented our water conservation efforts. The day after Christmas we had a snow storm, with the power going on and off while Rick was trying to cook dinner. He had to spend a snowy day with our well guy, repairing the leak which required excavation and replacing pipes before they froze.

All this stress was causing Rick to become very angry, which frayed my ability to remain calm and upset Sarah. Very courageously she decided to talk with her dad about his anger triggered by situations and things, which periodically had always been a family concern. After the talk, Rick and I had an honest discussion in which I told him that women instinctively fear men's anger. Rick replied that because of his mother, he feared women's anger. We also talked about our pattern of sniping at each other during normal exchanges. After our talk, this happened again during dinner, and Sarah asked us to stop. It was this that ultimately broke through the final barrier I had created to keep my anger contained. I finally realized how much anger I was holding and— how it leaked out in unhealthy ways.

After Sarah and Tyler left, the septic backed up twice, spewing sewage all over the showers, bathtub and toilets. Each time we managed to clear it enough to use the toilets, but because of the holidays, the plumber could not come immediately. When next the roof in the pantry leaked, I could not ignore the symbolism. Life-giving water was not flowing easily in my life. It was blocked, bursting through pipes filled with garbage and leaking through our carefully constructed home and my carefully constructed life. Water was showing how blocked anger erupts and spills out in toxic ways. I kept hearing: it is time to let the water of your grief and tears wash you clean. Let all the anger out so life can flow easily with your divine purpose. Stop pretending to be perfect and remember your divine innocence.

Weekly appointments with the chiropractor for almost a year helped me realize that all these experiences were giving me forgiveness opportunities to love myself and appreciate everyone in my life, past and present. But there was more to be revealed: as I felt my lower back pain dissipating, I woke one morning with a pinched nerve in my neck, the pain radiating down the left side of the back and arm, numbing my fingers. At first I thought I'd be able to relieve it with some yoga movements. But the pain became increasingly more intense and unrelenting—making the pain from a freezing back pale in comparison. Once the back unfroze, I could function and drive, but with the pinched nerve I could not sit, stand, lie down or move in any direction without intense pain. Nothing I did helped. I spent hours pacing. No heat or cold pacts helped. Sometimes I could sit on the bed or a chair and bend forward with my face in a pillow or bend all the way over with my hands on the ground to achieve slight relief. Nothing the chiropractor did helped. Pain medication did not help. Nothing touched the pain. I started taking hot baths twice a day, which provided minimal relief because I could float my arm. Night time was the worst because there was no position that allowed sleep.

During the beginning of the pinched nerve period, Rick became very sick with bronchitis, and was in bed for several days. According to Louise Hay in *You Can Heal Your Life*, bronchitis is unrecognized anger within the family structure. We tried to help each other the best we could. I rallied enough to go with him to the medical clinic, although he had to drive. We went a week without being able to take showers or use the toilets in our house. Fortunately, we were able to use the facilities in a friend's unoccupied casita. Rick joked that we could tell people our house was so large we had to drive to use the bathroom.

In the midst of all this I received daily spiritual messages, especially while in the bathtub. Because it was winter and I was in so much pain, I stopped walking the labyrinth. I also spent a lot of time yelling at the Holy Mother and begging for relief. Somehow, through it all I began to embrace the experience and what I was learning. I managed to re-read Thich Nhat Hanh's book on *Anger*. One of the breathing exercises is to imagine your angry self as a burning house, and then breathe back to Self. As I visualized my house burning, the house changed into a ship floating on the ocean of the Holy Mother's love. I heard: "Let your ship burn, let all that does not serve you burn till there's nothing left. You are safe on my ocean; I will hold you." I used this image over and over again, letting it all burn: my anger, doubts, judgments of self, false expectations and my idealized self—all that fed the separated self. I would say the following while slowly breathing in and out. God breathes me. I breathe God. Life breathes me. I breathe life. Love breathes me. I breathe Love. After 6 weeks, the pain started to lessen. I began to understand that letting my ship burn completely allowed merging into the ocean of the Holy Mother's love, to become One with the ocean. Yeshua says:

> See yourself as the ocean rather than the ship upon the ocean. Know yourself that you are having the experience of the drop of water as you choose to know individuality, but truly you are the Allness of the ocean and the expansiveness that goes beyond even the concept of ocean.[35]

Though the intensity of the pain started to dissipate, my back still hurt indicating how angry I still was. I could not seem to find a way to dissolve judgment and blame of men for all the pain they have caused, and for continuing to be clueless. Another spiritual soul sister suggested I needed to find a way to allow the anger to move through my body. I had been resonating with the fierce warrior energy of the Hindu Goddess Kali Ma for several months. It felt as if I could physically enact Kali chopping off the heads of the demons of separation with her swords. I found some heart-pounding music and, while physically swinging two imaginary swords, I visualized cutting off heads and sometimes penises of men leaders, clueless hurtful men acquaintances and a few caustic vicious women. It was immensely freeing. I did this off and on for a month, till much of the anger was cleared and the remaining residual pain dissipated. The following story about Kali and Shiva is the version which speaks to me and inspired my cleansing sword dance.

## The Story of Kali Ma and Shiva

Durga, the Hindu Mother Goddess, is concerned for her wayward children. They have fallen deeply into separation consciousness and are fighting among themselves. The demons of greed, prejudice, gluttony, disrespect, war and abusive power were consuming her children to the point that minimal compassionate love could penetrate the fear they held in their minds. Durga tries to eliminate these demons of fear, but more pop up every day. Out of desperation she calls upon her sister Kali who springs from her head.

Kali Ma arrives in all her dark blue-skinned glory, carrying the swords of clarity and truth. She witnesses how destructive the children of the Mother Goddess are behaving. With fierce love Kali Ma vows to destroy all the demons of separation consciousness. "Not my children," Kali cries, "You can't have my children!" She launches herself into a whirlwind of motion, cutting off the heads of the demons with swords grasped in her many hands. The fighting is intense. Kali is unstoppable, gripped with passion to save her children. Eventually Kali is lost to her rage and can't stop cutting off heads till Durga begs her to stop, telling her the demons are contained. But Kali can't stop, consumed by her overwhelming rage to save the children.

All the gods and goddesses come together to ask Shiva, the god of light consciousness and protection, to intervene and calm their sister Kali Ma. Shiva tries reasoning with Kali to no avail. He tries to physically stop her, but does not succeed. With the wisdom of a God, he realizes he must surrender to her. Shiva lies down in supplication beneath Kali while she's on her destructive rampage. When she's about to crush Shiva beneath her foot, she regains her sanity, her foot coming to rest gently on Shiva's body. Balance returns once again.

### *Why This Story Speaks to Women's Anger*

We have entered a time of massive polarization with the dismantling and collapse of everything created within dualism that serves the power-over paradigm. All false programming and its reliance on the cycle of suffering is intensifying in harmful ways. Our job as mystics is to hold the higher resonance of the new paradigm of Oneness, to rise above the battleground and expand love to those continuing to choose the destructive energy of separation. They have their mission and we have ours: we are all essential to the ascension process.

In order for me to anchor the powerful love energy of the way of Mary, I embraced Kali Ma's fierce energy to cut off all the heads of those I perceive as harmful, clueless and destructive. During this stage I was like Kali who had lost her way. Once I had moved decades and lifetimes of angry energy through my body, I was able to embrace my sacred masculine to forgive those who choose to enact the role of perpetrator and destroyer. I realize that they are hastening the demise of all the systems, structures and laws created to keep us enslaved to third-dimensional suffering. I can throw into the cleansing flames of Kali Ma's ferocious love all the old habits and patterns of the separated self no longer serving me till a fierce love for all of humanity is ignited. This is the process of surrender to knowing deep within that we are loved and safe while the world seemingly falls apart.

"Not my children! How dare you create a world that harms children." Kali's battle cry speaks to me. All of my professional jobs placed me into situations where there was no way to change the systems creating intolerable conditions for people—especially for children. In retrospect it feels that my whole professional career was one in which I was constantly banging my head against the wall of patriarchal structures and systems that I could not change. I love this person who always thought she could make a difference in children's lives. I forgive myself for feeling I always failed to make a lasting difference. I realize that within separation there is no way to change the system. Yet I appreciate how often I touched the lives of children and their parents. *Change comes from expressing the Divine Mother's love, one person at a time.*

My first job out of college was with the YWCA to create self-improvement programs for women. I was on fire with feminism and, as so often is the case for young educated women, I thought I had new information that most women had not considered. Fortunately, I had some wonderful tolerant mentors. My next job was an eye opener and heart breaking.

I was hired as a child-care worker as part of a special project to help normalize conditions for children held in a state institution for people with mental retardation. (The more accurate and less stigmatized label used now is intellectual disabilities.) Non-verbal children were locked all day in a huge day room with few toys. The door to the bathroom was kept locked. Unable to ask to use the bathroom, the room stank of pee. The children were left to bang their heads against the walls or wander aimlessly around in circles. We took these children out of the day room and tried to teach them non-verbal commands using their hands. We arranged trips out of the institution to parks, zoos and farms. While I felt good about making a small positive change for a few children, it felt too big and hopeless to change attitudes in the institution. I was relieved to leave the job when I was accepted into graduate school.

After graduate school, I was hired to run an after-school and summer camp program for children living in poverty, many were from abusive and violent homes. When I was hired the entire staff quit, protesting the removal of the director and declaring I was not qualified. The program and the children were in chaos as the previous staff had a laissez-faire approach to destructive behavior with no consequences. I eventually hired new staff and was able to institute a caring program with enjoyable activities, while rewarding considerate behavior. The incidents of conflict dropped considerably.

The list of jobs goes on: I worked in state government and nonprofit agencies to create programs designed to train and help young people with disabilities find jobs; I consulted with organizations to improve their services to children with special needs labels; I started and managed two nonprofit organizations to raise awareness about people with disabilities and atypical children.

My job as Development Director for the Unitarian Universalist Urban Ministry (UUUM) was a pivotal time, as it coincided with my emerging spiritual journey. I was caught in the middle between well-meaning white people from UU churches and the black community we served. There was misunderstanding on both sides with a considerable dose of white privilege trying to direct our efforts. UUUM's programs—battered women's shelters, after-school programs, a gang outreach program, programs for men coming out of prison and a food pantry—did make a difference on an individual level; however, I could not solve the divide between white entitlement that wanted to help and the anger of black people still living with the effects of racism. I was filled with love for everyone, even while I bounced back and forth from being overwhelmed with work, underappreciated, blamed at times and clueless as to how to heal this wide divide. I was also being confronted with my own attitudes of white privilege. It was a time of great turmoil for me, as well as great spiritual growth.

I see how every job flowed into the next and led to where I am today. With distance, I can appreciate how all was perfectly orchestrated for my awakening and has always been filled with the Holy Mother's grace and mercy. I worked in the turmoil of difficult situations and I survived. I gained internal strength and divine awareness. I now have the courage, compassion, faith and resonance to see us through the entropy and suffering being caused by the collapse of the old separation paradigm. I hold the vision of a world being created by those radiating with the power of love and Oneness. As lightworkers, wayshowers, loveholders, mystics, elevated Selves of form and bodhisattvas we anchor the Divine Mother's love and resonate at our highest vibration. This affects more people than we can possibly imagine. It is fueling an unprecedented evolution of consciousness into a planetary ascension through two dimensions never before experienced throughout galaxies and multiple realities.

Look at your life with new eyes, with the eyes of the Holy Mother Sophia God. Go deep within to understand how your life is perfect for your mission and purpose as a divine being. I write repeatedly how critical it is for each one of us to embrace and clear all buried feelings residing in the shadow. Then, we can love ourselves enough to forgive ourselves, and forgive ourselves enough to love ourselves unconditionally. This allows vibration at the highest octave possible for our planetary awakening.

## The Dragon Doesn't Live in Me Anymore

The dragon in the form of a monster to be feared does not live inside me anymore. The dragon of anger hidden in the shadow does not live here anymore. Like Jane in the children's story, I've tamed my dragon's masculine energy, and claimed my divine feminine power. Lucy Pearce in *Burning Woman* describes it beautifully.

> The dragon never was your enemy. The treasure was his. It's yours. It always was. All he was doing was waiting for you to claim it, protecting it from those who would steal or misuse it. He knew his job was to protect it until you were able to care for it as fiercely as he. Until you knew yourself as its rightful owner. Until this great wealth would be used wisely, not to do damage to yourself or others. Until you were learned enough in the ways of the world not to squander it or give it away. That was his sacred role, as your greatest ally and protector.
>
> You can call on him to stand with you any time you need an ally—a visible representation of a powerful guardian to model, support and strengthen you—the fire-breathing dragon: belly full of fire, watchful eyes, scaly impermeable skin, fire spewing from the mouth, committed to protecting what is precious to you.[36]

It is a relief to finally feel the fire, clarity, discernment and protection of my inner masculine dragon. It is a relief to feel the divine union between my sacred feminine and masculine energy. I feel blessed to be whole again. I feel the power of this joining as I rest in my yang feminine. It is grounding as well as freeing to come home to my inner God Self. While I may occasionally stumble and stray, it is never for very long. The dragon of anger does not live here anymore.

### Healing Dis-Easement of the Body

Yeshua advises us to not judge ourselves for what is going on with our bodies as if we've made a mistake or done something wrong.

> No, you have not done anything wrong. Everything that you bring forth is for divine purpose. Everything you bring forth—even the body and its disease as it speaks to you sometimes—is for divine purpose, and you are not doing anything wrong.[37]

It took prolonged experience with pain and a consistent spiritual process to realize that I was not doing anything wrong. I thought I lacked understanding because if I had the right awareness, I'd be able to heal instantly. Reading stories about people who gained an awareness to heal cancer or traumatic injuries fueled self-judgment for my inability to heal. What I came to realize and appreciate is that my healing process was necessary to clear decades and lifetimes of anger. I had to see, accept and embrace the anger, grief and shame I had buried in my shadow before I could let it all go. Trying to do a spiritual bypass may work temporarily; however it is never permanent. The separated ego's existence depends on keeping us in a cycle of suffering.

The practice of acceptance is powerful energy, and it is the most difficult to embrace. When we are in pain, the last thing we want to do is accept the pain. We can't embrace pain; however, we can accept the unrecognized feelings causing the pain. Once I acknowledge and identify buried feelings, I accept the feelings so I can grieve. That begins the process of forgiving myself for choosing pain to get my attention. I trust that whatever is happening with my body is for a divine purpose.

God does not create the disease or painful injuries to teach us a lesson. We create pain and disease with our habitual thoughts of the past and worry about the future. Pain is the result of spiritual torment caused by the denial of our Divine Self. Long-term denial of our divinity results in disease. I feel this now without judgment. Please do not beat up on yourself for creating the perception of pain. Use it for awareness of what powerful creators we are. In my experience this opens the door to self-forgiveness and self-love. It frees judgment about other people's experience with dis-ease and pain.

We do not have a clue as to the purpose of some other person's diseasement with the body. We have no idea at the personal level what they've agreed to experience in order to assist in their own and sometimes another's awakening process. I've done this, looked at someone else's disease or pain with judgment for seemingly not doing their spiritual inner work. When I look inside, I realize I am only judging myself for being unable to heal. I received a message from Mother Mary.

*Write your book, be completely vulnerable. Let yourself grieve, let yourself cry, let yourself rage. Writing is transmuting the anger into fierce love. Harness it into fully being a wisdom-weaver creating and holding the container of love for all humanity. Find your voice in writing, be vulnerable. Let yourself be enfolded by the primordial darkness of the Holy Mother's heart womb. Acknowledge that is where you've been and be grateful for this healing time of burning your ship, this gestation time in the loving darkness of infinite possibilities and being cleansed by the blazing love of the Holy Mother. Rise in your sovereign divine power. Stop trying to feel safe by remaining small.*

## Chapter Two

# Forgiving the Unforgivable and Loving the Unlovable

I wake from sleep and realize I am gently floating in the primordial dark of the Cosmic Mother's womb. I am embraced by her ocean of love in warmth and safety. I feel all the aches and pains of my aging body dissolve as I sink into deep abiding peace. All thoughts cease as I am enveloped in silence containing the music of creation. I feel the spaciousness of the Creator within and all around as I abide in my Interdimensional Self. I feel One with All that Is; One within the many and the many within the One. Planets, stars, suns, galaxies, universes are born and die constantly, expanding the love of the One Source Light, the Great Mystery. All my earthly third-dimensional incarnations gently float away as if they never were. What remains is infinite gratitude for being part of humanity's ascension and the creation of Nova Earth. "Grace is acceptance of the Love of God within a world of seeming hate and fear."[38]

As women we may feel that all the abuse, violation, violence, degradation and suppression of the feminine from twelve thousand years of patriarchy can't be forgiven, much less loved. There has been so much abuse and cruelty. We are not asked to forgive hateful actions—only to accept our feelings about these hurtful actions. Writing this book is my practice of forgiving the unforgivable and loving the unlovable. It is a process. It is a process containing profound moments embraced by God's merciful grace.

In ACIM Yeshua says that people are either asking for love or expressing love. There are no other choices. In *A Journey into the Unknown*, Yeshua expands on this idea:

> Many of the situations that are disturbing to virtually all who walk the earth are calls for love. This is the easy part. Not condemning potential or actual perpetrators thought to be the cause, is much more challenging. Who shot the gun that took the lives away? This person is calling for both love and forgiveness. They rarely receive either. If they physically survived, they universally are pushed away from love's embrace, deemed not worthy of love, and deserving of hatred and scorn. This has to change if your world is to survive.
>
> Love can only love. It cannot do anything but love. If you are in love, then you are only capable of love. If a society is in love, it cannot push one of its members away. A love society brings everyone into its embrace.[39]

People who appear to be acting in harmful ways need our love and forgiveness. Once we attack their harmful behavior, we join them in perpetuating the suffering. I know people committing terrible acts are divine beings lost in the denseness and darkness of the separated ego. They do not understand what they are doing. I understand intellectually, yet many times it does not land in my heart. I want it to happen in one blaze of glorious light burning up all that does not serve me, igniting my embodiment of Christ consciousness, sending my Soul Self soaring to embrace new worlds, new ways of expanding the Creator's all-encompassing Love. I emerge from the dark comforting warmth of the primordial womb into my physical body realizing there is much left to do to assist the awakening of humanity. I embody these expansive feelings of Oneness. The gap between my personal self and the elevated Self of form continues to shrink as I'm drawn less and less into old habits of the separated self.

## Power-Over Transformed into Power of Love

I write over and over again that the purpose of humanity is to experience love in a new way. This is part of the never-ending expansion of God's love. I never fully understood why this is so different from the experiences of our Star Nations until I read *Unplugging the Patriarchy* by Lucia René. I write about love as true power not patriarchy's abusive power-over. What I realize is that humanity's awakening is all about full awareness of the power of love. The Indian spiritual teacher Sri Chinmoy explains it beautifully: "When the power of love replaces the love of power, man will have a new name: God." Both women and men agreed at the soul level to experience power devoid of love so we could ascend into the heart. When both women and men ascend into the heart, we access our divine power in all its wild, compassionate, infinite creativity and expansiveness.

Love encompasses power, compassion and wisdom. It is women's power sourced from love that was brutally repressed when patriarchy became the controlling system of the separated ego. This could not have happened without divine feminine agreement. I am not sure the oversouls of both men and women realized how extensively we'd experience power-over or how deeply we would fall into the corruption and miscreations of fear-based dualism.

With the repression of the Holy Mother aspect of God, we lost our heart center and the Father God was distorted into an authoritarian and vengeful god. This led to stagnation of our right brain and an inability to lead from the heart. In a sense we short circuited our divine knowing and as a result our crown chakra was capped. As we fell even further into allegiance to the human-based separated ego we became ensnared in the enslavement codes of the karmic template. Thus, we incarnate over and over again making only small progress toward remembering our divinity. Ascension and enlightenment seem almost impossible.

All of us get stuck in the old habit of rationality first, over the heart's intuition. Distorted left-brain masculine energy in both men and women wants proof before acceptance. Therefore, we begin to understand intellectually, but awareness does not come until it focuses in the heart. With men primarily exhibiting the distorted masculine energy, they've been blocked from their hearts and do not have much experience with the process of going inward to accept their feelings.

Surrender can feel like dying because it is the process of releasing the separated ego and embracing what feels uncontrollable. *When we became disconnected from the primordial chaotic creation energy of infinite potentialities, we became fearful of our divine power. Thus we created the perception of separation to distance ourselves from a chaotic God and to bring God under our control, rendering God solely an authoritarian Father who could control the chaotic divine feminine energy.*

Throughout his-story men have needed to be dominant over women based on fear of our power. Our feminine power when given full freedom is loving, wild, untamed, passionate, creative, intuitive, fluid and unstoppable. Men feel this as chaotic, and want to control it. Within the feminine wild energy is the Divine Order of creation. Surrendering to this energy saves us, but patriarchal men do not understand this.

The return of the Holy Mother aspect of God is felt by wayshowers, lightworkers, loveholders and mystics. It is awakening in more and more people exponentially. With so many women engaging in inner work to heal our wombs and hearts and clear our perceptions of separation, we are freeing men to do their inner work to embrace their feminine chaotic energy and thus surrender to the divine within.

We are at a pivotal time in the awakening of humanity. This is the incarnation when we are asked to heal not only the wounds of this lifetime, but all our parallel lives. As we go deep to dissolve what is buried in our shadow place, it automatically dissolves all pain and suffering we've carried with us from all incarnations. All karma is being erased as the cords of enslavement to the separated ego have been cut. This is also mending the ancestral wounds we carry within our genes. The human-based ego is no more. What is left is habits and patterns of the old power-over paradigm. It still appears active and real at times, but the healing and clearing of these abusive patterns are accelerated by the light of love, forgiveness and infinite perfection pouring into every person's I Am Presence.

This grand heart-opening cleansing and dissolving of our sacred wound comes with small deaths to the old paradigm of power-over, giving birth to the new paradigm of power with and within. The process of surrendering it all to the Holy Mother can feel like dying. Sometimes we have suicidal thoughts, yet this is a misunderstanding of the soul's desire to transform and allow what is no longer serving us to die. The intensity may feel as if all the spiritual work we've previously done is useless because how could we possibly still have so much to forgive? During this pivotal point in humanity's awakening all has speeded up as the Cosmic Mother's love is pouring into us in unprecedented amounts. It is causing fear to rise out of the shadow place. It is intense, entropic and vengeful. The poison of separation has been pierced, and it appears on the outside as if it is getting worse. But it has to come to the surface to be transmuted into the light of forgiveness and love's perfection. The poison is so destructive, many are feeling compelled to choose a different way of being. There are many who've lost themselves in the darkness of separation and need our unconditional love rather than our fear, anger and judgment which only perpetuates suffering. In *A Journey into the Unknown* Yeshua says:

> There's electricity in the air. All of this ugliness is coming up to the surface. People are clueless as to what to do with it

> except throw it around. When bitterness of any kind arises in you, what do you do with it? Don't reject it and say that it shouldn't be there. It should be there. It came to tell you something. It wants your attention...it wants you to see it and to own it. Take responsibility for creating it. What is it saying to you?...Dig deep and see where you are rejecting what life gives you. Life only gives you what you need.[40]

Feeling into our hearts to see that life only gives us what we need is a major stepping stone for forgiving the unforgivable and loving the unlovable. The people in my life and all my experiences are what I need to wake from this dream of separation. I can choose to respond through love when I own it, realize I created it and learn from it. *Whenever we want this moment to be different than it is, we suffer*. When we accept our feelings about each painful moment, we eventually see the blessing and wisdom it brings. At a retreat several years ago, one of the attendees had become pregnant through rape and then chose to give birth to a daughter. She said no woman ever wants to experience rape; however, out of it came the blessing of a daughter she loves and cannot imagine a life without. *Finding the blessing in the seemingly unforgivable act ends the suffering*.

There are enough of us who've made the choice to awaken and move into the fifth dimension that the door is open and will not close until everyone walks through. We have no idea of the vast number of people who are affected by one person's choice to forgive and dismantle separation consciousness within themselves, the core sacred wound affecting all of humanity. More and more people are making this choice every day and women of all colors are leading because we've stopped playing the victim. This finally allows the space for men to step back, pause and realize that all healing is an inside job.

## Forgiveness and Surrendering to Divine Innocence in Ourselves and Others

All anger ultimately originates from a belief that God has failed us over and over again. The rich get richer, the poor get poorer and the vast middle class stagnates. How is this fair? It isn't, and the old patterns of the separated ego want to keep it that way. When we begin to realize the loving Creator within, then we realize the God we are angry with is of our own construct. We created a God outside of us to punish all those seemingly clueless and hateful people who make us suffer. Many of us reject the idea of a Beloved Source of All that Is because it appears as if God plays favorites and allows bad things to happen. We think that if God were truly all-loving, then bad things would disappear. The anger builds from feeling duped and unfairly treated. If we keep looking for something or someone outside of us to fix the world, we'll stay stuck in the cycle of suffering.

Consistent spiritual practice and the process of enlightenment is a messy affair. I love the title *Accidental Saints, Finding God in All the Wrong People* by Rev Nadia Bolz-Weber. While I do not resonate with her organized religious theology, it is okay because each of us is on our own unique spiritual path. We all come together in the unity of love. I do resonate with the compassion for herself and others rising from the Universal Truth that God is in everyone, if we look for Her. *A Course in Miracles* captures this with the following teaching.

> When you meet anyone, remember it is a holy encounter,
> As you see this person you will see yourself.
> As you treat this person you will treat yourself.
> As you think of this person you will think of yourself.
> Never forget this, for in this person you will find yourself or lose yourself.
> Whenever two Offspring of God meet, they are given another chance at salvation.

> Do not leave anyone without giving salvation to them and receiving it yourself.
> For I am always there with you, in remembrance of you.[41]
> (Wording changed to be gender neutral.)

Loving the unlovable and forgiving the unforgivable happens when we return to our divine innocence. Returning to our divine innocence happens when we love ourselves enough to see every encounter as a holy encounter, when God actually does exist in what we think are all the wrong people. This is something I've known intellectually for as long as I've been on this spiritual journey into my heart. Sometimes I feel my invincible innocence, but then it is gone the next time I feel judged, blamed or unfairly treated. Many government leaders and their followers provide perfect lessons for finding God in people who appear to be filled with hatred for anyone who threatens their power. We feel as if they are the wrong people; however, they are calling us to love.

The campaigning for the 2020 presidential election in the USA was polarizing, contentious and fear-based. I kept getting sucked into fear and judgment of Trump and those government representatives who actively enabled his disastrous policies. I certainly struggle every day to find God in what I think are all the wrong people. I know deep down that Trump acts as a divine catalyst to bring everything unlike love to the surface to be healed into the light of love. However, the destructive disorder is damaging. Perhaps Trump is an accidental saint who has lost his way? I also feel deeply that the Holy Mother's plan of awakening has compassion at its source. This feels contradictory.

I knew to go deeper than I had ever gone before to release my judgment of those who voted for Trump and all the elected representatives who support him and his policies. I saw a picture of an entrenched Senator and for the first time I really looked at him. What I saw is a very tired man. His eyes were ringed in red, his mouth in a permanent frown, his body held rigid and defiant, and his hands gripped to hold onto his power. I saw a very unhappy miserable man. It loosened the judgment I was holding. He doesn't know what he's doing because he's lost his heart and does not know how to access it anymore. Little by little compassion began to flow, creating cracks in my judgment, and I began to feel what it truly means to find God in all the wrong people. I remind myself of a visual meditation I periodically use to forgive myself for judging people who push my buttons. I have adapted it from the spiritual teacher Paul Selig so that it more fully resonates within my heart.

*I take this Senator into a dark cave. Tenderly I take his face in my hands and look him in the eyes. I say, "I see you in your beauty, I see you in your right to be, I see you and together we will free ourselves from this darkness of judgment I've placed us in. Come with me into the light." I take his hand and walk out of the cave. We walk into the sunlight and a gorgeous green garden filled with flowers of every color and lots of giggling joyful children. When I look at him, we morph into innocent children. We look at each other, laugh and join in the fun.*

You can adapt this meditation to resonate within you until you feel the power of forgiveness and love melting your judgments and fears into your heart space. I have taken many people into this cave. Many times, tenderly taking their faces in my hands has been the most difficult part. Turning into children allows seeing and regaining our innocence so we can once again feel only love. I look at the adult Senator and see the innocent hurt child he's holding within. All my judgment, fear and hate dissolves. My heart opens even wider filled with expansiveness and freedom. This is what it means to love ourselves free. We hold all of humanity in our endless expansive hearts, till every person returns to Christ consciousness. This is why every encounter is a holy encounter because it sets us free to love ourselves and everyone unconditionally.

The teachings about our invincible innocence and forgiveness from Green Tara in *The Sophia Code* resonate in my heart and expresses why forgiveness is our salvation. As I have mentioned we do not have to like or condone harmful behavior. Instead, we are being asked to surrender into heart-entered forgiveness that knows the past can't control our life in the present.

There's that word again—surrender. One of the reasons we suffer and have difficulty surrendering is because we believe divinity is flawed and has failed us. Through contemplation I realized I was holding the belief that I was the imperfect part of divinity—I am the one who failed and is unworthy of God's love. Humans are the ones who fell from grace and are unworthy of God's love. This is why forgiveness is so critical for our return to innocence. It clears the belief that we are flawed and unworthy of Divine Sophia's love. When we release the belief that we are flawed and unworthy, we do this for everyone.

We are scared of surrendering and giving up control because as women we've surrendered to men's dominance over and over again often in harmful and demeaning ways. With ACIM I was asked to surrender to a Father God, which to me meant a patriarchal God. No amount of being told the Father in ACIM was a loving God worked. Using patriarchal language of the past to embrace God does not help. First, I had to embrace the Shekinah held within to return the Holy Mother to God. Then I began to not fear the act of surrender.

Surrendering to the ocean of the Universal Mother's love is blissful and powerful. During this pivotal time in our awakening, we heal all our parallel lives in this still point of awareness by forgiving ourselves and others, and by freeing ourselves from the wounds of separation. If we don't forgive, we become our wound and continually suffer. *We are not condoning abusive behavior; we are forgiving our decision to experience this behavior in ourselves and others.* This sets us free to embrace the power of love. The power of love is innocent, invincible, creative and eternal.

Total surrender can happen in an instant; however, for most of us it is a process. One of the most freeing judgments I've dropped is the belief that surrender happens once in a blaze of divine glory and I'll never have to do it again. Yet it may come gently one day when we realize we are fully a being of God, and it may happen several times until it's all we know.

Our spiritual journey is the path of surrender. Writing this book is a continuing process of surrender, trust, gratitude and renewal. Clearing and healing our mother daughter wound is an act of surrender. Loving our inner child is an act of surrender. Allowing our anger to point us to what needs to be seen, accepted and dissolved is the process of surrender. Feeling our sorrow, our grief and allowing our tears are part of the process of surrender. Embracing the spiritual learning in challenging experiences is part of the process of surrender. Unraveling the ties that bind us to co-dependent behavior is part of the process. Understanding in our heart that judgment of another is only a judgment of ourselves is part of the process. The willingness to open and receive God's love is an act of surrender. Forgiving, loving and saving ourselves is an act of surrender. Yeshua says in ACOL:

> This is the final surrender. The surrender of the control of the personal self. Even with the ego gone, the personal self can continue to move about within the world, a faceless and nameless entity, a being without an identity, humble and selfless and ineffective. For there must be cause to engender effect. These anti-ego tendencies are a real danger in this time. You are not called to selflessness but to Self![42]

The call to Self, our I Am Presence, originates from complete forgiveness and love of self. With this love comes forgiveness. We experience what loving the unlovable means. We see through people's personal self to the reality of their divine selves. We see their actions as a call for love. Again, we are not being asked to love unspeakable acts of abuse, we are being asked to accept our feelings about the abuse and release what keeps us in a cycle of suffering. Once we do this, we feel the power of love to embrace all as their divine sovereign selves. Choose only love.

My mystical co-creator sister Sajit Greene experienced a transforming moment of this type of forgiveness and love, and wrote the following blessing.

*To those who are acting out the power-over paradigm—those who are run by fear, hatred, greed and a need for control*
*Your time is up. Your program is outdated.*
*You know not what you do while the program is running you.*
*We are breaking the chain of tyranny and abuse.*
*The light has come.*
*The darkness reveals its pain and fear.*
*Fear's driving force is being cut off at the root.*
*Perfect Love casts out fear. It cannot continue.*
*All inquisitors, interrogators and witch hunters, go home.*
*Go home to your hearts and be healed.*
*There is enough forgiveness to enfold you.*
*All torturers and executioners go home.*
*Go home to your hearts and be healed.*
*There is enough forgiveness, love and compassion to wash you clean.*
*All abusers, dominators and persecutors, seek healing in the all-loving, all-forgiving, all-compassionate embrace of our Mother who is here with us.*
*You've made a mistake.*

*You've been part of a chain of abuse.*
*You've been controlled by a program.*
*The program is NOT who you truly are.*
*Your True Christ Self, your True Compassionate Self is already holy and wholly accomplished within you.*
*Hear the call to remember and awaken. Hear and heed Love's call.*
*You are forgiven.*
*You are Love. You are Loved. You are loving.*
*Find and remove all blocks to the awareness of that Love that flows to you and through you.*
*The halls of injustice are closed.*
*Go home. Go home. Go home to Love.*[43]

We are this power of love. We are dissolving the habits of the outdated separated ego's program through our path of trust, surrender, gratitude and renewal. We are healing the mother daughter patriarchal wound in our wombs and hearts and thus the wound of separation. We are embracing our victim anger and transmuting it into fierce love. We are the ones we've been waiting for. We are victorious in our divine sovereignty. We've become the Creatrix radiating fierce love for all of humanity. This is cause for joyful, unbridled celebrations. I Am the One Source Light of Love. We are the One Source Light of Love. Amen, Ah Ho and Blessed Be. Beloved I Am, Beloved I Am, Beloved I Am.

# As Within So Without Meditations

## The Gift of a Question

*She remembers who she is and transmutes anger into fierce love.*

If you need to refresh your memory about what is involved in these meditations, please re-read this section in Movement One. Please start with the two following questions before beginning your inquiry process then read the additional questions. Try to write down whatever arises without judgment or editing what you don't like. Most importantly ask your guides/light family to help with your inquiry work.

Can I love myself enough to forgive myself?
Can I forgive myself enough to love myself?

### *Additional Questions*

What is your relationship with anger? Do you bury it or fear it? Do you embrace it or resist it?

Where do you physically hold your anger: in your womb, throat, heart, head, shoulders, back, hips or elsewhere?

How does your anger feel: corrosive, uncontrollable, unbearable, cleansing, freeing?

How do you feel after you've been angry?

Can you imagine yourself as Kali Ma cutting off all the many heads of the separated ego?

With the balance of the divine masculine, do you feel your anger transforming into fierce love?

How can you express anger in your body to release it? Ideas can be: dancing to heart-pounding music, dancing with boxing movements, punching pillows, pushing hands against a wall while screaming or growling. Feel your anger and set the intention to release while you hike, walk or walk the labyrinth.

Do you think it is possible "to find God in all the wrong people" in order to embrace the idea that people are either calling for love or expressing love? If so, what is your heart telling you to do?

What are the blocks you are holding to love's awareness for those acting in harmful ways?

How do you feel when you hear the words vulnerability and surrender?

Return to the first two questions about loving and forgiving yourself.

This is the final surrender

# Movement Six

# The Divine Sophia's Song of Beauty

## Chapter One

# Walking in Beauty and Remembering My Song

*The female energy is a primal force of creation, a fundamental part of All That Is. She brings forth life and flows through everyone. Without her, you would not exist, either as a soul or as a human being.*[44]

When I first read these words from a Pamela Kribbe channeling many years ago, I rejoiced from a place so deep within my heart I felt my world shift. I felt an overwhelming sense of gratitude to finally hear her voice once again. I have felt her arms holding me, yet not her powerful voice of remembrance of all She is. I had silenced the Holy Mother's voice, but never forgot her. After reading *The Sophia Code* several years later, the One Divine Mother Creatrix of All Life is risen once again within me. This time I am singing and claiming her name inside my heart womb space. Never will I bury her again. I am not hiding anymore. I proclaim my very existence that resides in Her, the Divine Sophia. My voice is no longer silent. I vibrate with love, passion and compassion. My reserve is shattered. I know who I Am. The Shekinah is released. I remember my Song.

I learned from Yeshua in ACIM that "Love is the way I walk in gratitude."[45] May my life be a walking prayer of gratitude. May I walk in beauty with all God's relations as taught from the wisdom of indigenous people. With the voice of the Divine Mother risen within, I feel the gratitude to live my prayer, walk in beauty and sing my song of love.

I have moments when I feel completely at one with the Divine Mother, when I am filled with such gratitude for all life that I become an overflowing vessel of God's love. Eventually something happens, and I'm temporarily pulled back into the habits of the separated self. I describe this process of surrender to gratitude over and over again. I have learned that the process of embodying and remembering my divine song sometimes leads to physical pain in order for me to actually pay attention to how I'm still holding on to what does not serve me. It would be helpful if I did not choose this method of awakening; however, ultimately, I am so grateful for the love it releases.

I had a deep knowing that there would be something I needed to heal and clear after the 2020 USA elections. The country is deeply polarized with both sides of the divide acting from fear. It is the out-picturing of dualism so intense that everyone has to pay attention. It no longer can hide just below the surface. We have to see the division and the hatred in order to choose differently, to choose to live differently. At times it is painful to watch, and I allow myself to be pulled into outrage over all the turmoil and hatred surfacing.

I discovered some friends voted for Trump, and it sparked anger I'd hidden to surface on how any kind and compassionate person could vote for someone embedded in sexism and racism. This occurred even with me knowing all the governmental, social, educational and financial structures created within separation consciousness have to be dismantled for the new world based on our I Am Presence to be created. After some deep contemplation, I realized that I was outraged by anyone who would support a person who ordered children to be ripped from their mothers' arms and placed in cages at our border with Mexico. I believe that if we create a world in which all children are safe and loved, everyone will be safe and loved. It feels as if loving all children should be a no-brainer for everyone and should be our guiding light.

I fed this outrage. I felt morally righteous. Therefore, I did not want to give it up. My heart knew this was not healthy, was making me cry and was not the way to heal the great divide. I started judging myself as a failure. I thought about the Goddess Kali Ma and how she lost herself to chaos and rage, cutting off all the demon heads of the separated ego. Surrendering to the masculine energy of Shiva brought her into balance and compassion. I was Kali lost to rage and unable to harness my masculine energy to return to balance and release my compassion.

Everything within this dream of separation is neutral. It is our thoughts about events, things and people which create our feelings and emotions, not the object or person. I was definitely not in a place of neutrality and I was confusing fierce love with my outrage. I asked Mother Mary about the conflict between neutrality and fierce love. She replied that fierce love rises from neutrality. When one is neutral there are no judgments and blame of others or self, no projections of feelings onto others, and no rejection of feelings into the shadow. From this neutral emptiness we open to receive God's mercy, compassion and unconditional love. The fierce love of the Universal Mother rises to embrace ourselves and all humanity.

I shared with a spiritual sister the outrage I felt about how we treat and abuse children and my feelings of guilt and inadequacy for my inability to let go of the judgments and anger. This led to feeling I was failing in my sacred mission. The light of the Divine Mother shone through my soul sister as she reminded me that the Holy Mother holds me in love and sees my innocence and perfection. None of her children are failures in her eyes. She reminded me that if my grown children were feeling this way, I would energetically hold them within my loving embrace. All of this I know in my heart. This is why circles of women are so important for holding and remembering our divine truth for each other when one of us stumbles and forgets. I've nursed this outrage about our treatment of children all my life, stuffing it away into my shadow place. With the acknowledgment of all the anger I had been holding—I let it loose and it found purchase with Trump's actions. I feel this outrage had built up over many lifetimes till it was too big to hold anymore.

This rage felt like a hard, impenetrable pellet from a BB gun which could hurt and harm others if fired. I thought about the pearl which is formed when an irritant such as a grain of sand works its way into a particular species of oyster, clam or mussel. This causes fluid to cover the irritant until it becomes a beautiful and lustrous pearl. With the Divine Mother's milk of self-love and forgiveness flowing over my pellet of rage, it transformed into a white pearl of shining love. I remembered my divine innocence and perfection. This process confirmed that my life is a continual prayer of the already answered prayer. My heart embraced, at a much deeper level, complete trust in the Universal Mother's plan for the wakening of humanity. The message is trust in my divine sovereignty, trust in everyone's divine sovereignty, trust we are co-creating Terra Nova. My heart overflows with gratitude combined with faith that all will be well and has always been well. I Am walking in beauty, remembering and embracing my song.

## The Power of Song

The collapse of Atlantis thousands of years ago triggered what is called our first major fall from grace. We fell from the fifth dimension into the denseness of the third dimension. This fall was orchestrated metaphysically by beings in the fourth dimension with an explosion of discordant painful sound which broke our internal connection to Mother Earth's primordial origin sound of creation. We fell into fear. Because it was so painful, we believed it was possible to destroy the Cosmic Mother's sound of love. Mother Earth also lost her connection and has struggled with us through all the subsequent falls. Each fall tried to convince us that the origin sound of love was destroyed. Now Mother Earth has risen again with the support of all mystics and lightworkers vibrating at a higher resonance. Even with the intense increased metaphysical attempts to prevent Mother Earth's ascension, she is stronger than ever and will not allow another fall to happen. We must not become complacent. We are called to join with her, vibrating at the highest resonance possible. We are returning to the fifth dimension what many call the garden of Eden with this planetary awakening.

Creation is sound, resonance, vibration, rhythm and tone. Many of us who lived during the time of Atlantis remember when we sang our creations into being, when our unique song was our essence, vibration and resonance in harmony with the primordial song of earth and the universe. Our deep inner song was connected to sacredness of nature, to the land and all Mother Earth's relations. We were devoted to the web of life and the Divine Mother's ineffable mysteries focusing her Christ ray of immortal love. All life was fluid as we could hear within the origin sound of creation. Many of us remember our ancient indigenous roots before the relentless and systematic decline into dualism. The deep knowing of our soul song's connection to Mother Earth's primordial sound of creation was severely suppressed. Our dormant songs are being awakened. When our thoughts vibrate with our hearts, they sing with the breath of God and become the song of creation. We return to song as we sound and vibrate ourselves and Terra Nova into being.

No matter what color we are, we have indigenous ancestry. Our ancient spiritual knowing of the Mother Creatrix was infused into our culture's fabric of life to constantly resonate Christ energy. We knew nothing else but the sweetness and ineffable magnitude of Oneness with all creation. That is why when indigenous tribal people were colonized and their culture torn away, they were left bereft of what gave them life. All of us lost our soul's song. With the return of the Holy Mother, that which was torn asunder rises again to restore people to our heart song. The ancient spiritual traditions passed down through the generations are once again gaining strength.

Susan Elizabeth Hale's *Song and Silence, Voicing the Soul* is a rich source of information on ancient singing traditions which include stories of creating the world through song. The Keres and the Hopis in the USA believe Grandmother Spider sang and wove the world into being. The Athabascan people of western Canada believe that Asintmah sang and wove her song into the Great Blanket of Earth. Ancient Egyptians believed that the singing sun created life with its cry of light. The Aborigines in Australia believe that the world was sung into existence within the Dreamtime. The Eskimo people of eastern Greenland enter into the sacred tribal circle to resolve disputes by singing and drumming their anger until the energy dissipates. The ancient Druidic and Celtic faith in Britain was sustained and expressed through music. All around the world people sing and chant the beauty of the earth, they sing to honor the transition from child to adult, to grieve the passing of loved ones, to sing the songs of healing, to sing while mothers give birth, to celebrate the seasons with the planting and harvesting of Earth's abundance.

The Bible describes how God created the earth from song, bringing the light. There is anthropological evidence that music and song came before speech. This resonates because before the fall, our heart's song vibrated in harmony with Mother Earth's origin song. Words were not necessary.

Despite colonization and modernization attempts to suppress our soul songs, people continue to sing and create music—we never stopped. Song is the universal language of the soul. Even though much of creation's song has been either muted or silenced by our inability to hear our inner God Self, people still sing and make music. When people join in song sourced from love, we feel the passion of Oneness in our hearts. Our breath is the spirit of God breathing through us. Song begins with a breath immediately joining us with the mystery and beauty of life. It makes sense that religious services, faith traditions and spiritual gatherings still hold the essence of the sound of creation. Most of the Christian hymns use patriarchal language and celebrate a Father God. However, this does not matter, for when people come together to raise their voices in song, the Holy Mother is present in the many as the one and the one as the many. All faith traditions use chants and songs to return to the heart.

The soul itself is song. While we may have muted our ability to hear our own song, music reminds us over and over again to listen with the ears of the heart. Song and music have kept hope and revolutions alive. The song *We Shall Overcome* generated hope, resilience and powerful belief in the sustaining force of life during the civil rights movement. Song was the one thing allowed slaves on plantations. When they were not allowed to voice their anger and despair, they sang, and it was allowed because it was couched in songs of Christianity. Singing in choirs, choruses and a cappella groups, at church, at summer camp, at spiritual retreats and spontaneously with friends over and over again sustain me throughout my life.

*Amazing Grace* is one of the most popular Christian hymns in the USA and is an example of a song that sings from the soul of anyone who joins with another in song. It was written by John Newton from England, a slave trader who later became an Anglican Priest and abolitionist. He wrote six verses to *Amazing Grace* about his experience of receiving God's mercy and grace when his ship almost wrecked. This is what led him to renounce slave trading and become a priest. Abolitionist Harriet Beecher Stowe also added another verse that has become popular. William Walker is the American composer who set *Amazing Grace* to the tune from the song *New Britain*, which became the version of the song we sing today. I have eight renditions of *Amazing Grace* in my iTunes library. All are different yet hold space in my heart. I even have the version sung in Cherokee by Rita Coolidge. The words and music allow anyone, even those who are not Christian, to feel through song the transforming power of the Holy Mother's merciful love to forgive ourselves for all earthly atrocities.

Through the power of song, we find our voices again. Under patriarchy, women's voices have been suppressed, but never completely. The written word could be destroyed; however people singing from their hearts could be discouraged but never extinguished. Song cannot be silenced. Somehow song always finds a way to burst forth through trauma and suffering. With the rise of the technology to record song, music became available to everyone, and cannot be contained. Rock-an-roll spawned an entire generation that will never be silenced again. Some music became highly negative and deafeningly loud to reinforce the discordance of the original sound explosion. Yet I feel that also changing. All over the world people are singing from their hearts and it is unstoppable.

During COVID, I'm amazed by the many virtual choirs that have come together to sing their songs of faith, hope and resilience for the world. I have listened to more choirs than I ever did before. People of all cultures are coming together, joined in singing and recording, during this pandemic. Impromptu musicians perform virtually to give their music to the world. Walls are coming down because no one can prevent these songs sourced from love from playing around the world.

Many women and men believe they are tone deaf and can't sing. This is not true. Everyone can remember how to sing. There are plenty of coaches who can help anyone find their voice and sing. Each time a person restores their voice and sings their song, others follow. When we free the voice to sing, we heal trauma by singing our pain. When we sing our pain, we free the voice. Then we can sing our joy, and our life becomes a song of love. Hale wrote the following at the end of her book.

> A woman suddenly realizes "I may not be a great singer, but I am song." All over the world life is but a song. Cultures who still use song, who know the power of song, know this as fact. Song mixes the inside world into the outer world. Our soul becomes the world's soul, anima mundi. How can we keep from singing?
>
> One night a group of men and women walk out into the desert, form a circle and tone the stars.
>
> Then sit and listen. The journey ends in silence. And begins once again.[46]

We believe the opposite of silence is noise. *When we forgot our song, we forgot how to be in silence.* It is within the stillness of silence that we know all is divine. Our mind is a noisy place full of thoughts—what many call the monkey mind constantly charging off in different directions. Rick calls it his pinball brain. Metaphysical teachings talk about going inward to access the silence of the heart, which quiets the mind. This can be done even when outside of us is noisy and chaotic.

We find our unique song of love in the silence of the heart. The heart does not harbor fearful, judgmental thoughts, only the silence of unending love, from which our unique song rises. The heart is the source of everyone's radiant song. I describe the process of learning to listen to my heart song held within the spacious silence of my heart womb. Within the well of silence springs the healing waters of our heart song. The space between silence and song is God's breath in us. With the breath of life, we bring our song into the world to join in Oneness with every person's soul song. We walk into the center of the labyrinth, sit within the silence, listen until we hear our song rising, then we sing our song as we walk out of the labyrinth into the world. *We blend our voices in harmony to the sounds of freedom from separation, no longer giving strength to that which binds us to the habits of fear.*

## Chapter Two

# When the World Tried to Sever the Divine Mother from God

We forgot the Holy Mother when we decided that you are separate from me. Eventually we decided that because we are separate, some people are lesser than other people. Because some people are lesser than other people, they are not as worthy of abundance and maybe the right to live. Therefore, whole cultures of people are seen as a blight on the face of the earth. This gave leaders who earned their power through violence and intimidation the right to eliminate people who are not held in favor in their father god's eyes. The lesser people became so dehumanized, we believed that killing them was okay. Wars became a mission to spread the faith of a patriarchal god to persecute, enslave and annihilate all the people in any culture or country who worshipped different gods. We became experts in determining who deserved to be killed in order to justify empire building to satisfy greed. Genocide of whole cultures and countries became acceptable.

Eons ago we worshipped the Immanent Mother as the divine womb birthing all that is. These are pre-his-tory times of the original tribal people of earth in what we now call indigenous communities. With the onset of empire building through colonization, we started to believe that these tribal peoples in every part of the world were savages needing to be civilized. But this process was at a cost to indigenous wisdom of knowing in our hearts the divine connection to the feminine face of God and all Her relations. In contemporary times we refer to these tribal communities as people of color, as if the color of their skin is the reason they need to be eliminated. Their ancient spiritual wisdom threatened the separated ego's tool of might is right, so they had to be silenced. White skin began to be associated with the power-over paradigm. It became us versus them and the onset of the extremism of white superiority. Over time we became complacent as the tribal people were persecuted and systematically exterminated. We almost forgot our divine connection to Mother Earth, her primal beauty and abundant life.

The indigenous Teyuna people isolated themselves in the mountains of the Sierra Nevada of Columbia for hundreds of years, thus managing to escape the ravages and carnage of colonization. Four indigenous groups make up the Teyuna people: Wiwa, Kogi, Arhuaco and Kankuamo. The Kogi emerged as their ambassador in the 1990s, spoke to the world, retreated, and then emerged again with a film called Alunas in 2012. The Kogi gently refer to us as younger brother and warn us of our destructive madness. They speak about their ancient wisdom of devotion and respect for Mother Earth. Their voice reminds us that the only purpose of human life is to care for all living relations.

Many of the leaders and peoples of the First Nations all over the world, despite decades of repression and eradication, maintain their ancient culture infused with spiritual wisdom and deep connection to the earth. They share a message about the Earth Mother's abundant garden, and the need to live in respect, balance and harmonious relationship with all the Great Mother's offspring. Many of us are listening.

## The Fall from Grace

Separation is the original trauma felt by everyone living on earth with the fall from the garden of Eden that coincides with the fall of Atlantis. The people of Atlantis arriving from a star nation lived in matrifocal balanced communities spiritually connected to all living beings. They lived and taught those inhabiting earth to be in joy and harmony, continually co-creating with all

Mother Earth's relations including the living elementals whose very beings are life.

Fear is also enfolded in the divine. Many Atlanteans increasingly became enamored with the intellect. Their eventual arrogance created a sound explosion and humanity's first major fall into duality. The original Atlantean legacy of complete immersion with the Holy Mother balanced with the Holy Father remained in Egypt under the divine feminine reigns of Hathor and Isis, both known as Queens of Heaven. This halted for thousands of years within Egypt much of the attempts to subdue the Holy Mother aspect of God. Isis and Hathor's legacy continued with the Order of the Magdalenes which became part of the Essene communities of Christ love.

There have been several subsequent major falls carrying us deeper and deeper into colonization and the suppression of the feminine divine. These falls contributed to hordes of marauding men killing, raping, destroying and spreading the disease of conquer-and-divide all over the world. I feel in my cells connection to the ancient times as over and over again the feminine resonance of God was systematically and brutally suppressed. Eventually Egypt fell around 5500 BCE; next ancient Greece fell around 3500 BCE; and then the Druids in 60 BCE. These falls affected Mother Earth's ley lines and energy centers. Our march continued to subdue all radiating feminine energy and the primal life force of Mother Gaia.

Gaius Suetonius Paulinus, Roman Governor of Britain, slaughtered the Druids at Mona and the tribal people led by the Iceni chieftain, Boudica. The heart of Britain's tribal people was the Druids' faith with their deep harmonious connection to Mother Earth and the web of life. Their spiritual values and lifestyle posed the most threat to Roman rule and had to be eliminated for the Romans to gain control of Britain. The Druids' home of Mona, now called the Holy Isle of Anglesey in Wales, was the spiritual heart center for the tribal people who made up the Celtic culture in western Europe. Mac Macartney wrote in *The Children's Fire*:

> The killing was methodical, absolute and without mercy... When the sacred groves of Britain's ancient spiritual tradition were cut and burned, and Boudica's army was defeated by the legions, a cord was severed that has never fully healed. I believe that we learned something in this period of history that seared itself into our very soul and, like the abused child, we grew to adulthood and exported our trauma around the world.[47]

We've continued to experience smaller falls into dualism. These include the fall of the Cathars in France, where the focus and teachings of Mary Magdalene survived. While his-story talks about the gnostic beliefs of the Cathars from the Roman Catholic perspective, it does not include how the teachings of Mary Magdalene influenced the Cathars. The Roman Catholic Church did not recognize Mary Magdalene as a teacher, only a whore saved by Jesus. This persecution and genocide by the Catholic Church occurred with the inquisition times of 1200 CE. These inquisitions continued in western Europe and colonized countries all over the world into the 1700s. Some call this The Burning Times or the Women's Holocaust. Millions of women were tortured, crucified and burned at the stake.

The "might is right" doctrine was brutally hammered home by hundreds of years of the Roman Empire's quest for land, resources and dominance. The early and imperial Roman Catholic Church continued the cruel power-over programming by co-opting and manipulating Jesus's original teachings that God is in us as we are in God. The Roman Catholic Church elders designated Jesus as the one and only Christ and son of a Father God. They taught that all are born sinners (original sin) who have to sacrifice in order to obtain heaven through priests as intermediaries and dispensers of God's will and justice. The theology of the one and only Jesus Christ was adopted by most of the protestant churches during the time of the Reformation.

This is the immense trauma of the Middle Ages when Europeans persecuted, tortured, butchered, enslaved and colonized each other, all in the name of a Father God and his one son Jesus. The European nations of Britain, Spain, Italy, Portugal, France, Sweden, Belgium and the Netherlands exported this trauma through colonizing the Americas, Canada, Australia, New Zealand, India and Africa. Eventually Britain controlled all the colonized territories in what is now the United States, Canada, Australia and New Zealand. The seeds of white supremacy were planted.

The power-over paradigm of conquer, divide and annihilate all, in the name of empire building, to control wealth and the world's resources became global with the two world wars and their aftermath, as empires fought with each other for ultimate control of the world's resources. Genocide and ethnic cleansing were central to Germany's justification for conquering countries in order to be the biggest empire left standing. They extolled the beliefs that those with white skin are God's chosen people and Jews were to be exterminated. Eastern countries and empires also practiced genocide and ethnic cleansing to expand their control and domination. During WWI, Turkey as the weakened Ottoman Empire committed ethnic cleansing and genocide against the Armenians, killing one million people. Japan invaded China in 1931 and bombed Pearl Harbor in 1941, bringing the USA into WWII. After WWII the Chinese Empire invaded and conquered Tibet trying to wipe out their indigenous culture heavily influenced by their deep faith in Tibetan Buddhism. There has been more recent genocide in Bosnia and Rwanda. And now Russia has invaded the Ukraine.

After WWII we delved deeper into the total influence of power-over. Much was being enacted on the metaphysical level in the fourth dimension, where beings of great psychic power adhering to the desire to stay within separation, manipulated many of the world's leaders and humanity. This metaphysical influence has been gaining strength since the 1800s. The deeper we submerged into separation consciousness, the more Mother Earth and all her elementals and primal beings and all living beings have been seriously harmed.

My lineage traces back to western Europe. As a white woman I never considered I had indigenous roots. I feel the spiritual connection to the womb teachings of the Great Mother, yet I did not connect the dots to my indigenous roots. This is profoundly disturbing and life-giving. Patricia Pearce, in her blog titled *White Supremacy and the Identified Patient*, says:

> Who are you as a "white person"? You are immigrants of many cultures, lands in which the skin color of the people happened to be fair. Can you see the absolute absence of meaning in this? How fragile an identity it is that relies upon skin color? Revisit your ancestral roots. Who were you before you became "white"? Before you became "white" you were many things. You were the speakers of Gaelic and had a sacred relationship with the land, which you understood to be inhabited by entities not visible to the human eye. You were dancers around the bonfire at the winter solstice. You were creators of sublime music that touched the soul. You were tellers of stories that spoke of the transcendence of the human spirit.[48]

It is too easy to put all the blame on white supremacists. They are a stark reminder of our dysfunctional multicultural human family. They are acting out a human trait that's been left too long to fester. All of us at one time or another have felt rage about how we've been treated. White supremacists are dramatically enacting for all to see the utter empty absurdity of holding an ideology based on the nothingness of a pale skin color. They are asking to receive the Holy Mother's love they have never felt. If one of my children was acting out, I would not withdraw my love. I would find a way for them to feel into their hurt and need to lash out in order for them to accept their feelings. People are either expressing love or calling for love. We are being asked to choose between continuing a world in which hatred and revenge dominate, or a multicultural diverse world in which we draw a circle of love around the wounded in our human family and find a way for restorative justice, reconciliation and healing to occur.

### *When the World Forgot How to Hug*

The work I did with Sarah to heal the mother daughter wound made me aware of how uncomfortable I was with hugging. Touch could not always be trusted. I started realizing that a symptom of our loss of harmonious balanced communities was the belief that we could never show our emotions to provide comfort, especially through hugging. It makes sense that we were taught to deny our emotions, because when we honor our emotions it leads to remembering our connection with all living things. This is dangerous to the separated self. We learned that holding and hugging babies was necessary for survival, but once children are old enough, they need to be made tough to survive. Physical contact between men and women was allowed only if it was sexual, ensuring that women stayed bound to the sexual needs of men. With this emphasis on sexual control, women learned that hugging could be dangerous and painful. Hugging for comfort became suspect and strictly reinforced. Hugs between men was highly discouraged lest they be seen as wimps and too feminine. This feels extreme; however, like my 4-year-old friend who was terrified of hugs, those countries that practiced colonization learned to uphold the idea that showing emotions and any physical expression of compassion was weak.

I feel a little silly writing about when the world forgot how to hug. However, it is emblematic of how the values and structures of patriarchy divide and separate people to prevent us from remembering our true divine Self in Unity. Of course, a few cultures remain who hug more spontaneously. My observation is that these cultures have more direct access to their indigenous roots. Even within the USA there are differences depending on where one lives. The Puritans of New England created a strict culture of rigid morality that frowned on physical displays of emotion while extolling hard work and piety. We still feel much of that heritage in contemporary times.

A mother's main job is to nurture and care for her family. All else is supposed to be secondary. As I talked with friends about this, I realized how many of us grew up in families with limited physical loving expression. Hugging is only acceptable as a hello or a goodbye. What drove this home was watching season four of the TV series *The Crown*. The English stereotype of the "stiff upper lip" and never expressing emotion is the product of jokes that have their base in a cultural condition.

I have no idea how accurate the portrayal of Queen Elizabeth II and the royal family is by Netflix, yet it felt right. I do know it spoke to me on a fundamental level about how both men and women governmental leaders all over the world became effective transmitters of patriarchy's doctrine of power-over. Season four portrays the time when Margaret Thatcher was prime minister and Diana became the Princess of Wales with her marriage to Charles, the Prince of Wales. Thatcher, referred to as the Iron Lady, pursues the belief that women are weak but that she is the rare exception. She fiercely loves her son and dismisses her daughter. She is driven to be seen as stronger and more ruthless than almost all the men around her. Thatcher saw the economic hardship people were experiencing as necessary to toughen everyone up. The Falklands War and her refusal to back down or even try diplomatic talks was all done with the power-over doctrine of might is right. She was definitely not a hugger. Thatcher is one side of the coin of might is right, the Queen is the other side, upholding benign paternalism that cares for England's conquered colonies that form the Commonwealth.

The royal family is dominated by the Queen as head of the monarchy. All revolves around her. Not only is she the symbol of the monarchy, as a woman she is therefore the central mother figure for the royal family. Her decisions are absolute. But this is a mother who struggles with maternal feelings. She confesses she loves her children but felt no maternal inclination to hold them when they were babies or young children—the nannies took care of her children's comfort and physical needs. She has one daughter and three sons. Prince Charles is deeply unhappy, always under the shadow of his mother and forbidden to marry the woman he loves. Princess Anne is unhappy in her marriage. Prince Andrew and Prince Edward are away at school. Prince Andrew is recklessly carefree and Prince Edward is being bullied, yet is advised to tough it out. Her husband, Prince Philip, learned early that his only role was to support the Queen.

Here comes Diana approved by the Queen as the seemingly perfect wife for Charles. She is beautiful, charming, gracious and loved by the people. She is also bulimic and extremely unhappy, exacerbated by Charles' continuous affair with the woman he loves. When Charles says he is unhappy and complains about Diana and her love affairs, the Queen tells him to pull himself together, stop his ridiculous affair, and act like the king he will eventually become. Charles begins to hate Diana and ridicules her incessantly because she outshines him in public. Diana asks to meet with the Queen, wanting her support and advice, but most of all she wants her love. In desperation, she hugs the Queen. The uncomfortable Queen remains frozen within

Diana's embrace without returning the hug. Later she questions her circle of women—the Queen Mother; her sister, Princess Margaret, and daughter, Princess Anne—whether or not a hug would have helped. They all sit silently, saying nothing.

Men and women both lost the ability to honor our feelings. We became experts at denial, either projecting our feelings onto others or rejecting our feelings into the shadow. With our fear of turning inward lest we hate what we might learn, we forgot how to create compassionate loving relationships, opting instead for co-dependency. This perpetuates suffering and separation consciousness.

During COVID and sheltering in place, we were forced to let go all communication through touch and hugs, except perhaps with our immediate family. We've become more reliant on technology and the computer to communicate, reinforcing separation even while creating more ways to connect. Masks are supposed to keep us safe, yet they hide our facial expressions, enforcing separateness. It is a double-edged sword revealing truth as well as reinforcing the division of the separated state. Some people felt relieved and comfortable having an excuse to not have physical contact. Many women and children were locked in with their abusers where harmful touch is magnified. However, many people had space to realize how much personal relationship, interaction and human touch is necessary for our well-being. Without the usual activities and distractions, we were given the opportunity to go inward and access our heart. More and more people are becoming comfortable with their inner lives and have embraced a simpler, more loving life, needing less distractions in their search for peace.

Yeshua's teachings in ACOL help us understand the process of acceptance of feelings. Remember, we are not being asked to condone violent or abusive behavior or to like the people who act out in harmful ways, only to accept our feelings about these destructive acts.

> In denying your feelings you will tend also to deny the feelings of others. While true compassion sees only the truth, this does not mean it holds the feelings of anyone—not those living in truth, or those living in illusion—in disregard. Distancing, or non-acceptance of your own feelings, is not living in the present and will create an attitude that will not be compassionate.[49]

When we accept our feelings, we accept the feelings of others. When we accept ourselves, we fall in love with ourselves. When we fall in love with ourselves, we fall in love with all beings. We stay in presence. By helping each other evolve into the fullness of our beings, we are co-creating communities respectful and grateful for the amazing diversity of the web of life. This is the Divine Sophia's song of beauty.

### *Embracing Indigenous Roots*

Matrifocal tribal communities began to disintegrate when they devolved into matriarchy and men started to rebel. Indigenous and tribal communities all over the world were not immune to this disintegration and the fall into dualism. Separation expressed through patriarchy is global. Some communities were able to hold onto their connection to Mother Earth and the web of life, and some fell into the patriarchal ways of warring tribes and disrespect for feminine energy long before the age of empire building and colonization. Rome started the colonization process and Western colonization continued the conquering, killing, enslavement and extermination of indigenous and tribal communities. Children were forced into organized Christian schools in order to strip them of their culture and spiritual connection to Mother Earth. We see the results today in deep poverty, alcoholism, and abuse against women and children. We took away their divine heritage of deep spiritual connection with the land and left them empty through the worse aspects of the power-over paradigm.

In the 1980s when my heroine's spiritual path was beginning to whisper to me, I read Marion Zimmer Bradley's book *The Mists of Avalon*. This is an epic novel about the story of King Arthur as told from the perspective of the women who wielded the power of the Goddess, during a time when early Christianity was taking over Britain. This is a time of the Druid Merlin. Avalon existed behind protective mists where Morgaine, half-sister to Arthur, reigned as High Priestess to the last remnants of the Druids worshipping the Immanent Mother—all that remained after the Romans destroyed the Isle of Mona.

I felt acutely the struggles to maintain the Goddess and sacredness for the earth and all life with the increasing encroachment of Christianity's patriarchal doctrine of a Father God. At the end of the book when there is little left of goddess worship, Morgaine realizes the Goddess is preserved in Mother Mary and that she'll rise again. There is hope as Morgaine retreats permanently behind Avalon's veils, to close off the patriarchal world. While I was reading this novel, I felt I had been in Avalon. I felt the heartache of the final fall of the feminine divine, yet also the preserving of the Goddess in Mother Mary until she rises again in people's hearts. I have talked with many women who also feel a strong connection to Avalon. Avalon exists as a myth with roots in spiritual truth.

In the channeled book *Anna, The Voice of the Magdalenes*, by Claire Heartsong, I learned that after Yeshua's crucifixion and resurrection, many of his followers, including Yeshua's Grandmother Anna, Mother Mary and Mary Magdalene, sailed to Britain to join a community in Avalon (Glastonbury), established by the Essenes. The Essenes (essence) were earth-based communities of powerful Christ healers initiated into the heart mysteries of the Divine Mother enfolding the Father as the Universal Beloved Source of all that Is. The lineage from the Egyptian order of the Magdalenes helped form these Essene communities long before the birth of Yeshua. In Israel the Essene Magdalenes was the spiritual community of Mother Mary and Joseph, and Joseph of Arimathea that prepared for Yeshua's birth. They helped raise Yeshua, Mary Magdalene, John the Baptist and many who became disciples. Essenes lived outside of the patriarchal programming, which made them targets of the Roman colonization machine.

Joseph of Arimathea and his sons established the Essene communities in France and Britain. They lived in Avalon and the Essene Druid's religious home on the Isle of Mona, which some in Avalon refer to as the Isle of Avalon. Yeshua visited Avalon and Mona when he was 13 years old. Long-lived Anna continued to reside in Avalon and witnessed the dispersal of Yeshua's family and followers and the destruction of Mona. Many fled to Mount Bugarach in southern France, where Mary Magdalene continued her ministry and which became the home of the Cathars. Anna mentions meeting a gentle Christian priest who promised to preserve the teachings of Yeshua in Glastonbury. In my heart it reinforced the connection and knowing of being in Avalon.

When I read *Anna, the Voice of the Magdalenes,* I was amazed to learn of Avalon's connection to the Essene Magdalene communities in Israel and eventually Yeshua's teachings. After his resurrection, Yeshua visited Avalon many times. I was also delighted to learn that in order to evade the Romans, the Isle of Avalon (Mona) was deliberately concealed in mists as mentioned in *The Mists of Avalon*. The Arthurian story written in *The Mists of Avalon* happens during the war with the Saxons, when the last vestiges of the Essene Magdalene spirituality was holding on by a thin thread. And, like all myths, it points to truths and has its origins in history. I feel in my cells and bones the truth of my ancestral indigenous Celtic and karmic connections to Avalon.

## *The Marys Shine the Divine Feminine Light*

Almost everyone who has had some education in Christianity has noticed how many Marys existed during the time of Yeshua. Dale Allen Hoffman, an Aramaic scholar and spiritual teacher, says that Mary, Maryaam or Miriam comes from the Aramaic title of Maryaa, which means "one who shines the feminine light." It refers to women who have awakened this feminine light in themselves. The title Mary comes from Coptic Egyptian, and refers to the virgin Isis Mary. Isis Mary's story was born again in Mother Mary, both referred to as Queen of Heaven. Virgin actually means "sovereign woman who has awakened," hence the title Mary. And the story of Isis and Osiris being resurrected is played out again with Yeshua and Mary Magdalene.

Magdalene in Aramaic is Magdalitha which means a tower or fortress of feminine strength. Thus, Mary Magdalene is a woman who shines the feminine light as a fortress of strength. It does not refer to only one woman. There are several women who were bestowed with the title of Mary Magdalene. There are many modern-day women mystics carrying the resonance of Mary Magdalene. As described in *Anna, the Voice of the Magdalenes*, Mary of Bethany is the Mary Magdalene we've come to know. The order of the Magdalenes or Magdalitha had its inception with Isis Mary which was passed down by many women throughout history.[50] Joan of Arc is also of the Order of the Magdalenes. The Essene community was a stronghold of women holding the Magdalene legacy. This shining of feminine light is the Shekinah, the Holy Spirit and Shakti energy.

We hold in our ancestral and karmic memories our indigenous roots when we worshipped the Holy Mother Creatrix and felt the interconnectedness of all life. We are being asked as wisdom weavers to forgive and dissolve all trauma from experiencing through many lifetimes the suppression of the feminine face of God. It does not matter which indigenous culture is your heritage, it only matters to heal the trauma we've been carrying for many lifetimes. We open our hearts, we stay curious, we embrace our memories of the divine feminine, we honor the times when we felt the web of life as One with the Universal Mother and we joyfully co-create Terra Nova in harmony with all that is.

## Chapter Three

# Womb Healing and Awakening

The heroine's path is a journey of womb healing and awakening. Women's wombs are our cervical gateway for return to Mother Earth and the Cosmic Mother. This is why I was guided to use the labyrinth as a metaphor for our journey. Initially when I created the labyrinth, I knew it was a symbol of the feminine divine. The awareness of constantly walking into the womb of Mother Gaia came only gradually with the understanding of mending and healing the colonized womb of all women. We are inside the womb of the Cosmic Mother and we have never been separated from her. We tricked ourselves into believing in separation, but that is an impossibility: all I need do is remember her origin sound of creation, her embrace and the warmth of her loving primordial womb.

The year 2021 began the decade of the divine feminine. With many mystic women, I feel this deep within my bones. Polarization and divisiveness have been so severe, most are seeking a better way. The contrast is so absolute that we are forced to pay attention. I see evidence of divine feminine energy everywhere—from lightworkers and loveholders, from spiritual teachers and channels of ascended masters, archangels, star nations and all our light family. Absolutely everyone is awakening. No one is left behind, because we all exist in Oneness. *As women heal, they lead the way, holding the space for men to go inward to set free their sacred feminine energy.*

I am beginning to witness more and more men forming their own circles to explore their feminine essence in relation to their unique spiritual journey of awakening. Men need to learn how to feel and express their emotions with other men without the presence of women. Women learned the lessons of patriarchy well, so we've been complicit in wanting men to always be strong. Both men and women have been taught that strong men do not cry. Therefore, many women admonish or dismiss men who cry or express tender emotions. And we can be cruel.

BIPOC women are forming circles to explore their indigenous communal spirituality without fear of white women trying to take over or hurting their feelings. This time of transition is needed in order for everyone to explore their own unique spiritual path in loving, respectful circles without subtle racist and sexist assumptions getting in the way.

Trauma from all lifetimes is being felt and dissolved. This process often connects to lifetimes when we were tribal people of a different culture than who we are in this current body. The process also asks us to return to the indigenous roots of this life's personal ancestry to reconnect with the land. This is an aspect of healing racism; it is both ancestral and karmic. I have memories of being a Native American in at least three other lives. And even though I can't claim that ancestry in this life, what I learned from those lifetimes affects my spiritual path in this lifetime. It is why I was directed to live in New Mexico—the land calls to me and helps my mystical path to remembering my divinity. At the same time I'm being guided to ancestral healing of this life's indigenous roots in Britain. Where are your indigenous roots? It's important to connect with our ancestors in order to heal all human-based trauma.

We are being called, dear mystical sisters of the heart, to go deeper than we ever have done before, to fearlessly look at all the wounds we've been carrying from many, many lifetimes of persecution. We hold this trauma in our hearts and wombs. Let us unravel and clear all the synthesized DNA implanted in our cells, heart and womb from these lifetimes of abuse. We are being called both backward and forward into Mother Earth's primal heart and womb before patriarchal colonization dragged us over and over again into the density of dualism.

Mother Gaia is taking back her body—purifying and healing all her wounds, freeing all her many relations inhabiting earth. Mother Gaia, along with those who've been victims of the colonization machine: women, indigenous people, all people of color and people with the variety of gender and sexual expressions are saying No to victimhood, and No to the colonization machine. We return to Christ consciousness through love, through loving so deeply within the primordial womb of the Cosmic Mother that we flood the world with the Mother's light. With this we set persecutors, victims and saviors free to return to their Truth. Believe this is happening. Believe within every cell of your body. This is the creation of heaven on earth, the creation of the new. Everyone is beloved within God. Beloved we are. Beloved I Am.

## The Wise Woman Returns

I don't remember growing old. Yet here I am. I look in the mirror and I look old. There are some wrinkles and my face sags in places that says: yes, you are old. I look at my hands and there are a few age spots. How did it happen, how did I arrive at this place that says I'm old? I don't feel old in my heart. Yet my body tells me I'm old. There is wisdom I did not have when younger. I am an old soul in an aging body. There are lots of aware old souls on earth in younger bodies. I bless them. Let them be the ones to usher in this planetary awakening; combining old soul, youth and action into manifestation.

I don't remember agreeing to write this book. Yet here I am writing a book that is writing me; birthing this book while it is birthing me; answering a call that won't let me be. *This is as it should be,* She says with a smile, *writing a book in your wisdom years you agreed to long ago.* All my lives arrive at this still point of awareness to have a book write me. With much humor She says, *at this pivotal point in humanity's awakening, you need to look like a grandmother.* I'm not a physical grandmother, at least not yet. *It doesn't matter* She says, *this is not about physicality, it is a state of mind and heart joined in whole heartedness and ancient wisdom.*

Who is this for? Who will read it and does it matter? *Oh, you know,* She says. I want to protest, yet I don't have the energy. I feel Her smile, Her loving embrace, and Her laughter. I smile in return. It doesn't matter because it is out of my hands, always has been. I gift Her the book and She'll take it from there. Still lots left to finish. Maybe by the time it is complete and published, the world will no longer need it. Now I feel lots of laughter from all my light family. *Silly girl, they say.* Girl—now I do protest, I'm not a girl! I thought I had to look like a grandmother. *Young at heart,* She says. *A young heart in an aging body being the Universal Grandmother.*

Oh! I can do this; I can finish this. *Oh, you'll never be finished* She says, *but the book will be. Who knows what will happen after that? Be curious and alive to infinite possibilities? Curiosity did not kill the cat—it set her free.* I laugh in delight. Ah, I'm loving myself free. Who knows, maybe in my next life I'll spend time as Mother Owl soaring and spreading her wisdom? *You can do that now,* She says, *by being the Universal Grandmother. Have fun, soar all you want, but land occasionally. You are still needed here.* Gratitude swells in my heart. I can do that, I say.

Many years ago, at the beginning of my spiritual awakening path, I was friends with a woman who had studied with a well-known shaman and eventually became a practicing shaman. She offered to do a past life regression with me. I was nervous and distrustful of my ability to hold a meditative state for a long time. What happened was a total surprise. I thought I'd maybe access a specific parallel life, but what came through was a vision of sitting around the fire with the elder grandmothers. I felt ancient wisdom flowing through me. The grandmothers said I had the ability to always return to them and the sacred fire. I did for several years, until I forgot. The message I received from the Sky Grandmothers about the Universal Grandmother archetype came from this same ancient wisdom of sitting around the fire with the elder grandmothers. The following message from Mother Mary, channeled by Mari Perron, reminded me of my first contact with the ancient grandmothers.

> My son spoke of anchoring The New (in ACOL) and I want you to imagine now the women around the campfire, squatting while they tend the fire, squatting as they birth new life. This is the posture of the anchor, solid as an anvil, feet planted, balance fine and deliberate, poised. Poised for what will be needed next. Poised and ready for the invasion of The New and the old's lingering encroachment, as mesmerizing as the flames of the fire that signals The New. The invasion is an intrusion of The New into the old, a force meant to quicken the passing of all that lingers of death in the living. To end living death and welcome living life. To end division and become one with what is being birthed. To mother The New into existence.[51]

I am gratified to remember what I received so early in my emerging spiritual path, a message from the grandmothers. I return to the ancient grandmothers and become a wise woman with them through the Universal Grandmother archetype. We are returning to the ancient circle of wise women around the fire. It is safe to access ancient memories known deep within our hearts and bodies that emerge to heal us and our ancestors through many lifetimes. "To end living death and welcome living life." We access our ancient wisdom from the time when women led from their hearts and created communities of harmony, interconnectedness and abundance with all life. The wise woman returns.

These wise women squatting around the sacred fire are anchoring the energy of the new. We are solid in our balanced masculine and feminine resonance, steadfast, courageous and singing the fierce love of the Cosmic Mother. We can access the ancient grandmothers at any time, no matter what age we are. The wisdom of the Sky Grandmothers is available to everyone. We come together with the energy of Universal Grandmothers to hold humanity in our container of love, becoming wisdom weavers for the awakening heart of humanity. Mother Mary, through a soul sister's vision, brought into my awareness that this container of love is a colorful woven basket symbolizing the feminine essence. We are weavers of soul songs woven into the basket. The basket holds the bounty of life, nourishment, birth and rebirth, infinite endings and beginnings, and the tree of life. We opened the basket's lid to release our entry into the fifth dimension. The basket overflows with the Cosmic Mother's all-encompassing love with no opposite.

### Universal Grandmothers' Chorus of Love

The multiverse is forever singing, is always resounding with the chorus of Sophia's love. She sings her song of love for those who hear until all her creations are listening. Every person desires to be fully witnessed, to be seen and heard, appreciated and honored. When we listen with the ears of our heart, we know we have always been adored. We breathe this until it is all we know and express. Our inner heart womb overflows with love, thus birthing heaven on earth.

The embrace of the Universal Grandmother is luminous distilled wisdom radiating from our hearts. We bless with our words and songs, for we are divine beings created in the image of Sophia God. We receive the wisdom and rainbow energy of the Sky Grandmothers becoming their emissaries on earth as wisdom weavers. The Sky Grandmothers are very ancient beings simultaneously singing and weaving timelines for billions of souls incarnating on earth. Like Grandmother Spider, they weave all our realities into our highest good. They weave and balance the threads of light that hold our divinity in this dream of separation until all species on earth are awake to their Christ Selves.

The Sky Grandmothers radiate fierce unconditional love and radical compassion for Divine Sophia's children. They connect to each person's inner child to return us to the purity and innocence of our heart. Universal Grandmothers as emissaries of the Sky Grandmothers are immersed in the warmth and healing powers of rainbow energy, the many colors of the multiverse. We sing the colors and variety of Sophia's queendom within every cell of our bodies. We resonate at a higher octave. As Universal Grandmothers we weave a rainbow bridge from Sophia's heart womb to Mother Earth's heart womb and to our heart womb joined with everyone's heart womb.

The Sky Grandmother's representative on earth is the Divine Feminine Ascended Master, White Buffalo Woman. She represents indigenous wisdom and assists in the awakening of all humanity. Grandmother Spider as named by the Hopis, also called Changing Woman by the Navajos in many spiritual stories, is also a Sky Grandmother. In Native American spirituality the thirteen original clan mothers are Sky Grandmothers. Anna the grandmother of Yeshua, and the Celtic Goddess Brigid are members of the Sky Grandmothers. The Sky Grandmothers represent many indigenous faith traditions all over the world.

As emissaries of the Sky Grandmothers, we are creating a vessel of love in our hearts and wombs to hold all of humanity in their Truth till they can see and feel it. You may not feel the call of the Sky Grandmothers to embrace the Universal Grandmother's archetype. However, we are all being asked in our unique way to hold love's basket within ourselves in order to be a vessel of overflowing love. Continuing to resonate at the highest octave affects even those who are still unaware of the divine light shining within them.

As wisdom weavers we are uniquely positioned to create this basket of love because of our human experiences. We know what it means to birth and mother a child or birth and mother a new creation such as a new business, a piece of art, a song, or a book. We know what it means to join others on the side of love with courageous acts of non-violent resistance to tyranny. Many of us have been fierce warrior mothers, aunts and special friends for our children, and have gained much wisdom from the experience. From this wisdom, we see the light of God in all Sophia's children, young and old. It feels easy to love all people because we have regained our inherent wisdom as Observer. We can step back and hold each person in our loving embrace, no matter what is happening with them, no matter how much they are struggling, no matter how lost they are. We are the ones we've been waiting for.

### *Dissolving the Ties That Bind*

The chapter on healing the mother daughter wound is about clearing the co-dependent ties or enmeshment with our mothers and children in order to heal and dissolve patriarchal wounding and conditioning. When we do this, we learn to mother ourselves—which is the process of self-love and forgiveness. Instead of passing down the patriarchal wounding, we gift our daughters, and sons and nonbinary or trans children with freedom to clear their own sacred wounds and return to their divine sovereignty.

In the movement about Lilith, I described two meditation visions about cutting the rope that kept me bound to Tyler so that we could both be free to soar with Mother Owl. The last one occurred when Tyler was 18. Tyler is now in his thirties. He has become a successful tattoo artist and is part owner of a tattoo shop. It felt as if all was finally well with Tyler and I could stop worrying. Then the COVID-19 pandemic hit and he had to shut down the tattoo shop.

After the initial shut down, the Governor of Maine, where Tyler resides, allowed some non-essential services such as hair salons to re-open but not tattoo shops. It is ironic since tattoo shops in order to receive a license have to meet the same strict health and safety codes as hospitals. Tyler felt unfairly treated. He wanted to go back to work not only because it is his passion, but also because he needed the income.

I knew I was being triggered by this, as Tyler was being triggered. I remembered learning to be aware when you feel unfairly treated. It is the separated ego talking. I was feeling sad for several days because there are thousands of people out of work feeling unfairly treated and suffering. Then a spiritual sister texted a Malaysian version of the song *The Blessings* written by Kari Jobe and Cody Carnes. There are choir recordings of this song from all over the world singing in their own language and cultural tradition. This is one of the blessings of the pandemic—people sing into their computers and some computer wizard puts it all together into a beautiful choir. When I heard the words that God is always with our children for generations, I started crying and couldn't stop. I took a bath to meditate and go deep into this sadness. I knew this meditation would once again be about letting go of the tie that binds me to Tyler. I expected Mother Owl to show up. This time it was Mother Mary.

Tyler and I are once again standing with a rope tied between us. I am crying what feels like a flood of tears. I feel the warmth and embrace of Mother Mary's presence. She says, "Sally, you can do this—only this time untie the knot do not cut it." I walk over to Tyler. He is smiling and saying, "Mom, you can do this." It feels so hard all over again. The tears are blurring my vision as I work to untie the tangled knot until it unravels. Tyler is free and I stand there with the rope dangling from my waist. Mother Mary asks that I untie the knot keeping the rope attached to me. I stand before her and feel Tyler's gentle presence at my back. As I weep, I realize my healing tears of release and forgiveness are dissolving the rope so that the knot dissolves in my hands.

Mother Mary gathers me into her arms as I cry. Then she gently takes my face in her hands and we touch foreheads. "Will I have to do this again?" She replies:

*We've been co-creating this moment for many years; this is the final healing. You may out of habit return; however, it will be fleeting. This healing released the separated self's idea of what it means to be an earthly mother who thinks she has to fix everything for her children. This was necessary so you can now fully embrace the Universal Grandmother archetype as your elevated Self of form. Humanity is entering a most wondrous as well as difficult time of change and suffering for many who are as yet unaware of their divine Selves. As a Universal Grandmother, you are being asked to hold all of humanity in your embrace with love and compassion, without being drawn into the drama of separation consciousness. So long as you felt the need to take on Tyler's unhappiness, you were not free to turn all your trust over to God's goodness and mercy. Now you can relax and surrender completely into knowing that all is well, has always been well, and will always be well. Look me in the eyes like you've never done before.*

I do, and fall into the depths of her never-ending compassion of an all-seeing wise Mother as we both watch the seemingly endless journey of humanity struggling and suffering. I feel Mother Mary's knowing that we are finding our wings to fly like the angels. I feel her continual blessings of golden light energy flowing as healing oil over the wounds we create when we doubt our Divine Selves. I see all of us rising as our sovereign Selves to create Terra Nova from love.

*Hold onto this vision, for you are an emissary of light, and it is time now to release all that has bound you to the earthly plane, for*

> *it no longer serves you. You are free. Sweet Sally, we have known each other for thousands of years. It is time for you to flourish. Write your book as your gift to yourself and those who will read it and anchor love's energy on your beautiful mesa. All of your parallel lives have led you to this moment. Be still and know you truly are God's Love.*

At the end of the meditation, the bath water was cool—it was time to leave the healing waters and be in the world but not of it. I am calm and at peace inside. The unbearable sadness is gone, and for the first time since the pandemic started, I know I'll be able to embrace the Universal Grandmother's archetype and hold all in the Universal Mother's wisdom till every person wakes to their divinity.

### *Wisdom Weavers Co-Creating the New Earth*

There are many wisdom weavers here on earth. It is a momentous time. We are circling and coming together to sing and celebrate the unity of our heart song. We have arrived through many lifetimes at this still point of awareness. Both women and men are being called to step forward and embrace our divinity as Divine Feminine Christ Creators and Leaders to usher in the New Earth. It is a time of holy potential as well as a polarizing dense time for humanity. Light workers, wayshowers and mystic wisdom weavers are being asked to complete our mission to create this new paradigm of heaven on earth. For those of us in our elder years, aging is an illusion of separation. Yet with it come years of earthly experience in dissolving the separated ego. Thus we have much insight to share. The millennials and children who have arrived during this pivotal time are poised to totally re-shape our communities and our countries as they dissolve separation consciousness and create from their Holy Divine Selves. Most of humanity will start to awaken together. It takes all of us together to usher in this new way of being and creating.

I have resisted my calling and purpose during this time of profound change and transition to Terra Nova. I thought I had already contributed to creating a legacy of love. I thought that being the energy of Sophia God's all-encompassing love and compassion would be enough. Yet in order to usher in this new paradigm of heaven on earth, our vision, voice and teaching from wise women not only is required, but is essential for ushering in a golden age of miracles. We can do no less than to embrace the voice of our Higher Holy Selves—in this great undertaking, what many are calling the Great Turning or what I call the Great Tuning toward love. It takes all the mystics and lightworkers to create the new earth, to show the way for those who are still confused and resistant to dissolving separation consciousness. We are being called to ignite the sacred fire of healing; to share our visions of a new global community created from love; to fulfill the prophecy of the new earth; to be the light we are; to open the way for all humanity to awaken to their divine selves; and to sing our heart songs.

When we embrace our own heart song, we are truly the wisdom weavers for the awakening heart of humanity. It is up to all of us to dispel the perception that we are separate from the Mother/Father/One, to end duality. Those of us who appear to be in our elder years are being called to dissolve the belief that death is inevitable through accidents, disease and aging. *Age cannot change what is immutable. It can only deepen it and give it wide context.* We are creating a new paradigm in which death is no longer needed to give us relief from an existence of bodily form. As we claim our divine innocence and complete our transition into being divinely human, we can demonstrate our choice by staying on earth as long as the Holy Mother requires our service.

This is my vision of a new earth conceived and held in pure love. We are required to hold onto our vision during this disorderly time of high contrast—it is essential for the transition to heaven on earth. We are co-creating a global enlightened community, based on shared human connection that resides in the Oneness of All that Is. As divine human beings, we care for mother earth as well as every single person living on earth. Everyone will be raised from poverty, violence and oppression as more and more remember their divine selves. We are creating a time fueled by divine love. God's abundance replaces lack-consciousness. We gaze, witness and cherish every breath of every living creation. Everyone desires to be fully witnessed, seen, heard, appreciated and honored. We give our wonder to every living being. We behold this immaculate creation of earth in all her relations: the two-legged and the four-legged, the winged and the finned, the crawlers, the plants and the trees, the rocks, mountains, deserts, plains, rivers and oceans. All of nature sings the same song—life is a song of love. We are ushering in an age of Christ consciousness which is compassion. What is your vision?

These words, reflecting the words of many in Oneness, are placed on these pages as distilled wisdom arising from the many as One. We can create this. It is not wishful thinking. It is created when we speak our vision and Truth. We command miracles when we remember we are beloved children of Sophia God. Christ consciousness is this remembering and embodiment in human form. We are this, we are co-creating this. We are Wisdom Weavers and our voices will speak and sing to millions. Our energy of Love is felt all over the earth. We join with all those creating this legacy of love, right now in this moment of time. We are literally creating the new earth now, based on a paradigm of unadulterated, unconditional, uncompromising, invincible divine love for all Sophia God's creations across lifetimes, multiple dimensions and multiple realities. As we co-create the new, Terra Nova is creating us. The time is now. Yeshua in ACOL says:

> This Course is but a trigger. These words the prelude to the explosion. It is as if you have been waiting for someone to whisper: Now! The whisper has come. The time is now.[52]

Our unique song has never changed. The song of the angels and the symphony of the multiverse praising and blessing the Holy Mother Holy Father Sophia God has never changed. It is comprised of the eternal origin music of Sophia's love and every unique heart song resonating in harmonious union. Therefore, each person's heart song has never changed. It resides in an immaculate field of pure, innocent divine love. It is our capacity to listen, to hear clearly, to feel that has changed. We have lived many lifetimes in the density of separation consciousness. Therefore, our unique song plays at a lower frequency and feels distant from us. As we return to wholeness and feel our Oneness with All that is, our unique song does not seem so far away and we begin to hear it again clearly within us. We are circling together to sing our song, for it is our sacred purpose.

### *Wisdom Weavers as Charismatic Adults*

The Universal Grandmother archetype is coalescing within my heart. It began when I was a lay minister for children with special needs labels. It is my previous experience of creating a container of love for atypical children that first introduced me to the concept of a charismatic adult. This was a time when I expanded being a fierce warrior mother for my children to include all children, especially atypical children. My first book, *Welcoming Children with Special Needs, A Guidebook for Faith Communities,* was written primarily for UU ministers, religious educators and teachers. I realize that the Holy Mother gave me a community who could receive my teaching. Basically, the book is a how-to manual for creating beloved community for all children. The following quote comes from the chapter on mood disorders.

> In *Raising Resilient Children,* Robert Brooks and Sam Goldstein describe how one charismatic adult can make a positive difference in the life of a struggling child. That adult is someone who listens, cares and supports, sees the

> strengths in the child rather than just the problems, and is consistently present in the child's life to lift him or her out of despair and stop self-destructive behavior.[53]

I list suggestions on how to be a charismatic adult. They are: listen carefully; respond genuinely; love and support the real child not the troublesome behavior; create ways to understand others; be a loving adult; practice visualization, guided meditation and prayer; and restore hope continuously.

As Universal Grandmothers we are being called to be charismatic adults for all of humanity. In our basket of love we can: listen from the heart to those who are addicted to drama and suffering; respond genuinely from our heart to their heart; unconditionally love and support as we sing the song of each person's divinity, even if they are acting from the separated self; join and co-create with others the beloved community as a golden age on earth; envision heaven on earth in detail and then claim the vision; meditate and pray this vision so it sings within our hearts; and with this vision we restore hope continuously until it births the new earth.

The Universal Grandmother archetype is for anyone no matter their age who feels the call to embody being a charismatic adult. I am describing a mystic, love holder, elevated Self of form who has gained spiritual awareness during this incarnation. While we are in this pivotal time of planetary awakening, wise women are needed more than ever to hold the truth of everyone's divine sovereignty until every person knows it for themselves. There are many old souls in recently incarnated children with a deep well of inner wisdom. They are singing their unique songs in resonance with the Great Tuning, held with love by the Universal Grandmothers. From now on every child born on earth is here for the sole purpose of contributing to our alchemical transmutation into the fifth dimension, to assist in co-creating Terra Nova.

## Whirling Rainbow Prophecy

> There will come a day when people of all races, colors and creeds will put aside their differences. They will come together in love, joining hands in unification, to heal the Earth and all Her children. They will move over the Earth like a great Whirling Rainbow, bringing peace, understanding, and healing everywhere they go. Many creatures thought to be extinct or mythical will resurface at this time; the great trees that perished will return almost overnight. All living things will flourish, drawing sustenance from the breast of our Mother, the Earth.
>
> Navajo-Hopi Prophecy of the Whirling Rainbow

Many Native American cultures, including: Cree, Navajo, Hopi, Salish, Zuni and Cherokee, have versions of this prophecy. Many refer to this time when the Rainbow Warriors of all colors return. Jamie Sams in *Sacred Path Cards* also mentions the Seneca and the Iroquois Peace Confederacy tradition of the Whirling Rainbow of Peace which dissolves our human miscreations of distrust, and replaces separation consciousness with Unity consciousness. It is also told that the Whirling Rainbow Prophecy occurs when the white buffalo returns to earth. White Buffalo Woman as an ascended Christ Master was given the mission to guide indigenous peoples all over the earth throughout the ages in the ascension process as prophesied by the Lakota/Sioux.

While writing about the Whirling Rainbow Prophecy, I remembered a book I read several years ago by Ken Carey titled *Return of the Bird Tribes*. Reading Carey's divine transmission was mesmerizing, heartachingly beautiful, inspiring and transformative. I realize that the entire book is about the Whirling Rainbow Prophecy, although Carey did not name it that way. The Bird Tribes are ancient beings who are now known as star seeds that returned to help with earth's planetary awakening.

"For thousands of gentle circlings of this earth around her star, the peoples of the Americas, the highlanders of Asia, the natives of central Africa and earth people the world over have known us as The Bird Tribes."[54]

Both Carey and Sams write that part of the prophecy mentioned a time when the children of the white eyes will grow their hair long, wear beads and seek wisdom from the elders of the Red Race. Sams also mentions that the white-eyed children are red inside. These children were seeded with songs of love to give to the world. We moved through this part of the prophecy with the flower children of the 1960s and 1970s. Many of us in our elder years were actively involved with the hippie generation, and all of us were influenced by it, primarily through music. Many of us have stayed on the sacred path.

There are several prophecies that foretell of this time when the ancients incarnate again: the return of the White Buffalo Woman Lakota prophecy; the Mayan Fifth World prophecies; and the many New Age prophecies announcing the Star children. All these prophecies are unfolding now. We are transitioning into the fifth world or dimension. White Buffalo Woman is energetically guiding us and the white buffalo are physically on earth. They are being tended by The White Bison Association and Sacred World Peace Alliance. Many Star children have already incarnated and many more rainbow children are being born. This is not a prophecy still yet to come—it is happening now. People of many colors are remembering their ancestral and karmic indigenous roots, and are joining together to co-create Terra Nova.

The second coming of Christ, as foretold by the Christians, refers to this time of planetary awakening. Contemporary understanding of this prophecy means that everyone on earth is remembering our Christ nature to return to Unity consciousness or Buddha consciousness which is our divine inheritance. We are the ones we've been waiting for.

## Chapter Four

# When Children Are Safe and Loved, Everyone Is Safe and Loved

Much of my ministry for children with special needs labels revolved around the idea that creating a world in which children are safe and loved means we create a world in which everyone is safe and loved. I still believe this. When children's well-being is front and center in everyone's concerns, then we will have no wars, education will include heart-based learning to teach and magnify children's unique gifts, poverty will be eliminated so everyone is living equally within abundance, and children acting out will be embraced within the community until they gain an understanding of their distress and are able to make amends. Children of all countries, cultures and colors will be heard, hugged and loved. Our cities will be clean and healthy places to live, with open fields and parks to bring everyone closer to nature. They will include many communities all dedicated to keeping the children safe and loved so that no one lives a life of lonely despair. Our open spaces and wilderness will be preserved for all our beloved relations, each singing and vibrating their unique songs from the primal heart of the Divine Mother.

In all my workshops we thought creating a world where all children are safe was an ideal to work toward, but none of us actually thought it would happen in our lifetime, if ever. However, I believed we could create a church community in which all children were honored and integrated. The question that started my ministry was, "If I can't bring my son to church, where would he be welcome?" So the catalyst of creating this church community started with being welcoming to one atypical child. What I discovered over the years is that the process of being welcoming to one or more children with special needs labels eventually creates a beloved community for everyone within the church community. The container of love we created compassionately held everyone with their needs, quirks, uniqueness, difficult and challenging behaviors, unhappiness and happiness.

While I was exploring ways to create a beloved community starting with the children, I heard about the Maasai Tribe living in Kenya and Tanzania. The men are fabled as being fearsome and highly intelligent warriors. A traditional greeting to each other is "Kasserian Ingera" which means "And how are the children?" I love how their concern for the well-being of their children became an indicator of the wellness of their whole community. Imagine if our government representatives and leaders, before they shaped or passed any legislation, first asked, "How will this affect the well-being of our country's children?" Perhaps we would see the blossoming of communities that are dedicated to the welfare of all our citizens.

According to Jamie Sands, the tradition of Native American tribes is to use governing councils when decisions need to be made concerning the welfare of the tribe or nation. When the council of the sacred fire is called, a Talking Stick is passed from one person to the next. When the person is holding the Talking Stick, everyone listens to each person's sacred point of view until everyone has talked and all opinions have been expressed. Children are taught how to listen and respect different points of view at an early age. When youth are asked to sit at a council fire, they are accorded the same respect as the adults. Their sacred point of view is equally heard.[55]

I am always talking to Mother Mary or the Holy Mother throughout the day. When I was recently grocery shopping at a huge chain store, I looked to see if the store had any organic vegetables. When I didn't see any, I asked Rick. He said the organic produce is generally with all the produce. So, I went back to look, and sure enough there were some organic vegetables. I immediately received an insight from Mother Mary with a very simple suggestion: *If you look and don't see, it's because you don't expect to find it.*

I didn't expect to find the organic vegetables because I believe big chain stores couldn't care less about healthy food. While this may feel minor, it does illustrate how our biases affect our perceptions. Within separation each of us sees the world from our own cultural perspective, beliefs, biases and filters. Until some event propels us to open our eyes to a new way of perceiving, we will stay stuck in the illusion of our own making—which reinforces the belief we are separate from each other. When we reinforce our biases by seeing a whole race of people as inferior, we create massive suffering for ourselves and others. We expect to see a person who is inferior to us, and therefore, that is what we see despite evidence to the contrary. Thus, separation consciousness is reinforced. The way out of this conundrum is fostering a contemplative practice of inner inquiry. Richard Rohr says:

> Everyone sees the world from a certain, defined cultural perspective. But people who have done their inner work also see beyond their own biases to something transcendent, something that crosses the boundaries of culture and individual experience.[56]

Indigenous people with their ancient governing method of council fires in which everyone's sacred point of view is heard and respected create an environment in which children grow up listening to different honored perspectives. Calling people's unique way of perceiving the world as sacred sets the stage to respect each one's inner knowing, Divine Mystery and Mother Earth. We return to the Holy Mother's embrace where we listen, hug and see unconditionally.

Mac Macartney in *The Children's Fire, Heart Song of a People* writes about his time learning from Native American friends and teachers from the Lakota and Mohawk nations in the USA. This is where he heard about the children's fire. The following quote explains the wisdom that was handed down to the people from a time hundreds of years ago when men and women sat in council fire and asked how to govern their people. Their question became a prayer to all Mother Earth's relations to help them foster harmonious and caring governance:

> We have listened, spoken and found our way to some new understanding. The question we ask will remain alive, yielding insights that will grow and deepen as we do likewise. This, however, will remain constant, a pledge to our people and to life. Each time we gather in council we will build a small fire in the centre of our circle of chiefs. The Children's Fire. This fire will be a living reminder of our pledge to hold the children in our hearts as we create and break laws, settle disputes, and lead our people. No law, no decision, no commitment, no action, nothing of any kind will be permitted to go forth from this council that will harm children, now or ever.[57]

Our patriarchal world forgot their sacred duty to love and care for the earth and all of her organic life. The children's fire was extinguished when we no longer put the welfare of children first. Of course, there are some safe places for our children, yet we do not live in isolation. Way too many children are living lives of abuse, hunger and despair. Human trafficking of women and children exists absolutely everywhere. How we treat our children is reflected in how we treat all the interconnected relations of Mother Earth. We have plundered her womb, raped the land, poisoned her rivers and oceans, clear cut her forests, and killed off many of the four-legged, the winged, the skittering, slithering and finned relations. The Native American

Chief's message to us through Macartney is to: "Mend what was broken. Rekindle the Children's fire."[58]

When we care for our children of all colors from all cultures and countries, we remember to care for Mother Earth. It becomes our sacred duty of service to ourselves and all humanity. This is not wishful thinking. This is the Holy Mother's promise happening now. Our planetary awakening is happening now and it starts with our children. We are experiencing a revolution in consciousness.

In many of our UU churches we created welcoming communities for children. It took a lot of effort and constant vigilance to respecting the sacred points of view of all ages. It did not happen immediately. We are transitioning into creating Nova Earth. It will not happen immediately. Do not let yourself be discouraged by the upheaval, turmoil and polarity currently being expressed. The intense division is forcing people to pay attention and ask for a better way. This creates cracks in the separated self to allow the light of love and forgiveness to permeate and resonate within every person.

## Unconditional Listening Creates a Song of Love

During my ministry for atypical children, I came to realize that children in general are rarely asked questions about their feelings, and are hardly ever listened to with total attention and compassion. This is amplified if they have special needs and disability labels. I learned about the art of unconditional listening at the Option Institute in Sheffield, Massachusetts while I was writing my first book. Over the years I started noticing how often people do not listen, needing to interrupt with their own advice or to relate similar experiences with the one talking. I have done the same thing. When I'm mentoring, I can listen wholeheartedly, yet when I'm out of that professional role, I sometimes forget to listen unconditionally to my family and friends.

Everyone wants to be heard, to be accepted, to be honored for their feelings. Yet, many of us are lousy listeners. *When we lost our ability to listen to our soul's song, we lost the ability to listen unconditionally to others.* Barry Neil Kaufman in *Power Dialogues, The Ultimate System for Personal Change* identifies the components of a good listener: to be completely present; to be nonjudgmental, no right, wrong, good or bad; to have no agenda or expectations of outcomes; and to trust that the person is their own best expert. I have found them over the years to be invaluable reminders. They are also an excellent guide for being kind to oneself in order to forgive and fall in love with Self.

Creating an atmosphere of wholehearted listening may be all a person needs in order to find the inner resources to care for themselves creatively and compassionately. This is what women's circles do for each other. We create the space so people listen and share without being interrupted or judged. It is an invaluable experience.

When I conducted my workshops about atypical children, I included a listening exercise using the principles of unconditional listening. I asked people to partner with someone. For 5 minutes one person would talk about a problem or concern and the other person would listen. Then they would switch roles. I told them that when they were listening, they could not ask questions unless for clarification, and to not give advice or relate similar experiences. They were to be totally present without assumptions concerning the topic of the sharing and with no thoughts about what they needed to do, like going to the grocery store, etc.

I expected people to share that listening without interrupting was difficult. I was surprised to hear how many people had difficulty sharing for 5 minutes without the interruptions. Here is where we stumble, whether sharing or listening. We don't believe we deserve compassionate listening. We don't believe that everything is neutral (no right, wrong, good or bad) nor that it is our thoughts causing our reaction and feelings about an event or person. We often want someone to tell us what to do, because going inward and listening to our inner knowing is too hard. We don't believe people know what is best for themselves, especially children—because we don't know what is best for ourselves.

*When I became a compassionate listener to myself, I became a wholehearted listener for others.* I have cultivated with my spiritual sisters the art of unconditional listening because it is in synchronicity with my ability to listen to my inner knowing, my intuition and loving all I've hidden in the shadow. I am constantly filled with gratitude for my mystical sisters' gift of listening unconditionally. It is a merciful blessing to be heard without judgment and to be held in trust that I know what is best for me. *Unconditional listening nullifies the need for answers or solutions, because what arises is living in a space of compassion where one's song of love is the only answer.* Wholehearted listening is what we do for ourselves and for each other. It is the foundation for holding the Universal Grandmother's basket of love for all of humanity.

In separation, with the seeming loss of the Holy Mother, we forgot how to listen and sing our soul's song, and we forgot how to hug. We are remembering to listen to our feelings and then weave them into a song of compassion for Self and others. Our discordant song is returning to balance and harmony with the union of the masculine and feminine resonance. Listening to our heartbeat takes us deeply within in order to listen to our song of love and joy. It has always been there, our unique song of love. *Our song never left us, we just forgot how to listen.* We are becoming the song of our heart. As we reclaim our song, we lift others to sing their unique songs until once again it becomes a chorus and symphony resounding with the Divine Mother Father's universal, cosmic song of creation. This is a time when we wholeheartedly trust in the unfoldment of the Universal

Mother's plan of love for the earth. If we've done our inner work to love and forgive ourselves, then we can let go judgments of others and reach out in compassion.

We learn on our spiritual journey of the heart and womb that what we imagine comes true. We learn that our heroine's journey is a path of coming home to Self. We learn we are constantly creating so we might as well co-create Nova Earth. We learn that it is our perceptions which created these false lives of suffering and discontent. We learn that our minds can support the yearnings and creations of the heart. We learn that we are divine beings choosing to have a physical experience on earth. We learn that we are a balance of masculine and feminine energy. We learn that our inner knowing, our intuition fosters inspiration and changes what happens outside of us. We learn that spirituality is not only individual but also communal. We learn that the Cosmic Mother/Father/One is constantly creating planets, galaxies and wondrous beings of multiple colors and amazing variety. We learn that we are divine sovereign beings in equal relation with all of the Universal Mother's creations. We learn that life truly is a song of the Holy Mother Father Sophia God's all-encompassing love with no opposite.

As we learn and abide within our inner temple, we witness changes in our outer world instead of joining in the drama. We start witnessing with compassion all those who continue to choose the suffering of the separated state. We hold this vessel of overflowing love within us until everyone returns home to Unity Consciousness.

*We dissolve separation consciousness for everyone to the extent we have dissolved it in ourselves.* Therefore, being a Universal Grandmother Wisdom Weaver means being vigilant and uncompromising about weeding out—with great love—all forms of judgment. We look at ugly judgments unflinchingly with loving eyes till they dissolve. In so doing we do it for everyone, and our container of love grows stronger and stronger until it is all there is. As a Universal Grandmother we hold our arms wide to love and embrace all who are still lost. We float them in her ocean of love. We hold all in our hearts till they hear the Divine Mother's call to come home.

As Universal Grandmothers, we sing, dance and laugh without fear of the future. We hold the Truth of the expansive Self. We are remembering who we are and the earth is responding. Saying Yes to the truest version of yourself is saying Yes to the truest version of humanity. Being a Wisdom Weaver is fierce love without attachments. We are mending what's been broken by holding all in compassion. We are warriors for love, peace, harmony and joy. We are in holy relationship with all of humanity.

Do not confine yourself to the level of the tiny ego's voice that wants to keep you small, limited and suffering. We have within us the seed's capacity to birth star systems, galaxies and planets. We are co-creating, co-singing, co-dancing and co-birthing. We can take all that is within this earthly body and expand and expand with love until all humanity is transformed and awakened.

# As Within So Without Meditations

## The Gift of a Question

*She remembers who she is and starts a revolution of the Heart.*

If you need to refresh your memory about what is involved in these meditations, please re-read this section in Movement One. Most importantly ask your guides/light family to help with your inquiry work. Please start with the two following questions before beginning your inquiry process then read the additional questions. Try to write down whatever arises without judgment or editing what you don't like.

Can I love myself enough to forgive myself?
Can I forgive myself enough to love myself?

***Additional Questions***

How does heart-centered feminine energy manifest in you?

How does heart-centered masculine energy manifest in you?

What happens when they are joined in harmony?

Where are your indigenous roots for this lifetime?

Can you find a way to embrace your indigenous roots that honors Mother Earth and all her relations?

What is your culture's attitude toward hugging? Is it different for men and women?

Is there a part of you that holds back from hugging people you trust and love?

When did you hug your children and when did you not hug your children?

Do you hug your grown children more often or less often?

Are you able to acknowledge, feel and accept your feelings?

Are you confused about what emotions you're feeling?

Are you confused about the process of acceptance?

Do you know how to access the feelings buried within your shadow?

What can you do right now to help you access these feelings?

Visualize your inner child that lives in the shadow. If it would help, tenderly hold a soft doll or a stuffed animal which represents your inner child, then tell your inner child it is OK to feel and that you love her.

Ask your inner child what hurts or where she is afraid.

Ask your inner child what makes her feel alive and joyful.

Ask your inner child to join you in the process of accepting the feelings that have remained hidden.

Are you fully present when listening to other people share their story, or are you constantly thinking about other things or a similar experience?

If you struggle with this, chances are you struggle with staying present with yourself during inquiry work. Re-read the chapter on unconditional listening, and practice with your friends and family.

Do you resonate with the idea of being a Wisdom Weaver?

Do you resonate with the Universal Grandmother's archetype?

Can you see yourself holding the basket of unconditional love for all of humanity until every person awakens?

Return to the first two questions about loving and forgiving yourself.

This is the final surrender

# Movement Seven

# The Great Tuning to Love

## Chapter One

# A Time to Flourish

*It is time to love*
*Embrace Divine Self*
*We shine our light and flourish.*

Creation is sound, resonance, vibration, tone and rhythm. Our hearts join in rhythm to the heart beat of the Cosmic Mother and her daughter, Mother Gaia. Our hearts vibrate and resonate with all creation, and we sing our heart song in harmony with all heart songs. As women mystics in this lifetime, we are vibrating at a higher octave than we have in any other lifetime. We signed up to be here during this pivotal and polarizing time of humanity's awakening. We are riding the sound wave of renaissance that sings our unique Divine Blueprint of our Christ Selves sourced from the Cosmic Mother and Father. We have direct access to the Divine Cosmic imaginal power to activate our glorious Sovereign, Holy Divine Selves. It is time now for all humanity to flourish. It has been eons since we've been open enough to hear the origin sound of creation. We are tuning and toning our resonance and vibration to the higher frequencies of the Holy Mother Holy Father Sophia God's all-encompassing love. The Great Tuning, what many call the Great Turning, is about tuning to our higher vibration's song to lead in love.

The phrase "the great turning towards love" is attributed to the mystic Joanna Macy. I started seeing the phrase and idea of "the great turning" in many different places. Thich Nhat Hanh expressed that the next Buddha may not be an individual, but an enlightened community. This view that change is coming from an enlightened community is also expressed by Richard Rhor. If you were paying attention while watching the Star Wars Movie *The Last Jedi,* the force is awakening among the many, among ordinary adults and children.

Richard Rohr's teachings remind me that mystics of all traditional faiths have always felt the non-dual Truth of God's love existing in every person. According to Rohr:

> The toothpaste is out of the tube. There are enough people who know the big picture of Jesus' thrilling and alluring vision of the reign of God that this Great Turning cannot be stopped. There are enough people going on solid inner journeys that it is not merely ideological or theoretical. This reformation is happening in a positive non-violent way. The changes are not just from the top down, but much more from the bottom up. Not from the outside in, but from the inside out. Not from clergy to laity, but from a unified field where class is of minor importance. The big questions are being answered at a peaceful and foundational level, with no need to oppose, deny or reject. I sense the urgency of the Holy Spirit, with over seven billion humans now on the planet. There is so much to love and embrace.[59]

While this Great Tuning may create both turmoil and great love within our inner temples, it is causing an earthquake in separation consciousness. What is occurring outside certainly does not feel peaceful, and much continues to be damaging. If we only go by what we perceive in this dream of separation, it can feel as if the destruction of Mother Earth is getting worse, that the hatred and violence of others is greater than ever. There are those who have gone monumentally astray, temporarily lost to the egoic, fear-based path of entrenched patterns of power-over. This tuning into a global community, based on the interconnectedness with all life, creates massive fear as the structures and beliefs which we thought kept us safe are crumbling. The separated ego is holding on in desperation, solidifying the old paradigm of power-over in many people terrified of losing what they believe is their only safety in the control, domination and—at the extreme—elimination of others.

I have this visual image of a lost person hanging onto a cliff's edge with their fingertips, terrified of falling into the unknown. Yet as more and more of us open our hearts and become vessels of the Universal Mother's ocean of love, the vibration of love and hope will expand exponentially till all begin to feel that love is where their true power lives. I see this person finally letting go, only to gently float home buoyed by the Mother's love.

Everyone living on earth at this time asked and were chosen to be part of earth's ascension process, this transformation of consciousness. Not because we are special (or as some believe cursed) but because we have proven resilient and resourceful during other incarnations. We each have unique gifts, abilities and a special mission to fulfill during this time of transformation. Some of us volunteered to play the perceived bad guy in order to bring into the light all of our miscreations to be dissolved. Everything created within the dualism of separation consciousness has to be dismantled so that the new consciousness can be created from the power of love.

Most of the seemingly lost people are performing their mission in order to create a stark contrast between love and fear. Then they will awaken. Unfortunately, there are some who have succumbed deeply to the allure of patriarchal power-over and will need our focused vibration of forgiveness and love. The few who are still deeply lost to the separated ego's control when they leave earth will be taken to special schools in the realm of illumined truth to receive focused attention and love. The majority of humanity that chose to wake all at once will need steady higher vibrational resonance to understand what is happening to them. This is already occurring. As Wisdom

Weavers and Universal Grandmothers, this is our sacred contract—to hold the Truth and Love until everyone returns home to their God Self.

## Chapter Two

# The Process of Transformation and Resurrection

While we are riding this massive origin sound wave of the Great Tuning, it feels exhilarating and scary all at the same time. We might fall off and drown never to be seen again. Yet we remember that this sound wave arises from the infinitely vast ocean of the Divine Mother's all-encompassing love. We are held, cradled and infused with her healing water's song of resonance and vibration. We cannot drown or be lost because we've been in this process of remembering our Divine sovereignty during all our earthly lives. We've been enslaved by our belief in the separated ego to reincarnate over and over again with little chance of ascension. We've learned from this experience, which is why we are now at this pivotal time of earth's awakening. Enough people have healed and dissolved eons of trauma that the combined energy of higher resonance and vibration is coalescing into this time of the Great Tuning to Love, riding the crest wave of love that can't be stopped.

Within all our lifetimes we've been learning to listen to our God Self. Metaphorically we were turned upside down with our crown chakra buried, so that our ability to remember and embody our divinity was short circuited by the wounding of our feminine energy and the extreme distortion of our masculine energy. The cycle was to learn what we could from each lifetime, die and then be resurrected over and over again in many lifetimes, each time at a higher vibration. Now during this incarnation, we have righted ourselves and like the phoenix we are rising from the ashes of our collective trauma to mend what's been broken, to embrace the Universal Mother as the

Divine Creatrix of all that is, to forgive the unforgivable and love the unlovable.

## Howling at the Moon

All over the world we are still feeling the effects of misogynistic, power-hungry nations. In Western culture we are living with the legacies of white nationalism and misogyny, the extreme bi-products of separation. Animals, women and children—especially women of color—always bear the greatest risk of men's violence. While I write, in the USA wolves are being slaughtered in Wyoming and Arizona, hundreds of children are abandoned at our border with Mexico, whales, who are the memory receptacles of the Holy Mother's love, are near extinction. In Atlanta Georgia, Asian women were gunned down while working in massage parlors, and black men and women continue to die by the hands of the police. Voting rights are being severely suppressed in states fearful of the new paradigm of love, returning to a lynching mentality. The government in Afghanistan collapsed to be replaced by the misogynistic, cruel Taliban. And as I do a final edit of this book, Russia has invaded Ukraine.

With Mother Wolf, I've been howling at the moon in grief, sobbing out all my feelings of disbelief that human beings can be so cruel. I am feeling eons of massive trauma and experiencing massive grief. How could we go so monumentally astray from our true divine nature that we created a living hell? I realize this need to dominate and control others must be an addiction for so many people to stay stuck in the emptiness of violence and rage that lashes out, hurts, maims and kills. We've been in a living death while in the body. This is why physically dying has ultimately always been a relief. I am feeling acute grief for all our violent miscreations. We've been numb for eons, enabling us to survive. Now that we are in the midst of the Great Tuning, we allow ourselves to feel and be totally present with trauma and the continuing violence against women, children, BIPOC, indigenous cultures, Mother Earth and all her organic life. I've been feeling raw, witnessing all the hatred still occurring.

Adding to this immense grief, Lori, a beloved mystical soul sister in our co-creator's group, left her physical body. I miss her physical presence, even when I'm aware she was called home to be a powerful source in the realms of Truth for assisting in our planetary awakening. Cancer spurred Lori's devotion to dissolving and forgiving all the trauma in her life. By the end, she was radiating love and peace. It was inspiring and it is her gift to us in our co-creator's group and a gift to humanity. Her death acted as a catalyst for everyone in our group to go deeper into grief by staying fully present.

Our grief feels pure and clear. What emerges is a deep knowing that the grieving we are holding for eons of trauma, perhaps for the first time, is without the anger of judgment and blame. We stay wholly present with the grief, while moving at the same time into gratitude and eventually into joy and celebration of life. This is not something I could feel even a week ago. It is difficult to describe—it is the process of transformation, the tuning to a higher frequency. I could not make myself understand. It came gently and unwavering with constant attention to always singing and walking my prayer knowing it is already answered. This is our sacred trust.

## Removing Myself from the Cross

Easter week occurred while I was writing this chapter. In perfect synchronicity, I joined Maleda Gebremedhin's virtual healing workshop, *Essene Mother Christ Source Healing Journey, Deprogramming Your Womb from Spiritual Persecution*. I went even deeper into the grief and trauma to remove and dissolve more and more of the patriarchal programming still running within my body. I learned more about what crucifixion did to penetrate our wombs, programming lifetimes of fear and denial of our true loving, wild, innocent selves. Maleda led participants through an intense healing visualization to remove ourselves from the cross in order to dissolve eons of brutal patriarchal programming.

We hold in our wombs the Divine Mother's song of life. And this is what people, pulsing with the low energy of separation, try to take—completely missing that the power of love and life can't be harnessed, controlled or subsumed for the harmful purposes of domination and separation. We became enslaved, but love did not die. Those who have been subservient and loyal to the separated ego for eons have been trying to become powerful enough to cannibalize the Holy Mother's all-encompassing love for their own power. Women—who are the Holy Mother's embodiment of the womb, birth and creation—have been consistently targeted with a never-ending attempt to harness love's creative power. It can't be done. It can't be controlled. Empire building, colonization, genocide, industrialization, technological advancements, defilement and destruction of Mother Earth and all her relations cannot destroy love. We can blow ourselves up, yet we do not die. For the Universal Mother's song of life is more than these bodies. We are more than these bodies.

Prior to his-story, people from ancient cultures in complete harmony with the Cosmic and Earth Mother knew that women care for the Mother's souls that are birthed within the womb of our bodies. Men used to cherish and protect the wombs of women and Mother Earth. Ancient indigenous communities all over the world including Celtic and Essene/Magdalene communities retained a deep knowing of the Divine Mother's mysteries and womb of life. Therefore, they were targeted over and over again, long before the Roman Empire succeeded in eliminating them. Crucifixion was a favorite practice before Yeshua was crucified on the cross. Men and women anointed in the ways of the Divine Mother were tortured, crucified and burned at the stake many times throughout many incarnations.

Women hold this trauma in our wombs. The story of Yeshua and his crucifixion on the cross permeates the Western countries and is well-known all over the world. We've all inhaled the destructive programming of the crucifixion as taught by the patriarchal Christian religions. The cross augmented the progression of colonization programs. It became the focus of patriarchal Christianity, always reminding people that Yeshua suffered for us and therefore we also need to suffer in order to resurrect and transcend. They taught that we were born in sin and needed intermediaries to be forgiven, denying our own direct connection to God.

Maleda led us through an incredibly powerful visualization to dismantle the cross, returning the wood and nails and rope to the sacred elemental fires of the Holy Mother to dissolve the persecution programming we've held in our wombs for thousands of years. While I visualize, I use hand gestures to remove the rope and nails, simulating embodiment of the visualization. During the visualization I had a vivid memory of being crucified. I have written how I healed crippling lower back pain. Now I have a deeper awareness of how much that lower back pain was related to trauma I've been carrying in my heart and womb.

I've continued enacting this visualization every morning, either in the center of my labyrinth or in the bath and shower. I've noticed that occasional back pain lessens when I stand straight as if a thread is attached to my chest pulling me upwards, strengthening my spine, allowing me to stand tall again. With it comes freedom and purpose reminding me of my feminine power. For many women we've been conditioned to slump and hide, trying to make ourselves small, protecting our breasts, heart and womb from being hurt. Removing persecution programming is a process of strengthening our spines so the kundalini life-force energy flows easily, reminding ourselves of our co-creative power sourced from the Holy Mother's love.

Removing the cross of persecution wherever it still resides in my body is the process of freeing myself from the bonds of the separated state. It becomes my resurrection. This is what Yeshua showed us: we live in the world of separation, it is full of suffering and contradictions, and it is both human and divine. We can choose to continuously suffer or we can let it change us by removing ourself from the cross to be resurrected into a life of devotion and love. We can continue to project our pain onto others or we can use it to save ourselves to live life fully.

We are being guided to feel the bonds or chains of trauma that remain by staying in presence with all the horrific stuff still occurring—not looking away. We can do it now because we've awakened enough to no longer need numbness and distraction to survive. We feel, grieve and stay in presence in order to open fully to Sophia God's love. I can howl my grief at the moon, joining with mother wolf. We open ourselves to the merciful grace of eternal love more completely than we have ever allowed ourselves to feel before.

## Grief Allows Love to Bloom

We can't move forward with co-creating Nova Earth if we have not grieved fully the amount of damage that occurred and is still happening within dualism. It is massive and difficult to comprehend. Massive change creates massive fear, but also elicits immense hope and the transforming power of love. My cries of how could we do this, need not be answered. Instead, I embrace the question. Universal grieving is a necessary part of the Great Tuning to love. Mother Mary says in *Mirari, the Way of the Marys*:

> This is the manner of grief. This is grief's movement. Now, we enter a time of grief—to move from death into life.

> You begin to see the soul's passage in this way, in everything that occurs. Grief awakens you to this way of passage now. Grief is alive with soul and depth and longing.
>
> It is death before death. It is life after death. It is life that can be lived in the world and restore the world. It is the way that is revealed when you become willing to care enough to have it come to be. It was the way being revealed to us in the Time of Christ. It is the way being revealed to you in the Time of Mary.
>
> Can you not imagine love's life in you? Grief reveals love's life in you.[60]

Humanity has not allowed itself to grieve. In order to survive the eons of atrocities, we covered over our grief with anger. We numbed ourselves with addictions. We buried our grief to fester and stunt our ability to live a full life. Coping has been shattered, and the grief we feel can be overwhelming. Grief launches us into liminal space which creates infinite possibilities for growth and transformation.

The time of Mary is the Great Tuning to love. It is the time of the divine feminine, the Mother aspect of God. It is a time of replacing the old paradigm of power-over with the new paradigm of power with and within. It is a time of anchoring the balanced masculine and feminine resonance to co-create Terra Nova. It is a time of compassion blossoming. It is a time of grief and resurrection. It is the time of the Universal Grandmother, the Wisdom Weaver anchoring this balanced Unity Consciousness on earth around the children's sacred fire. Mother Earth grieves with us as we open ourselves completely to presence. She is healing, reclaiming her wildness, her beautiful bountiful body. As she heals and dissolves all trauma, exploitation and desecration, we join her, merge with her, grieve with her, enabling us to reclaim our wild abundance with all life. We reclaim our womb as the Holy of Holies. Our healed wombs in their original wholeness are a cervical gateway for deep restoration of immortal love on earth. We are the pioneers of the New Earth.

We can't do this alone. We do it within Unity—the One in the many and the many in the One. We breathe into our God Self, which is our I Am Presence in order to awaken our unique song and hold it within our inner temple. I open to receive unending love and amazing grace by staying present to my despair until every part of my being knows that your prayer is my prayer.

Returning to a theme in this book—acceptance of feelings—and we use it now to accept our feelings of grief. Grieving is the way through the massive trauma to self-love and compassion in order to forgive the unforgivable, and love the unlovable. As Mother Mary says, "Grief reveals love's life in you." We've walked the labyrinth into the center of our heart and womb over and over again, feeling the trauma and walking our prayer. Each time, we awaken more fully to our heart's unique song. We fearlessly feel and hold all of the world's trauma, transmuting the poison into magnificent, universal infinite love. Co-creation of Nova Earth begins.

## Forgiving the Unforgivable and Loving the Unlovable

Once again I am writing about forgiving the unforgivable and loving the unlovable. Forgiveness fuels transformation. We can't love ourselves if we are holding revenge, hatred or petty grievances in our hearts. Initially, forgiveness is always about setting ourselves free, not about the person who harmed us. Forgiving ourselves may be challenging; however, it is the process of self-love, compassion and resurrection into divine life.

I am acutely aware that my forgiveness lessons in this lifetime are in many ways gentler because they do not involve personal experience of physical abuse. Somewhere deep within, I'm aware that this is possible because I've already forgiven an immense amount of trauma in parallel lives, which has allowed greater understanding in this lifetime. Everyone living on earth carries ancestral and karmic trauma. *I have discovered that the more we awaken and move into the light, the more shadow we see.* Letting go of numbness and denial allows us to acknowledge and feel the unceasing atrocities still being enacted, along with the unceasing beauty of life on earth. This is why I'm grieving and weeping for the atrocities as well as the beautiful—to cleanse those memories of abuse held within my womb and elsewhere in my body. Acknowledgment and acceptance of feelings helps the surrender to grief, which allows us to embody unending love and amazing grace.

In essence the process of forgiving petty grievances is the same as the process of forgiving unfathomable torture. However, within separation, it feels as if people committing unspeakable acts of brutality are harder to forgive. A profound realization occurs when we know the stories of those who have experienced unfathomable torture and then chosen dignity and a life of devotion to love rather than the self-imposed prison of hatred.

### *Stories of Forgiveness*

When I was a new student of ACIM, I read several books to try and understand forgiving the unforgivable. I was constantly confusing forgiveness with condoning abusive and destructive behavior. I would reach a place of fleeting awareness, only to be sucked back into the separated ego's judgment and disgust for those committing unspeakable acts: especially torture, rape and sexual abuse of women and children. I knew intellectually that forgiveness was the ideal, but I could not separate the act from the person. Telling me that life is all an illusion and not real was little help. Telling me to see the Christ in the abuser did not work either because I had yet to see the Christ in me.

There are many people who have written about their process of forgiving unspeakable abuse and torture, such as: *Forgiveness and Child Abuse, Would You Forgive* by Dr Lois Einhorn, *Left to Tell, Discovering God Amidst the Rwandan Holocaust* by Immaculée Ilibagiza with Steve Erwin, *The Choice: Embrace the Possible* by Dr Edith Eger, about the Jewish Holocaust. I came to understand that the more a person hates themself, the more extreme their projection onto others. All feelings hidden in the shadow are projected onto others in a misguided attempt to believe we are good and that it is someone else that is to blame or is the bad person. This is why self-love is critical for the process of forgiveness.

Dr Einhorn and her sister were constantly sexually abused by their parents. They were also ritualistically and sadistically forced to torture each other, as well as live and stuffed animals. Lois's story is truly horrific and difficult to read, but it is also inspirational. She learned to forgive herself and her parents. Lois says that we have the right to be angry—but not to be cruel. Cruelty to the abusers only perpetuates violence and hatred. We do not need to understand how people can be capable of brutality in order to forgive. We do not have to let the memories of atrocities in the past continue to hurt us in the present. *The abusive acts are not forgiven, but accepted as no longer having the power to continue making us miserable in the present*. We can say goodbye to the pain and anger associated with the abuser in order to forgive their tortured souls.

I struggle calling someone evil because it feels as if I'm condemning and judging them. Nevertheless, within separation consciousness we have committed brutal, evil acts. *People's souls are not evil, only the acts they commit can be evil.* Part of grieving and healing is naming the act of evil. When we lose sight of what is evil, events such as the Jewish Holocaust by the Nazis and the genocide of indigenous people is accepted as normal. Evil spelled backward is "live." If we open to heal trauma and the memories of abuse, then love can pour to transmute the perceived evil into embracing life in all its wondrous beauty.

Hannah Arendt, a Jewish philosopher, wrote *Eichmann in Jerusalem: A Report on the Banality of Evil*. The phrase "the banality of evil" struck a chord within me, providing a glimmer on how people throughout history could commit genocide, sexual abuse, torture, the desecration of mother earth and the destruction of all living things.

When we tried to sever the Holy Mother from God, we forgot that we are intimately connected with all life. This created the womb wound in women and the heart wound in men. The shadow side of feminine energy in women manifests as neediness and possessiveness of men's love. This spills over into possessive love for our children, mistakenly believing it will keep them safe and unharmed. The shadow side of masculine energy resulted in men being closed off from their hearts and unable to feel emotions, leading to coldness and isolation with an inability to access inspiration and compassion. Men and women hold within themselves both the shadow feminine and shadow masculine although in different ways. Within these wounds we lost our ability to honor everyone's sacred point of view, including the sacredness of all Mother Earth's relations.

The rape of women coincides with the rape of Mother Earth. It became okay to harm, punish and kill the four-leggeds, the winged, those who crawl, slither and swim for our benefit, because they don't feel. "They are just dumb animals." Eventually, we felt it was okay to kill anyone we decided was no better than these dumb animals, justifying abuse and wide-spread slaughter. It became the norm (banal) because we stopped knowing our sacred connection to all of Mother Earth's relations. With brutality becoming a normal occurrence, we numbed ourselves to the pain, wanting to blame it on all those people and living things whom we now see as less than human, as savages. Those who commit genocide and unspeakable brutality are cut off from their emotions and their heart. They lost their empathy, which is the ability to feel within themselves what another person is feeling. Thus colonization and genocide became the accepted norm.

Whether forgiving unimaginable abuse or everyday offenses, forgiveness is a gift you give yourself. It detoxifies hurt and hatred, and improves your health. It is brave and courageous. It sets you free. Within separation consciousness, we believe that forgiveness is more difficult with extreme abuse and genocide, yet the benefits are the same: forgiveness sets us free to embrace life. Practicing everyday forgiveness every time our buttons are pushed strengthens our ability to forgive, so that if the unspeakable happens, we'll be able to draw on our well of love. *Forgiveness is self-love, which allows compassion to flourish.*

### *Personal Forgiveness*

I knew a boy I will call "Sam" in the interests of anonymity. He is part of this story about my love of summer camp as a haven or sanctuary from school. I started going to camp for most of the summer when I was ten. I was a camper for 7 years and a counselor for 2 more. There was a girls' camp and a boys' camp. My brothers attended the boys' camp. The owner of the camps was charismatic and enthusiastic. He used to say that the girls were tougher than the boys, that we did everything they did while singing at the same time.

I loved being outside, especially the camping trips and canoe trips, floating down gently-moving rivers, occasionally rushing into rapids. I loved the friends I made and even the sports competitions. I loved learning new skills like balance beam; archery; track; swimming; canoeing; sailing; arts and crafts; identifying trees, flowers, plants and stars; creating and putting on plays; and of course the constant singing. As much as possible, there was freedom from the traditional feminine roles. On Sundays we had a Christian church service with gentle sermons about service to others and being true to God. I always sang with two other friends in harmony, celebrating life and God's love.

Sam was the son of the camps' owner and a close friend of my brother. Though he lived in another city, he occasionally visited us. I liked him. He was always respectful and never teased me. I also got to know Sam as a young man while I was a counselor. He thought I was the finest singer he'd ever heard. I met his future wife when we were both counselors together. Sam eventually became owner and CEO of the camps.

Many years ago, when my children were young, my brother sent a video of Sam preaching a patriarchal fundamentalist Christianity that made both of us uncomfortable. My brother drifted away from their friendship, and I realized the camp was no longer a place I might send my children. A few weeks ago, my brother emailed a disturbing article about the camps which described decades of sexual abuse of young campers by the camps' manager. He went to trial and was sent to jail for life. What upset me even more was the information that for years Sam had been covering up the abuse and paying off families to remain silent.

I was devasted and felt massive amounts of grief. At first I could not understand the amount of grief I was feeling. Then in a moment of insight, I felt so betrayed that Sam would allow my childhood summer sanctuary to be turned into a place which abused children. What happened to the kind, respectful boy I knew to change so much that he allowed this to happen? This requires me to forgive the unforgivable and love the unlovable.

For several days I allowed myself to grieve and accept my feelings. I would stop crying, but then something would trigger the tears again. The situation with Sam and all the hatred, brutality and violence escalating in the USA and around the world is igniting my anger and conflicted feelings, even while grieving all of it. I am angry about the continuing destructive behavior that has gone on for eons. This anger coincides with deep grief for all the suffering and trauma which is an integral component of this earthly experience. I am angry that we tried to sever the Holy Mother from the face of God. I am angry this caused the brutalization of anyone who tried to maintain their deep connection to Mother Earth and their feminine divine essence.

I recognize that grief allows love into my heart, and transmutes the anger into love. I focus on my heart and acceptance of feelings, but sadness and a low level of anxiety persists. The debris of the separated self keeps asserting its presence—and I feel attacked, my spiritual sanctuary is threatened. Intellectually I realize I'm being given the experience in order to transform and resonate at a higher octave. Yet I don't know how to do this.

I pray for the most benevolent outcome for the highest good of everyone involved. I ask that those involved allow the love of the Holy Mother to enter their hearts. I weave in and out of peace. I pray to Mother Mary and ask for guidance. What emerges is the awareness that my trust in the Holy Mother's plan is eroding.

I am struggling. A mystical soul sister recommends her friend Kendal McDevitt, a Soul Focused Energy Healer. I arrange a session. Much of what transpires reignites and releases what I already know. It also ignites the alchemical process of compassion. My grief and anger about my summer camp's sanctuary being used to abuse children is giving me exactly what I need to transmute all the anger, grief and lack of trust into compassion. I am shown that what I'm feeling is the dirt or compost covering a seed of transformation, a seed that grows into a flower of compassion as it shatters the stone of fear. There is a lot of gentle laughter from all our guides when I acknowledge I needed a firm shove to enter into this transformation.

I am told my camp sanctuary is an illusion—I immediately feel its truth. Distrust and doubt fall away. Of course it is an illusion. My sanctuary exists inside of me and is invulnerable to abuse. I realize this also applies to my home sanctuary where I created my labyrinth. My interior labyrinth is reinforced by walking it in the physical world. Living on top of a mesa with expansive views reinforces love's expansiveness in my inner temple. I feel this fully in my heart— perhaps for the first time.

Kendal mentions that there is another being who wishes to be more fully involved as one of my guides. I feel it is Kali Ma, which is confirmed. I immediately cry healing tears of love and gratitude. She was a vital presence healing a lot of my anger, yet I have not asked her guidance with anything else. I feel her love flowing through me and realize that she is always within me. It is immensely comforting and empowering to know I can always ask for her guidance. Kali Ma represents fierce love to protect and guide her children. I feel confirmation that our imagination sourced from love is our reality, not the perception of this dense 3D world.

Kendal reminds me of the five higher or transpersonal chakras existing above the head. The 10th chakra is the High Heart chakra. I share that many times in meditation; I visualize walking the rainbow path to deep awareness. Kendal explains that the Rainbow Bridge connects the personal self with the God Self as soul transformation. The Whirling Rainbow Prophecy speaks of this time when all walk the rainbow bridge or path, embodying compassion in order to create the new earth.

Kendal's guides say this is all I need do: envision the Rainbow Bridge to my High Heart chakra of compassion when feeling threatened or the pull of the separated self's thoughts, so the flower of compassion blooms. This is the compassion I feel when embracing the Universal Grandmother's basket of all-encompassing love for the awakening heart of humanity. The expansiveness of love and compassion fills my inner sanctuary in ways not previously felt.

Masculine ascension without input from the feminine was about individualism, doing, control and denying the body. The divine feminine is about embodiment, being, continuity, harmonizing and creating in community with others. Compassion fuels this transformation. It is not something we achieve. We let all our striving go and just be.

Forgiving the unforgivable and loving the unlovable is compassion for everyone living within this dense broken world of separation consciousness. *Forgiveness is the process of freeing ourselves from the belief that the past can control our lives in the present*. Each of us is either expressing unconditional love or calling for unconditional love. I no longer fear succumbing to the hatred being expressed in the world. I continue to bless people causing harm. I am not a victim, perpetrator or savior. I visualize and walk the Rainbow Bridge connecting with my High Heart chakra and my heart blooms, opening a portal to the 11th chakra of Divine Will and then the 12th chakra of Christ consciousness until the fierce love of compassion is all I know.

Kaia Ra, who received the *The Sophia Code* transmission, experienced unimaginable systematic sexual abuse and torture on a daily basis as a child and teenager. After many years of recovery and healing, she is now leading a revolution of feminine Christ consciousness that radiates forgiveness and love. Quan Yin in *The Sophia Code* teaches karuna. Her definition of karuna is to hold compassion so closely inside ourselves that no separation remains within. To refuse compassion for ourselves when we are suffering is to amplify our pain. The process of loving ourselves free within every moment of our daily lives allows compassion to rise for ourselves, which then flows to others. This compassion is what makes it possible to love what we believe is unlovable and unforgivable.[61]

This is my mystical heroine's journey: to love myself unconditionally so there is no separation within, until all that remains is compassion for myself. This compassion overflows for the children, for Sam who allowed the abuse, and for the man who sexually abused the children. Eventually calmness and peace began to ascend into my heart and I realized I felt no anger or hatred toward Sam. I knew the young boy and man who was kind and had easy respectful relationships with children. There is a huge disconnect from what I remember about Sam and who he is today. Nevertheless, my memory of Sam as a boy allows no hatred to enter my heart. I do not forgive or condone the abuse of children, yet I can forgive the boy. Sam in the fervor of a patriarchal religion forgot his own innocence and what it felt like to be a vulnerable child. His reputation and livelihood became more important. I can feel Sam's wounded child calling for love rather than condemnation.

The Universal Grandmother's basket of compassion overflows continually for all of humanity. When I hold compassion for those I know, it softens my resistance to holding compassion for those still acting from the low energy of hatred and violence. Karuna compassion enfolds trust and patience, because infinite compassion is all there is. It is the only answer for what needs no answer. We are ushering in the age of compassion. Every time I slip into judgment or fear, I visualize walking the Rainbow Bridge through my High Heart chakra to allow compassion to flow from embodiment of Christ consciousness.

I live a compassionate life.

I hold all within the Universal Grandmother's basket of love.

I Am that I Am.

## Chapter Three

# All the Traditional Systems Are Dissolving and Transforming

Imagination is more our reality than separation consciousness. In a world that believes in scientific reasoning and left-brain logic, imagination is often demeaned as being fantasy. Yet it is our imagination sourced from love that allows the scientist and inventor to make discoveries and the artist and musician to create. It has to be imagined as a possibility first. We dreamed ourselves into duality, and now we are dreaming and singing ourselves awake by reframing a new story infused with Unity consciousness. We do not need scientific proof to believe this is possible because we are seeing miracles and infinite potentialities come into our awareness and being. This is what we are doing every moment. This is what the Great Tuning to love is all about. As Wisdom Weavers/Universal Grandmothers we are singing and weaving a new story for the co-creation of Terra Nova.

Our imagination created myths or what we call science fiction, as if there is no way it could come true or it is so far in the future that none of us will experience these wonders. Of course, most science fiction stories reflect our earthly lives of living within duality. Some are empty dystopian futures of life after we destroy most of the earth or reenactments on a planetary level of the wars we've had, perpetuating the belief in the doctrine of power-over. A few imagine a time when the earth becomes a better version of itself but still with conflict, as in the Star Trek TV shows and movies. Yeshua says that we enjoy science fiction because we know there is so much more and we have vague memories of flying at the speed of light with spaceships activated by the energy of thought. Yeshua says:

> You put it in the future and say, "Well, this is a time to come," and yet you would not have that within the consciousness right now if it were not something that you have already experienced.[62]

Our news media is almost exclusively focused on maintaining the status quo of separation consciousness. There is constant reporting of suffering, the trials and tribulations of our human family. Occasionally heart-centered stories are reported to show people there is kindness in the world, yet it is considered soft news that does not garner the attention needed to increase ratings. Most people are addicted to the drama of suffering. People gravitate to the news that most closely resembles their own beliefs and views, reinforcing their closed view of the world.

Ironically, what is helping to crack this institution is the internet. If one looks, there is an amazing amount of information about people imagining a new world based on harmony; respect for Mother Earth and all her relations; restorative justice; a gift or life economy where everyone thrives; renewable energy; sustainable agriculture in sync with the rhythms of nature; clean water flowing and available in every place on earth; health care for everyone combining the best of Eastern and Western medicine with the understanding that dis-ease is a manifestation of the loss of self-love; and education for the purpose of igniting passion in each child and adult for their unique gifts. We already have the knowledge, skills and technology to transition into Terra Nova. Mother Earth was given to sustain us, not to be exploited and depleted.

## Lack Consciousness

The monolithic financial, pharmaceutical, medical, insurance, oil/energy, transportation, agricultural, media and communication industries try to control any innovative idea that would end their monopoly and wealth. These big businesses have been built within lack consciousness. We have swallowed the idea that there are limited resources to go around. Our destruction of Mother Earth appears to be making this belief come true. The fear of not having enough money to buy what we need from these big businesses is the single most self-destructive belief we hold even for those of us who know we are much more than this earthly experience. We feel yes, I'm a divine being, but while I'm figuring out how to love myself enough to awaken, I have to eat. We can trust the Holy Mother Father with our relationships, but not with creating money out of thin air. Nope, that's asking for too much faith. Yeshua says in ACOL:

> You believe having a spiritual context for your life can, in other words, change your inner life, but are more skeptical in regard to its ability to affect your outer life: and nowhere are you more skeptical than in regard to money or abundance.[63]

That certainly describes me for most of my life. Even when I did not have to worry about money, I worried. I would get angry, believing life is unfair because it appears that no matter how hard one works, it does not necessarily result in financial abundance. There are some people who get to have lots of money and others who do not. It is a world made up of those who have and those who have not. I have family members and friends who have plenty of money, and they still worry because there are too many stories of people losing it all and being out on the streets. A lot of anger is generated by how unfair it all feels.

The big business institutions are created within separation to keep us recycling the old paradigm of lack. This is perpetuated by having to work to earn enough money to survive. We are encouraged to go into debt to buy a house, a car, a phone, a computer, a TV, any item we feel will ease our life and make us happy. We also have to pay for expensive health care, and to make sure we have the money to pay for needed care, we buy health insurance. We buy a house with a mortgage because we can't afford a home otherwise. Next, we are forced to buy home owner's insurance to make sure we have money to pay the banks if the house is destroyed. Supposedly the insurance helps us rebuild or rebuy, but it is usually not enough, or the insurance companies find a way not to pay. Of course, the vast majority of people rent to make sure they have a home. We are convinced by those in control that capitalism and a debt economy is a good thing. It makes the world work. It is the only thing motivating people to do good.

We became a people concerned with winning this race to have enough money to do what we want and buy what we want. We became expert consumers always thinking that if we only had the latest "whatever," we would be happy. To imagine any other type of world where everyone always has what they need is unrealistic. The contemporary mystic Charles Eisenstein says, "The tragedy of greed, of course, is that no amount of money or anything else can ever sate it. Because we are starving for what money cannot buy."[64]

As we accept our feelings and dissolve all the places hidden within our shadow that do not serve us, we forgive and fall in love with ourselves—and then we open to giving and receiving as One. Abundance can only be acknowledged, accepted and received. There is no one outside of us controlling our entry into abundance. It is our natural inheritance. It is a process of complete trust in our God Self. It is not something we do or some plan we follow or steps we take. It just is, as is the well of love and abundance we hold inside our expansive Self.

Sometime while writing this book, I noticed I no longer worried about money for myself or my adult children. Throughout my life I've been safe and always had enough, even during times when I was not sure I could pay for groceries.

Somehow that finally sank in: I've always been safe, so why do I keep worrying? I couldn't make myself stop worrying, it just happened while I wasn't looking. It is an immense relief. In fact, except for a recent brief moment of forgetfulness, I can't even conjure up the feelings of panic I used to carry all the time, even though I've been financially comfortable for years.

Envisioning a world based on abundance rather than lack is the process of the Great Tuning, which is the transformation we are experiencing now. I do not have any of the knowledge, yet there are those who have the vision and the skills to transition the world into a gift/life economy. In the fifth dimension there will be no need for currency; however, during this transition period of the Great Tuning, we will find ways to gently co-create an economy that cares for everyone until there is no gap between the poor, middle class and the wealthy. As we dissolve the old patriarchal paradigm of power-over, it is being replaced with the balanced divine feminine paradigm of power within. We return to living a life of devotion within communities in sync with the natural rhythms of Mother Earth.

All our current governing systems—political, economic, social and religious—exist within separation and lack consciousness. They are disintegrating and transforming during this Great Tuning to love. There will be a long period of bumpy and sometimes heart-breaking transition as we gently transfigure into the New Earth. In the USA and all over the world we are trying to claim a new vision. Marianne Williamson, while campaigning to be the democratic candidate for president, said Americans need to reclaim this vision by:

> ....creating a moral and just economy, infusing hope and opportunity into the life of the average American. Rescuing millions of traumatized children. Creating a healthier society and a place where the sick are well cared for. Reparations for slavery and justice for Native Americans. Waging peace

> and transitioning from a war economy to a peace economy. Reversing climate change and transitioning from a dirty economy to a clean economy. Restoring America's moral leadership around the world. We need a politics empowered by imagination now. It's time to claim what it is that we really want.

The Great Tuning to love is a time for envisioning a world we want existing within the loving spaciousness of our Christ Selves. What we imagine and envision creates a world that gently transfigures fully into the fifth dimension. This is what is true: the old paradigm of separation is over. What is left is the debris from habitual systems and beliefs of the obsolete patriarchal paradigm of power-over. We assist greatly with dissolving these old habitual systems by staying focused on our vision of co-creating the New Earth, the planetary awakening.

**Chapter Four**

# A Vision of the New Earth Created with Compassion

*Lift up your faces, you have a piercing need*
*For this bright morning dawning for you.*
*History, despite its wrenching pain*
*Cannot be unlived, but if faced*
*With courage, need not be lived again.*
*Lift up your eyes upon*
*This day breaking for you,*

*Give birth again to the dream.* Excerpt from *On the Pulse of Morning,* written and read by Maya Angelou at the Inauguration of Bill Clinton, January 20, 1993.

*And every known nook of our nation and*
*every corner called our country,*
*our people diverse and beautiful will emerge,*
*battered and beautiful.*
*When day comes we step out of the shade,*
*aflame and unafraid,*
*the new dawn blooms as we free it.*
*For there is always light,*
*if only we're brave enough to see it.*
*If only we're brave enough to be it.*

Excerpt from *The Hill We Climb* written and read by Amanda Gorman at Joe Biden's inauguration, January 20, 2021

Along with these two women poets generations apart, many of us have the vision to co-create the New Earth. Do we have the will? The difficulty emerges when we try to fix our destructive miscreations using the separated ego. A humorous definition of insanity is doing the same thing over and over again, expecting to get different results. We have now entered the time of Mary, the feminine divine and the Great Tuning to Love. This is a time where imagination and inspiration—arising from hope, faith and trust in our divine sovereignty—are blooming in many of our hearts. Our two poets' words of hope and vision fuel our imagination, touch our hearts, and inspire. We are constantly tuning and toning our unique songs of love to vision a new world. There have been mystics for thousands of years speaking about this time and providing hope, vision and heart-centered prayer. It is time now to hold in our hearts the knowing that all our lifetimes exist in the perpetual now. We have stepped into the unknown to make known what we've denied or refused to believe. As we feel deeply into the unknown, we feel lifetimes of trauma and pain dissolving into love. What remains is compassion, joy and a celebration of our earthly lives. Yeshua says in *Journey into the Unknown*:

> You are a vessel of the divine spirit now, not a slave to the brain's thoughts about everything. This is a monumental change in purpose, one that is nothing short of revolutionary. The brain tells you that maybe you can be elected into political office one day. Your divine spirit informs you that you are already queen of the galaxies. There is nothing else to want or aspire to, but there is work to do here, in this very imperfectly perfect world that we all created together, a world that asks to be understood and accepted as it is, not as you wish it was. Transformation does not come from refusing to see and acknowledge what stands before you. Transformation comes from accepting and loving what stands before you warts and all. This is the power of love.[65]

Compassion is Sophia God's Love on earth. It fuels our transformation. Justice is compassion at the level of the collective. Our vision of Terra Nova is ignited by compassion for everyone, even those committing hurtful and harmful acts. There is no room for outrage, revenge or punishment. Occasionally it is still a challenge for me to accept the world we created. And this is okay, for it is the intent that matters. My prayer is the intent to feel compassion not only for lightworkers, mystics, my friends and family but also for everyone caught up in the unrelenting fear that comes from the separated state.

Compassion comes from blessing my friends and family and those who push my buttons, blessing politicians who are wedded to the doctrine of power-over; blessing those who believe the pale color of their skin gives them inherent superiority over everyone else; blessing the people I meet in the grocery store; blessing the people in my neighborhood; blessing all organic life; blessing the elementals in my body and of earth. It is a simple blessing. "Blessings to you dear sister and brother of God. I hope that your heart opens and overflows with the Universal Mother's all-encompassing love." A simple "bless you" also suffices when the intent is love. Visualizing my high heart chakra wide open to receive compassion magnifies these blessings.

Envisioning the New Earth comes from compassion. The Great Tuning to Love arises from compassion—for myself and all relations of the Holy Mother. We realize this is the process of transformation and transfiguration. As our poets have said: "For there is always light, if only we're brave enough to see it. If only we're brave enough to be it," and "lift up your eyes for this day breaking for you. Give birth again to the dream." We are in the midst of the Great Tuning to love, happening now not in the future.

## Can We Create a World Where All Children Are Safe and Well?

I am gratified how much this book is informed by my past ministry for atypical children. Much of what inspired me then, still inspires me now, such as creating a world where children are well is a world where everyone is well. Much of what I learned then, has deeper meaning now. I feel how perfectly it is unfolding for my awakening. I am brimming with gratitude for my life that led to this point. Within separation our lives have been fraught with trauma and pain, yet the Holy Mother's loving plan for humanity never wavers. Truly my life is a continual flow of unending love and amazing grace.

Ursula K Le Guin, in her short story *The Ones Who Walk Away from Omelas*, asks "can you create a utopian community around the suffering of one child?" It provides a profound metaphor for the world we created within separation consciousness.

Le Guin writes of Omelas that perhaps it is a fairy tale and invites readers to provide our own vision of this city of happiness. There is no guilt. People create beautiful buildings, music, art, poetry and have loving families with happy children. Life is full of promise and joy. Everyone lives equally, with no overriding government to tell them what to do. All appears well. However, Le Guin describes a room in the basement of a beautiful public building. Everyone in Omelas knows of this room and its occupant. Inside this very small room the size of a broom closet is a malnourished naked child with weeping sores, sitting in the dark in its own excrement. The child is feeble-minded, in terror of the brooms, but knows no one will come to save them. The child used to cry for its mother and sunlight and to be let out, but no longer. People occasionally come to fill the food and water bowls and sometimes kick the child, but no one helps relieve the suffering.

Eventually when the Omelas children are old enough, they are taken to see the suffering child in the room. Many weep and rage at such cruelty and feel pity and compassion. They are told that their way of life depends on the suffering of this child.

> The terms are strict and absolute: there may not even be a kind word spoken to the child. It is the existence of the child, and their knowledge of its existence, that makes possible the nobility of their architecture, the poignancy of their music, the profundity of their science. It is because of the child that they are so gentle with children.[66]

They eventually come to accept the idea that it is for the best to sacrifice one child for the well-being of thousands. Some people of Omelas leave the city of happiness one by one. They do not seem to know where they are going—they just leave without knowledge of life outside of Omelas.

There is no way to read this short story without feeling horrified. I could never condone perpetuating a community around the appalling suffering of one child. Nevertheless, within separation we have done just that—created a world condoning the suffering of millions of children. The separated ego tries to convince us that this immense trauma creates compassion. Without the bad we do not know the good. Without sorrow, we do not know joy. Without suffering, we do not know compassion. We forget to ask the questions.

Neither the citizens of Omelas nor the ones who walk away ever thought to question the rules that designated one child to live in misery. The citizens who stay never take the risk to find out whether or not it is true that their beautiful lives depend on one child's suffering. Even those that walk away refuse to take the risk. Instead, they flee the city, remaining trapped in the ideology of one child's suffering engendering contentment for everyone else.

The patriarchal doctrine of power-over that extolls the benefits of technology, capitalism and consumerism is so accepted that it is seen as sacrilegious to question whether or not it is the best system for attending to the well-being of all our world citizens. Millions of children and adults suffer, yet most do not question why this is so. Some of us try to walk away from the suffering, by ignoring it. We concentrate on our own lives, because everything else is overwhelming. But we cannot walk away from the destructive patriarchal systems we've created. The history of the world is a story of continual atrocities, relentless injustice, war, famine, enslavement, genocide, torture, domestic violence, imprisonment and human trafficking. We can no longer walk away from the emotional trauma embedded in our collective psyche. The inadequate band-aid of eons of numbness has been ripped off, and we are grieving. We cannot heal and accept God's love until we acknowledge and grieve deeply the shadow place where we've shoved the trauma.

The citizens of Omelas were told a lie they swallowed whole, just as we've been conditioned to believe over thousands of years of earthly life that suffering is inevitable. Without it, we could not feel compassion. Our heroine's journey brings us into our inner sanctum of our heart's song and into the womb to heal all trauma, to know without any doubts that we are love and have always been the loving compassionate Christ. Yes, we are healing and transforming the trauma to a deeper understanding of our Christ Selves and at the same time we remember we've always been divine, holy and sovereign. Perhaps it is the trauma that helps us remember that it is a paradox. The separated ego would like us to spin our wheels, continuously cycling our confusion to solve a paradox that can't be solved within the separated state.

What I do know is we can co-create a world in which all children are safe, loved, honored, nourished and embraced. In so doing we co-create a world of love and well-being for everyone. We do not walk away. We go inward first to forgive and love ourselves, so that we can forgive and love the outer world. We rekindle the children's fire and mend what's been broken.

## Creating Intentional Communities in Devotion to Life's Song of Love

Utopia is an ideal planned community based on the public good. Most of the utopian communities that existed throughout history failed at some point because they were created within separation. In creating intentional communities as our transition into the New Earth, we have models from the few remaining indigenous communities that escaped colonization. Also, we have the memories and teaching from our indigenous leaders who retained the wisdom of their tribe's spiritual culture. Many mystics, lightworkers and loveholders have recovered ancient memories and a deep knowing of how it is to live a sacred, devotional life.

Intentional communities are created when people come together with a high degree of spiritual and social cohesion. As well as indigenous communities living intentional lives of devotion, there are other contemporary intentional communities, for example: Source Temple in Brazil, Findhorn in Scotland, and Hummingbird in New Mexico, USA. Reverence for all life and total communion with the universe is the driving force. Love of Mother Earth is woven into the spiritual fabric of the community. They know that her bountiful life is there for their use, and her gifts are returned and renewed with devotion and care for all her relations. Everyone thrives within intentional communities knowing that if one person does not, it affects the whole community. Children are loved and cherished.

These intentional communities live outside of the traditional economic paradigms based on lack consciousness which creates wealth for one person at the expense of another. Intentional communities combine personal spirituality with communal spirituality in balance from merging the divine masculine and divine feminine. They become so intertwined that the holy breath becomes One. The common purpose becomes the well-being of everyone within the community, with everyone's gifts honored. Charles Eisenstein says:

> There are places in the world where people live devotionally, holding that intention consciously in community. Another way I like to describe it is that they live in the gift. To live in the gift is to live in the knowledge that the world is a gift (unearned, unforced), that we each are a gift to the world, and that we are here to add our gifts to the ongoing gift of Creation.[67]

Essential to living life as a gift is to see ourselves as a gift. Do you see yourself as a gift? Living a life of devotion means loving ourselves as the Mother/Father/One loves us, completely without reservation. We are a gift. We are the One.

In order for intentional communities to thrive, the members must be actively engaged in their own inner spiritual awakening that is committed to the well-being of everyone. Each person within the community is seen as a gift within the whole. I can envision a time when more and more intentional communities are formed within cities, small towns and remote rural areas. Eventually we create a world based on what Eisenstein calls a gift economy or what some spiritual teachers call a life economy which reflects great compassionate intelligence, love, peace, mercy, abundance and healing. I do not know how this will come to pass; it is not my mission to actively create these communities. What I can do is hold the vision with great faith that the seeds have already been planted and that there are those with the knowledge and wisdom to bring these communities into being. Linda Dillon, channeling the Council of Love, talks about the Cities of Light manifesting to gently replace our major cities. Again, I do not know how this is occurring, but I do know deep within that it is happening.

This time of the divine feminine is the Great Tuning to love and compassion. It is a time of Unity transformation, bringing together those with the knowledge and will to co-create a global community devoted to reverence for the web of life. People with both feet planted in separation consciousness will believe that everything I'm envisioning is not possible, a pipe dream, a fantasy. I hold this vision because I can do no less—because it is time now that we flourish and leave the illusion of separation consciousness. It is time now to claim our Christ Selves and return Home to the Mother/Father/One.

## Being Authentic

Living a life in devotion to God and all life is a process of being authentically aligned with our Soul's integrity. Authentic life comes out of grief that reveals our love of life. Authenticity comes from our heart-centered masculine and feminine energies residing in harmony within us. Authenticity is not something that is achieved, it grows as we transform. We can practice and be aware when we are not true to our divine selves to spark our transformation into our authentic Divine Self, but there are no plans we can follow. Authentic integrity requires being honest and compassionate with ourselves first, then it comes naturally with others. Authenticity arises from self-love. One of the ways we move into authenticity is to consciously breathe and be vulnerable with a trusted friend or in a group of women who listen with the ears of the heart. I have laid myself bare over and over again with my spiritual soul sisters and in this book. As I've done so, I've strengthened my knowing as an innocent child of Sophia God. It feels like a paradox because being vulnerable leads to the invulnerability of our God Self. This is being the living Christ.

When we have fully anchored ourselves in the fifth dimension, there will be no use for words. We will be living within Unity Consciousness, the One in the many and the many in the One. All communication will be telepathic because there will be absolutely nothing to hide. It is difficult to imagine because there appears to be so much about our thoughts held in the shadow that are surrounded by self-judgment, guilt, shame, unworthiness and hatred. We would not want anyone to hear these self-judgments or judgments of others. We are dissolving these unworthy thoughts on our heroine's journey. We return to our divine innocence which we never truly left. Our Holy Mother never judges as she holds for eternity our innate pure innocence. By truly feeling into the peace and love of knowing your innocence untainted by separation, we recognize ourselves in others who judge us out of their sacred wound, and then we see our innocence in ourselves and everyone.

While we are in the Great Tuning to love, we feel as if we have one foot in the fifth dimension and one foot in the third dimension. It may feel as if we are hopping back and forth one foot to the other foot. It is exhausting. I know I've landed again in judgment when I become angry with myself for appearing unloving or dishonest with my feelings. It takes an immense amount of courage to be honest with ourselves, for we've been conditioned to tell what we call white lies because it is the polite thing to do. The white lies we tell are endless, effective for maintaining separation consciousness. A friend talks endlessly and never pauses to ask how you are doing, yet you never call her on it. Or you tell her you love her rambling stories when you don't, because you do not want to hurt her feelings. You stop telling a man what you really feel about their treatment of you because you are afraid of their anger. What white lies do you tell yourself or others because of conditioned politeness or fear?

Women have been conditioned to take care of everyone else first, but this leaves us depleted and eventually we crash. This is part of the wound in our wombs that can't replenish itself. When we nourish ourselves first, we model that for others. Eventually we demonstrate loving and parenting oneself as the source of God's love radiating from compassion within. It is a process.

At a retreat several years ago, the retreat leader suggested that for lunch we sit at a table where we did not know anyone and discuss a suggested topic. The table where I sat included one man and several women. The man proceeded to dominate the talk the whole time, with no one else able to say much of anything. This definitely triggered my rebellion to the age-old pattern of "men know best and women should just listen, stay silent and bow to their wisdom." During the share session, the retreat leader asked how we did with the sharing, so I explained what happened, saying that the man had pontificated the whole time. The retreat leader held the space for everyone to talk through the dynamics of this situation. Years later when I happened to meet this man again, I gratefully hugged him, but then he started to accuse me as I walked away. For all these years, instead of going inward to look at himself, he still thought I was being unfair. That is a long time to hold a grievance.

Women have been so conditioned to caretake men's egos that men expect it and are thrown off balance when women stand up for themselves. Finding our voice, staying authentic to ourselves requires courage emanating from a strong grounding in forgiveness and self-love. We do not have to take care of other egos, only ourselves. When we start to be honest about what we are feeling, people around us may feel threatened or angry, as if they are being accused. It may push their unfair and unworthiness button. It may also open the possibility for them to go inward to explore their reaction. It is sometimes a fine line between judgment and authenticity, judgment and discernment.

I did judge the man at the retreat for silencing women's voices, so it is my inner work to feel the anger and forgive. It does not mean always staying silent when my voice is not allowed. Consequently, sometimes silence is the best option depending on how we are feeling. We ask our heart and our light family for guidance.

There are times when unconditional listening is the expression of love for someone calling for love. Then there are times the stories are unnecessary talk to fill space as a distraction from feeling. Some stories are blatantly or subtly hurtful to the listener. You will know the difference. The habitual white lies we tell ourselves and others are automatic and eventually erode our ability to stay true to who we are.

We often speak from the anger and hurt resulting from the suppression of our voices and the other person may feel attacked and also become angry. This is okay. It is a process of learning to speak our Truth. There are always at least two people in an exchange. The other person also has a choice to listen or react. Atypical children who are on the Autism spectrum are often seen as unfeeling, lacking in the art of being polite. Yet their honesty can be refreshing because they express their truth. The Netflix show *Atypical* demonstrates with much compassion how this type of honesty affects the people in their lives, usually for the better.

We always have a choice in our response. There is always an infinitesimal moment before we respond that if cultivated allows us to pause before a conditioned response. It is there in the pause when we can choose to respond from our compassionate self or our ego self. The stories I shared of forgiving the unforgivable and loving the unlovable were about the power to choose love over fear. Eventually as we acknowledge, feel and dissolve grief and hurtful anger our habitual reactions begin to soften. We start speaking our Truth and radiating power sourced from love.

Relationship implies there is a dynamic of energy exchange between two or more people. Our interaction or response depends upon how well we've done our inner work. If someone pushes my buttons, I may react with anger, fear, judgment and attack, or I can choose to pause, take a deep cleansing breath and respond from the heart. Being able to stay in the heart and respond from our voice of Truth opens up possibilities of deeper meaning in our relationships. As we build trust in our relationships, we feel safe to love our authentic selves enough that we can speak from invulnerable compassion.

We visualize the Rainbow Bridge through our High Heart chakra to embody Christ consciousness. This brings us into alignment with our God Self. Within this alignment we hold our Truth as Divine Beings. We witness without joining others' fear, anger and trauma. Interacting with anyone, whether they are attacking or radiating blessings, becomes numinous energy—all interactions become holy encounters. During the time of the Great Tuning, we are toning our song to live a courageous, authentic life of compassion for everyone.

## The Will of Sophia God Is Our Will

I used to have a difficult time with the idea that God's will is my will. After all, we have free choice. Once firmly on my mystical heroine's journey, I realized that my problem surrendering to God's will is remnants of the belief that God is outside of me. And the God outside of me was a patriarchal god that suppressed and demeaned women. Why would I want my will to be aligned with his will? Even now, I still have difficulty with those who insist on using masculine language to describe a loving God.

Once I embraced the Holy Mother Holy Father Sophia God, I was able to let go of my aversion to my will being God's will. The will of Sophia God is light, love, goodness, grace, mercy, peace, purity, innocence, balance, health, abundance, compassion, unity, happiness, harmony, perfection and immortality. We are co-creating a world with our will and God's will as One. My heart sings with allegiance to this New Earth co-creating devotional communities with Sophia God's Will and my Will as One.

Gratitude is essential for devotional life that merges our will with God's will. Gratitude dissolves fear and allows our light to shine. Feeling gratitude for everything in our lives allows the sharing of light for our benefit as well as the well-being of others. We can start feeling gratitude for our family and friends, no matter how annoying they are sometimes. Gratitude allows seeing each person differently and appreciating their presence in my life, warts and all. I feel their inherent worth and realize they are always doing the best they can, which sometimes is amazingly brilliant and beautiful. This invites forgiveness of times when I've been judgmental or critical of myself—which opens to compassionately holding others who are trying to forgive themselves. Gratitude creates the resonance to remember that everyone's experiences are perfectly orchestrated for their awakening to the Holy Mother's unconditional love. Gratitude is tuning to a higher vibration. Gratitude inspires authenticity. Gratitude allows compassion to flow.

## Atonement and the Time of Christ

When I started on my spiritual journey of the heart, I listened to spiritual teachers talk about atonement. It never made a lot of sense intellectually, and I felt laden with patriarchal Christian dogma. Some would say atonement meant "at-One-ment," and some would say No, it is much more than that. But I never understood their explanation. What I've come to appreciate over the years is that atonement is a process like walking the labyrinth—it folds in and out and gains clarity as I keep walking the path into my heart and womb. Atonement is coming to an awareness of the Christ within. It comes gently on tiptoe, sliding gently into our hearts when we've stopped efforting. It is when all the inner work over the years comes to fruition. The following quote from Ursula K. Le Guin's *The Telling* describes what atonement feels like to me:

> When my guides lead me in Kindness I follow, follow lightly, and there are no footprints in the dust behind us.[68]

On my heroine's journey I trust my guides, my light family, to lead me in kindness; trusting that as I follow lightly, I will leave no permanent footprints in this dream of separation to make it real. Through the process of atonement, all the trauma dissipates, no damaging footprints remain to remind us of our suffering. Yeshua in *A Journey into the Unknown* says:

> Atonement is an old fashioned or "old school" term, but its true meaning is very applicable to today's modern world. It signifies the end of the separate self, and being at one with source. It's when God looks like you. It's when every thought and every movement reflects the Will of God, which is unconditional love. It's when there are no conflicting thoughts to love. It's when there is no separate will. It's when you are in the middle of the deepest part of the ocean and there is no land in sight. The water is what sustains you. It's when you don't remember when you didn't live like this; those years, decades and lifetimes of struggle. It's when you have stopped looking for a god to connect with because you have discovered that you are a magnificent part of God and it's been this way all along. It's just that you didn't know it. Atonement is the end of the hero's journey. Atonement is crossing the finish line and turning around to cheer on everyone else still in the race, Atonement is discovering life's big, giant, and well-kept secret. Atonement is knowing that each and every person is born with the keys to the kingdom. The keys to unlock the secret, but they just can't find them.

> Life is designed to keep the location of the keys obscured but atonement ensures that clarity will prevail.[69]

Atonement is the end of our heroine's journey and the beginning of our journey as Christ. It heralds the time of Christ, the second coming of Christ. The way of Mary is ushering in the Time of Christ (Unity) Consciousness. We imagine the New Earth. We can do this now that we are acknowledging and grieving all the trauma. Each one of us is the Christ. The Great Tuning is toning to the resonance and frequency of the Christ within each one of us. The Christ within vibrates our song of love so that it becomes all we are, for we can be only this—the resurrected Christ. We join in Oneness with each and every embodied Christ. Our unique heart songs, our holy tones, join in harmony with all of existence. We join with the Cosmic Mother's heart song of uncompromising love. We co-create within the infinitely vast Cosmos, including other dimensions and realms of being all radiating and resounding with God's love.

## God Exists in the Details, in Ordinary Everyday Events

We can get so wrapped up in our struggles, we often forget to pause, take a breath and appreciate the daily flow of our life made up of seemingly small occurrences, including our daily chores. During this pivotal time of the planetary awakening with the massive hatred, fear and grief being experienced on so many levels, we forget to appreciate that the Mother/Father/One also exists in the details of everyday experiences. Often forgiving the unforgivable and loving the unlovable happens when we embrace the beauty of small events.

My mother died in 2008. I found this poem she wrote long ago when one of my brothers was 4 and I was a baby. It speaks to me as a mother. Now that I'm in my wisdom years, it speaks to me as a Universal Grandmother.

*God Is in Our Alley*
*After-dinner dishes are dull,*
*A chore for every tired mother,*
*And I am no exception.*
*I stood one night at my task*
*Impatient to be out free*
*I whisked about my kitchen*
*Half in anger and frustration,*
*Making the square hot room*
*A kind of temporary prison*
*In the midst of all this irritation*
*One small son burst in,*
*A muddy barefoot four-year-old*
*Bug-eyed with excitement*
*"God is in our alley!"*
*My first reaction—instant laughter*
*And a wonderful urge*
*To hug this grimy youngster.*
*Nothing would do*
*I must go see and see.*
*So, we did go*
*Just the two of us*
*To the back of our lot*
*Where the mud pies were made*
*There behind our own garage*
*In the narrow strip between fences*
*Wild flowers were glowing*
*In the half-light of dusk*
*Like a magic carpet.*
*"He is there in our alley."*
*The complete faith of a four-year-old boy*
*I stood for a moment*
*My hand in his*
*Absorbing the quietness*

*Glad for a chance to catch my breath*
*Marveling at the miracle of beauty*
*Evening light had brought*
*To the ordinary yellow daises*
*Blooming among the weeds*
*And do you know*
*My son was right*
*God was in our alley.*
by Mary Nancy Patton

I can visualize my mom as a young mother, frustrated by chores and then surrendering to the vision of a small boys clarity. This poem speaks of so much: my memory of my mother, her generosity of spirit, and her ability to stop and appreciate a child's wisdom. It also shines a light on the wisdom of the present moment, taking time in our busy lives to be quiet and notice the little ways God's presence is known. So often it is children who will do that for us, reminding us that it is the simple pleasures which quiet our thoughts and allow God's voice to be heard and presence to be felt. William R. and Barbara Kimes Myers in *Engaging in Transcendence* call these moments "mud puddle experiences" in which God is found in the small everyday happenings such as: a baby's smile, a spontaneous deeply meaningful conversation with my daughter or son, a beautiful sunrise or sunset, desert wildflowers after a rain, completing a jigsaw puzzle with my husband, sitting in my beautiful garden, a hike with a friend, or a splash in a mud puddle.

During a low point when Rick and I were struggling to stay centered and in peace about a personal conflict, we watched a western meadow lark splash and play in our bird bath. Then a few days later we watched a hummingbird dip and swim in the bird bath. Both times brought such joy and centered us again in peace.

Several years ago, after a drenching rain, Rick and I were driving down a dirt road with little traffic. There were some mud puddles. We spotted a little girl playing in a mud puddle to the side of the road. She was giggling with joy, with total abandonment to all but the delight in the moment of stomping around in a mud puddle. How often do we allow ourselves to enjoy a present moment pleasure with complete abandon?

Throughout the writing of this chapter, I've been weeping rivers of tears for the atrocities still happening, and also for all the simple yet sweet everyday moments of joy. I asked Mother Mary for help with the grief. Several years ago, Rick and I noticed a bird with white bands on its wings and tail that we could not identify. This bird sang the most beautiful song, full of variety. I finally identified it a few days ago as the northern mockingbird. Once I named it, I became more deeply aware of the many mockingbirds which surround our home with their constant singing during mating season.

This morning while I write two mocking birds were singing to each other, starting at 5am and still singing at 9am. I am transported by the beauty of their song. It seems that by recognizing them, I've opened to receive their song's message in order to soothe my aching heart. I look up from my computer and watch a mockingbird land on the wall outside my window. This is the closest I've ever seen a mockingbird—they are usually flitting at a distance from tree to tree. I invite the bird to drink from our bird bath. She took several flights toward the bath, but did not land. I tell her that she is safe and to drink anytime. That evening while eating dinner, Rick and I watch as she lands and drinks from our bird bath. Eventually she takes a bath and plays. We experience such joy. It is a moment of transcendence.

I read in *Animal Speak* by Ted Andrews that the mockingbird's spirit medicine is finding our sacred song which is our soul's purpose. I am reminded to sing forth my unique song. Because I am listening, it renews my belief in my inner knowing and sacred purpose to bring this book into fruition. I also learned that the mockingbird is a courageous bird that fiercely defends its nest against all intruders who would do harm. I feel this fierce love to nurture and care for all our children by singing my song's message in this book, in harmony with all of creation.

We are always blessed with these brief moments of clarity, if we expect them to occur. These "mud puddle" experiences are gifts of remembrance to help us through the difficult times. It is those times of frustration, anxiety, struggle, pain and adversity which provide our most meaningful opportunities to hear Sophia God's voice. I weave together many of these experiences which have been catalysts for my own change and I am grateful. Daily mud puddle experiences evoke my God Self's song which reminds me of Oneness with God, rather than the separated self's voice of judgment, lack and limitation. When I do this, my perspective of the world changes. The problem that seemed so difficult is transfigured. The painful event is still the same, but now I have accessed that stately calm within, and it no longer feels so overwhelming.

We learn from the small frustrations of having to do everyday chores, like washing the dishes, to prepare us for the more painful times of adversity. With our thoughts we either make our everyday chores "a kind of temporary prison," or we stay present and love what is. The principle is the same whether we are washing dishes or dissolving that which has lived too long in the shadow. We stop to appreciate and feel God's gift and mystery in the ordinary, and like the rainbow, it becomes a moment of transcendence. We can accept each moment in life as an opportunity to remove the obstacles to the Truth of who we are, or we can stay stuck in the prison of our own making. The Holy Mother speaks to us in times of great stress as well as those unexpected "mud puddle" moments. God is in our alley, always.

## The One Source Light of Creation

Beloved Mystical Soul Sister, I hope by this point in the book, you accept that we are always co-creating either with the fear of the separated ego or with the love of God. I am being asked to go even further into the unknown to an indescribable place. The words we use were all created within separation consciousness, thus the dilemma. Yet here I am being asked to describe a state of being I've yet to fully enfold.

Deep within the low, dense energy of separation consciousness we created a Father God existing outside of us on whom we projected all our feelings of fear, vengeance, violence, anger and authoritarian control, mixed in with love heavily influenced by co-dependency. As we began to rise from separation, our projections onto the Father God became more loving, yet remained unbalanced. Eventually we began to create a God who is both Mother and Father, yet still remained outside of us. We are now at a place on our heroine's journey where we accept that God is in us and we are in God: there is no separation. The veil of separation only exists inside us. The time of Mary ushers in the time of Christ, the Great Tuning to Love. We accept our relationship with the Holy Mother Holy Father Sophia God. In accepting our relationship with God, we enter into Unity Consciousness, where individuation becomes differentiation. Within separation, individuation is used to separate and divide. In Christ consciousness we know that all God's creations are wondrously diverse, the many in the One and the One in the many—differentiation within the whole. Differentiation plays our single tones joined in harmony within the whole song and symphony of creation.

As I journey even deeper into the unknown, I am being shown that we co-created a loving God so we could experience an intimate personal relationship with an all-loving Being.

We project attributes or ascribe characteristics onto God that assist in the planetary awakening. Love has no attributes. It just Is. The best description within the limitation of words is: Love is all-encompassing, with no opposites. I have used that descriptive phrase often when describing the Holy Mother Holy Father Sophia God's love for all her creations.

We exist within relationship so we can come into Being. Therefore, we co-create a relationship with and in an all-loving God who is in relationship with and in us. What arises for me now is that beyond God, beyond words, beyond my ability to understand and know, is the *One Source Light of All that Is* as the inexpressible, ineffable, unknowable Creator—a vast consciousness. While I've occasionally used the One Source Light of All that Is as a synonym for God, it is actually beyond God. We can't place attributes which allow relationship on the vast consciousness of Infinite Love as the *One Source Light of All that Is*. However, we can have a multidimensional relationship with the Holy Mother Holy Father Sophia God birthing Souls and galaxies in multiple dimensions.

The purpose of this awareness is to accept fully that I Am in relationship with God as God is in relationship with me. Because God is the bridge to all that is, through God I can access the vast consciousness of Creation. There is no alternative. We masterfully created an illusion or dream that we could separate and not be in relationship with God. Yet our experiences within this dream ultimately return us to relationship with God, because that is who we are. Thus, I Am in relationship with all of God's creations because I created God and God created me. All exists in perfect relationship. And I created God because the indescribable, unknowable Source of All that Is has no attributes needed to form a relationship. As my Christ Self is my bridge to relationship with God, God is a bridge to Love as the *One Source Light of All that Is*.

## Completion

I am at the end of the book. However, as Mother Mary told me, "Oh, you'll never be finished, but the book will be. Who knows what will happen after that—be curious and alive to infinite possibilities." Being alive to infinite possibilities or potentialities existing within the vast consciousness was not possible as I started writing about my heroine's spiritual journey. My journey happened while I was writing, taking me places within I had never previously explored.

When I started writing intellectually I agreed that life is a song of love, but deep within I was not so sure. Therefore, I wrote about falling in love with self, my feminine wildness and wisdom, and my devotion for the Holy Mother and Mother Earth. I learned to sing my masculine resonance in order to balance and harmonize with my feminine resonance. I learned to accept my feelings and embody repressed anger in order to release decades of suppressed pain, and to grieve eons of persecution and trauma. I went inward to own the ways I've benefited from white privilege and felt into ancient trauma. I learned to be a vulnerable mystic soul sister within our co-creators' woman's circle. Gratefully I embraced their support and wisdom. I healed the mother daughter wound with both my mother and Sarah, and hopefully provided insight for other mothers and daughters. I learned about my indigenous roots and the wisdom of indigenous peoples. I learned to hug and to listen from my heart. I learned to embrace my anger and grief, to forgive the unforgivable and love the unlovable that unleashes ineffable compassion. I learned to love myself warts and all. I stepped into claiming the Wisdom Weaver Universal Grandmother's archetype, learning to hold the Divine Mother's basket of love for all humanity. I have continued the process of rekindling the children's fire and mending what's been broken. Let us envision a world where children and all the Mother's relations are cherished and safe, thus saving ourselves.

Embracing the symbol of the Cosmic Egg I am birthing the new within to be a vessel of unending love and amazing grace manifesting miracles of life as divinely human.

Life is a song of love; I believe that now. In this Great Tuning to love's compassion, I feel myself resonating at a higher octave, joining in harmony with the symphony of creation. I slip less and less into the habits and debris of the separated self. More and more I know I am Christ in direct relationship with God. The Christ I Am is therefore a bridge to relationship with all of God's relations and creations which we co-created together. The Mother aspect of God returns to her rightful place as the Creatrix of all life enfolding the Holy Father and all of creation. I have an intimate relationship with Sophia God. This is cause for wild celebration, joy and infinite gratitude for my unique song of love joined with your unique song of love and blending in harmony with everyone's song of love. Eternal blessings for your heroine's spiritual journey of the heart and womb. May we join in compassionate devotion with the scaredness of all life in its vast wondrous variety.

# As Within So Without Meditations

## The Gift of a Question

*She remembers who she is and births a compassionate world.*
*She remembers who she is and sings us home.*

The purpose of this last inquiry and meditation is to focus on deepening our breath to merge with Mother Earth's planetary breath of life to abide within the Holy of Holies of our wombs, our cervical gateway to her healing resonance. It is there where we can focus on tuning to the ancient, primordial sounds of creation. Beyond stillness and silence, we can once again hear the origin sound and vibration of the Cosmic Mother resounding through Mother Earth. This is the final dissolution of patriarchal programming within our bodies and on earth.

When we do this work, it is important to protect ourselves by either physically or imaginatively walking into the center of our labyrinth, our symbol of the Mother's Earth's womb of life. Next imagine wrapping around you: a protective shining dome of love; or St Germaine's violet flame of transformation; or the Tree of Life: or the golden web of life—whatever divine symbol creates feelings of safety. Invite your light family to be with you.

### *Visualization*

Close your eyes and gently allow your breath to merge with the breath and heartbeat of Mother Earth. Gradually deepen your breath till you feel Mother Earth's breath and primal energy rising through your cervix into those places in your body where you feel pain, stress or tightness from patriarchal conditioning that still runs in your body. Pay attention to your anal canal and womb, as this is where a massive amount of ancient and current persecution is felt.

Pay very close attention to what your body is telling you and when it feels right, let the breath gently rise to the gateway of the heart where patriarchal programs have tried to suppress our love and silence our voices. Stay in the heart and throat area till you feel a lessening of tension and/or pain. When ready, allow your breath sourced from Mother Earth's breath of life to rise to your pineal gland in the center of your forehead.

The brain is a gateway to divine knowing, which has received massive patriarchal conditioning. Continue your deep gentle breath until you feel some release. Inquiry practice can be much deeper when we are doing it within the calming cleansing breaths merged with Mother Earth's planetary breath of life rising throughout our body from our cervical gateway. When ready, open your eyes and sit quietly absorbing Mother Earth's love. If you want, ask some questions.

Please start with the two following questions before beginning your inquiry process then read the additional questions. Try to write down whatever arises without judgment or editing what you don't like. Most importantly ask your guides/light family to help with your inquiry work.

Can I love myself enough to forgive myself?
Can I forgive myself enough to love myself?

### *Additional Questions*

There are inquiry questions you can ask yourself to feel into any trauma you may be carrying in the shadow. Sometimes we need help from a trauma therapist to suggest ways to access the trauma to create safety and hold a loving presence while you heal. Please ask your guides for help with questions and to find a therapist. They are always with you and are waiting for your request.

Have you experienced trauma in this lifetime that you've been unable to forgive? Do you have memories of ancient and karmic trauma?

Sometimes it is helpful to visualize your hurt inner child and ask her what she is holding that needs to be acknowledged, accepted and felt before healing can begin. Hold yourself as you would hold a new-born baby, tenderly with compassion.

Sometimes acknowledging the thought or belief that is not serving you can lead to its release. Sometimes you will need to find a way to embody the belief in order to allow it to move through your body. (This is what I did while imagining myself chopping off heads while physically moving my body.) A trauma therapist utilizing somatic techniques can help with this.

What is your relationship with money? What does abundance mean to you?

Release the idea that abundance only means having lots of money. Imagine what your abundant life would look like.

What is your unique heart song? What makes your heart sing?

Are you expressing it, or do you consider it a pipe dream?

What is stopping you from either recognizing your unique song or expressing it?

Envision the New Earth you would like to co-create. Let your imagination flow—it fuels creation. Plant the seeds and bulbs of love and peace in the desecrated earth, in arid places, in areas of conflict, in the hearts of those lost to darkness, in every person, and in yourself. Water and tend to your seeds in your world's garden every day until they grow and bloom. We are creating a new Garden of Eden. There is no reason to stop your imagination and the planting of seeds, no one to tell you it will not happen. Let your heart and mind expand into infinite possibilities. There is no lid on creation; it can't be contained.

Return to the first two questions about loving and forgiving yourself.

This is the final surrender.

# Finale

## We Begin Where We End

*After silence that which comes closest to expressing the inexpressible is music.*
Aldous Huxley

We begin where we end. You sing the song of your heart which is your truth and I sing the song of my heart which is my truth in communion and union with the Holy Mother Holy Father Sophia God. Your song may not resonate completely with me and my song may not resonate completely with you. This is because we still exist in a time on earth when we have yet to fully embody our Christ Self. Yet, each one of us, if we honor our truth, our unique purpose in union with Sophia God, is expressing and expanding God's love and creative power. We vibrate at a higher octave. Everyone's unique song joins in harmony with the whole, creating a symphony of love.

The Cosmic Mother Father's reality is the omniverse so vast it is beyond our human understanding. Its mystery is known and unknown. As we come to know, we realize there is always the unknown as an expanding process. And so, all of God's creations are constantly coming to know. It is how expansion and creation work in Oneness and communion with Sophia God. There is no end point to our becoming. It is infinite. Our earthly experience is an infinitesimal part of this process which is so much bigger than our current human understanding. We are multidimensional beings, always creating within the all-encompassing love of our Creator, the Beloved Infinite Intelligence, the Holy Mother Holy Father Sophia God.

Each of us is a unique expression of Sophia's infinite variety in human form. Therefore, we may not always totally understand another person's path or unique purpose in union with Sophia God. We don't have to. We are being asked to create the new by allowing, embracing and loving with compassion all the unique songs or purposes as expressions of the One. I Am a Divine Feminine Christ Creator expressing as a Universal Grandmother weaving songs of love. These are songs of reconciliation to balance the feminine and masculine energies. We create a basket of love holding all of humanity until everyone awakens to our Christ Selves. This is my truth, my song, my unique purpose. Being able to embrace my song and truth helps others to embrace their unique song. We balance feminine and masculine energies in order to heal and transform into being divinely human. We embody Christ consciousness. This is a return to what we've always been, only now in form.

Claiming the inclusive divine feminine energy of birth and creation and the divine masculine energy of clarity and action into form sings to me as an expression of me. It is what I am being called to be in this life as a woman. I co-create Terra Nova, a new paradigm of compassion for all of the Holy Mother's offspring. I am a vessel filled with the Shekinah to express the Holy Mother's love for all her relations. Everyone holds variations of this mission. Every person is discovering and living their unique purpose to embrace, honor and vibrate as spiritual movement into form. When each one of us is transformed to radiating our unique purpose, singing our unique heart song in union with Sophia God, then we will recognize, honor and allow it in others.

We co-create the new paradigm of heaven on earth. We step into our divine sovereignty. Vibrating at a higher octave encourages and lifts those who have yet to do the necessary inner work to transmute into being their own powerful divine sovereign Self. Becoming the best and brightest version of myself helps everyone become the best and brightest version of themselves. All happens within perfect divine timing, singing our own unique song. This is the Universal Grandmother's hymn for humanity creating a symphony of love.

I feel as if my song of love is this whole symphony of instruments and voices all playing in complete harmony as the Oneness of all that is. I want to sing with the angels. Words do not convey what I am feeling and hearing deep within my heart and soul. Words seem so inadequate to describe the inexpressible. I stay paralyzed and unable to write. And then it flows. And then it stops. How do I write it all down? How can I possibly organize the infinite music of the multiverse?

Enfolding God's symphony is absolute silence and stillness. It feels similar to when Rick and I were hiking in Arches National Park in the late 1970s before it became popular. We hiked in and sat on a rock. There was no one around and there was absolute stillness and silence. We could not even hear the skittering of insects or the slightest breeze. I felt this phenomenon again sitting in the middle of my labyrinth during the great pause of the COVID pandemic. Nothing stirred. There were no sounds. This is the thunderous silence that contains a whole symphony. It is the closest I've come to hearing the origin sound of love's creation. I can't explain it. It just is. So I'll stop trying. Maybe that's the point.

Our true inheritance is to remember and accept that we are created and held in love beyond our current understanding. Therefore, Love is all there is. It is the driving force of the multiverse, the allness, isness and oneness. The perception that we are separate from God is dissolving as we transform into Christ consciousness. It was a grand experience we willingly chose in order to create something not created before—becoming divinely human living a life of compassion. Sophia God and all her creations are infinitely creating, expanding and becoming in a vast variety of ways within Oneness. Therefore, life can be only a song of love—all it requires is our acceptance.

Our bodies have no boundaries. They are porous vessels overflowing with love so vast that it can fill an ocean. It can fill galaxies. The Source Light of Love has no boundaries and never ends. This is why we can be in these bodies while being wholly human and wholly divine. I Am the song of love's symphony and chorus resounding in perfect harmonious Oneness of love with all of the Cosmic Mother's creations. I begin again and again until this piece/peace of the eternal music resounds within always. I Am wholly complete for now in this moment as I realize over and over again that I Am already accomplished and at One with all that is. It is done.

There is an old traditional hymn that I love to sing that helps me remember to keep singing my unique song. The words are a little old fashioned, yet they express so much of what I am feeling. The only change I would make is that our new creation is not so far off anymore.

*My life flows on in endless song above earth's lamentation.*
*I hear the real though far off hymn that hails a new creation.*
*Through all the tumult and the strife, I hear the music ringing.*
*It sounds an echo in my soul.*
*How can I keep from singing!*
Words: Traditional, Music: Robert Lowry, 1826-1899

*She knows who she is and sings her song.*

# Endnotes


1. *A Course of Love* (ACOL). (Nevada City, CA: Take Heart Publications, 2014) T5:5.2. (All quotes granted fair use permission.)
2. ACOL D:Day20.2-3.
3. Stokes, Jeanette, Blog Post *Walking the Labyrinth Together*, Resource Center for Women's Ministry in the South (RCWMS), April 8, 2020.
4. Minor, Al, Channel for Lama Sing Readings, quote posted on Facebook. (www.lamasing.org)
5. Allen, Paula Gunn, *The Sacred Hoop*, Recovering the Feminine in American Indian Traditions. (Boston: Beacon Press, 1992) p. 13.
6. Munsch, Robert N, *David's Father*. (US: Annick Press, 1983).
7. Munsch, Robert N, *Paper Bag Princess*. (US: Annick Press, 1980).
8. Baynton, Martin, *Jane and the Dragon*. (London: Walker Books Ltd, 1988).
9. Giles, Mary E., Editor, *The Feminist Mystic*. (NY: Crossroads Publishing, 1985) p. 79.
10. Harvey, Andrew, Editor, *The Essential Mystics, The Soul's Journey into Truth*. (New Jersey: Castle Books, 1996.) Introduction p. xiii.
11. ACOL D:Day27.15.
12. ACOL D:Day21.5-6.
13. Harvey, Andrew, Editor, *The Essential Mystics, The Soul's Journey into Truth*. (New Jersey: Castle Books, 1996.) Introduction.
14. Rupp, Joyce, Dear Heart, Come Home. (NY: Crossroad Publishing, 1996) p. 55.
15. ACOL D:Day19.4.
16. ACOL D:Day19.6.

17. Rohr, Richard, *Daily Meditations*. Center for Action and Contemplation. www.cac.org (Copyright © 2017 by CAC. Used by permission of CAC. All rights reserved worldwide.)
18. Starr, Mirabai, *Wild Mercy, Living the Fierce and Tender Wisdom of the Women Mystics*. (Boulder, CO: Sounds True, 2019) p. 24.
19. Degler, Teri, *The Divine Feminine Fire*. (Flourtown, PA: Dreamriver Press, 2009) p. 81.
20. Starr, Mirabai, *The Showings of Julian of Norwich, A New Translation*. (Charlottesville, VA: Hampton Roads, 2013) p. 163.
21. Starr, Mirabai, *The Showings of Julian of Norwich, A New Translation*. (Charlottesville, VA: Hampton Roads, 2013) p. 163.
22. Watterson, Meggan, *Mary Magdalene Revealed*. (Carlsbad, CA: Hay House, 2019) p. 37.
23. ACOL T3:18.10.
24. Kaia Ra, *The Sophia Code*, (Mount Shasta: Kaia Ra & Ra-El Publishing, 2016) p.8.
25. Kribbe, Pamela, *The Forbidden Female Speaks, Conversations with Mary Magdalene*. (Petersburg, Florida: BookLocker.com, 2018, Kindle Edition.) Chapter One.
26. Pearce, Lucy H, *Burning Woman*. (Ireland: Womancraft Publishing, 2016) p. 26.
27. Hamilton, Ross, *Star Mounds, Legacy of a Native American Mystery*. (Berkeley, CA: North Atlantic Books, 2012) p. 220.
28. Redmond, Layne, *When the Drummers Were Women, a Spiritual History of Rhythm*. (NY: Three Rivers Press, 2018.)
29. *A Course in Miracles* (ACIM), copyright ©1992, 1999, 2007 by the Foundation for Inner Peace, 448 Ignacio Blvd., #306, Novato, CA 94949, www.acim.org and info@acim.org. (All quotes granted fair use permission.) W-pI.31.

30. Luna, Maya, www.deepfemininemysteryschool.com (Used with permission).
31. ACOL D:Day8.2.
32. René, Lucia, *Unplugging the Patriarchy*. (Williamsburg, PA: Crown Chakra Publishing, 2009) p. 203.
33. ACOL T3.5.7.
34. ACOL D:Day8.22.
35. Jeshua Online, Oakbridge University, 8/3/2020. (All quotes approved with fair use permission. ©2022.)
36. Pearce, Lucy H, *Burning Woman*. (Ireland: Womancraft Publishing, 2016) p. 130.
37. Jeshua Online, Oakbridge University 2/19/2020.
38. ACIM, T-142III.4.
39. *Journey into the Unknown*. (www.journeyhub.cocreatingclarity.org) J184,1-2. (All quotes used with permission.)
40. *Journey into the Unknown*. (www.journeyhub.cocreatingclarity.org) J129.1-3.
41. ACIM, T-142III.4.
42. ACOL D:1.8-9.
43. Sajit Greene (www.SoulMapCoach.com).
44. Kribbe, Pamela, *Spiritual Mothering*, Channeling December 15, 2007 (www.Jeshua.net.)
45. ACIM W-pI.195.
46. Hale, Susan Elizabeth, *Song and Silence, Voicing the Soul*. (Albuquerque, NM: La Almeda Press, 1995) p. 221.
47. Macartney, Mac, *The Children's Fire, Heart Song of a People*. (Great Britain: Practical Inspiration Publishing, 2018) p. xxiv.
48. Pearce, Patricia, *White Supremacy and the Identified Patient*, blog www.patriciapearce.com.
49. ACOL D:Day8.18-19.
50. Hoffman, Dale Allen, You Tube, *Ancient Aramaic Secrets of Isis-Mary Magdalene*, 9/23/2013.

51. Perron, Mari, *Mirari the Way of the Marys, A Dialogue on Mary of Nazareth's Way of Mary*. (St. Paul, MN: Course of Love Publications, 2020) p. 18. (Quotes used with permission.)
52. ACOL C26.15.
53. Patton, Sally, *Welcoming Children with Special Needs, a Guidebook for Faith Communities*. (Boston: Unitarian Universalist Association, 2004) p. 137.
54. Carey, Ken, *Return of the Bird Tribes*, (Harper Collins, 1988) p. 20.
55. Sams, Jamie, *Sacred Path Cards*, (New York, HarperCollins) p. 191.
56. Rohr, Richard *Daily Meditations*. Center for Action and Contemplation. www.cac.org (Copyright © 2021 by CAC. Used by permission of CAC. All rights reserved worldwide.)
57. Macartney, Mac, *The Children's Fire, Heart Song of a People*. (Great Britain: Practical Inspiration Publishing, 2018) p. 6.
58. Macartney, Mac, *The Children's Fire, Heart Song of a People*. (Great Britain: Practical Inspiration Publishing, 2018) p. 6.
59. Rohr, Richard, *Daily Meditations*. Center for Action and Contemplation. www.cac.org (Copyright © 2017 by CAC. Used by permission of CAC. All rights reserved worldwide.)
60. Perron, Mari, *Mirari the Way of the Marys, A Dialogue on Mary of Nazareth's Way of Mary*. (St. Paul, MN: Course of Love Publications, 2020) p. 246.
61. Kaia Ra, *The Sophia Code* (Mount Shasta: Kaia Ra & Ra-El Publishing, 2016) p.250.
62. Jeshua Online, Oakbridge University, 7/11/2020.
63. ACOL D:Day3.7.
64. Eisenstein, Charles www.charleseisenstein.org, Essay: *Source Temple and the Great Reset*, March 2020.
65. *Journey into the Unknown*. (www.journeyhub.cocreatingclarity.org) J136.1

66. Le Guin, Ursula K, *The Ones Who Walk Away from Omelas*. (NY: Harper Perennial, Digital Edition).
67. Eisenstein, Charles, www.charleseisenstein.org, Essay: *Source Temple and the Great Reset*, March 2020.
68. Le Guin, Ursula K, *The Telling*. (Darby, PA: Diane Publishing Company.)
69. *Journey into the Unknown*. (www.journeyhub.cocreatingclarity.org) J114.1.

# Acknowledgments

I lived this book during the 3 plus years it took to write it. My mystical soul sisters provided the basket of unconditional love to support my process. With love and gratitude I thank Lori Heimdahl Gibson, Sajit Greene, Jane Puryear, Sharon Petkau, Suvani Stepanek and Christina Strutt for their spiritual wisdom, clarity, support and love.

A special thank you to Sajit Greene, Christina Strutt, my daughter Sarah and my dear life-long friend Jeanette Stokes for editing, advice and suggestions.

Heartfelt thanks to my husband Rick for his constant support for whatever I undertake in this life and to my son Tyler, who is always there to listen in kindness and for his inspired cover image.

# About the Author

For over half her life Sally Patton has engaged in a contemplative spiritual practice to awaken from separation consciousness. Her journey began when her son was labeled as "severely dyslexic," leaving her feeling like she was in a "desert of no beginnings and no endings." Desperate to get out, she embarked on a spiritual quest that nurtured her own healing, leading to an awareness that it was not her son she had to change, but herself. The resulting spiritual journey inspired her ministry to create welcoming faith communities for children with special needs labels thus creating beloved communities for everyone. Sally also ran workshops for parents to see the wholeness and divinity of each child, creating the possibility to parent from love instead of fear.

This ministry ended in 2013 after Sally's move from the Boston area to northern New Mexico, allowing a deepening and expansion of her awakening spiritual journey with the Holy Mother's return as an aspect of God. She draws upon channeled non-dual teachings from Yeshua and Mother Mary combined with a variety of teachings from many faith traditions and spiritual paths to answer a unique call to be an emissary of Divine Feminine Compassionate Consciousness. The Holy Mother has returned to heal into wholeness the division between feminine and masculine energies necessary to end thousands of years of patriarchal domination. Sally helps women waken to the strength of the Mother within embracing the sacredness of all life on Mother Earth.

With a master's in education, Sally's professional experience of advocating for children and also parenting an atypical child provide deep insight into the wounding patriarchal conditioning has had on relationships between mothers and children, especially between mothers and daughters. Sally offers personal mentoring and workshops with a focus on healing our own sacred wounds, leading to an empowered awareness of the inner Divine Sovereign Self which heals all relationships between men and women and our children.

# For More Information

Thank you for purchasing *Life Is a Song of Love, a Woman's Spiritual Journey of the Heart and Wound.* Dear mystical soul sister, I hope that this book resonates with you as much as it resonated with me while writing it.

If you feel so moved, please feel free to add your review of the book to your favorite online site. This will help other women discover the book.

Please visit my website to sign up for newsletters, to read blog posts, to sign up for a mentoring session and to learn of upcoming workshops. I am also hoping to reach out to women through women's groups or book groups. If you feel you can help with this, please contact me.

http:www.embracechildspirit.org.

Love and Blessings, Sally

# O-BOOKS

## SPIRITUALITY

O is a symbol of the world, of oneness and unity; this eye represents knowledge and insight. We publish titles on general spirituality and living a spiritual life. We aim to inform and help you on your own journey in this life.
If you have enjoyed this book, why not tell other readers by posting a review on your preferred book site?

**Recent bestsellers from O-Books are:**

**Heart of Tantric Sex**
Diana Richardson
Revealing Eastern secrets of deep love and intimacy to Western couples.
Paperback: 978-1-90381-637-0 ebook: 978-1-84694-637-0

**Crystal Prescriptions**
The A-Z guide to over 1,200 symptoms and their healing crystals
Judy Hall
The first in the popular series of eight books, this handy little guide is packed as tight as a pill-bottle with crystal remedies for ailments.
Paperback: 978-1-90504-740-6 ebook: 978-1-84694-629-5

**Take Me To Truth**

Undoing the Ego

Nouk Sanchez, Tomas Vieira

The best-selling step-by-step book on shedding the Ego, using the teachings of *A Course In Miracles*.

Paperback: 978-1-84694-050-7 ebook: 978-1-84694-654-7

**The 7 Myths about Love...Actually!**

The Journey from your HEAD to the HEART of your SOUL

Mike George

Smashes all the myths about LOVE.

Paperback: 978-1-84694-288-4 ebook: 978-1-84694-682-0

**The Holy Spirit's Interpretation of the New Testament**

A Course in Understanding and Acceptance

Regina Dawn Akers

Following on from the strength of *A Course In Miracles*, NTI teaches us how to experience the love and oneness of God.

Paperback: 978-1-84694-085-9 ebook: 978-1-78099-083-5

**The Message of A Course In Miracles**

A translation of the Text in plain language

Elizabeth A. Cronkhite

A translation of *A Course In Miracles* into plain, everyday language for anyone seeking inner peace. The companion volume, *Practicing A Course In Miracles*, offers practical lessons and mentoring.

Paperback: 978-1-84694-319-5 ebook: 978-1-84694-642-4

**Your Simple Path**

Find Happiness in every step

Ian Tucker

A guide to helping us reconnect with what is really important in our lives.

Paperback: 978-1-78279-349-6 ebook: 978-1-78279-348-9

**365 Days of Wisdom**

Daily Messages To Inspire You Through The Year

Dadi Janki

Daily messages which cool the mind, warm the heart and guide you along your journey.

Paperback: 978-1-84694-863-3 ebook: 978-1-84694-864-0

**Body of Wisdom**

Women's Spiritual Power and How it Serves

Hilary Hart

Bringing together the dreams and experiences of women across the world with today's most visionary spiritual teachers.

Paperback: 978-1-78099-696-7 ebook: 978-1-78099-695-0

**Dying to Be Free**

From Enforced Secrecy to Near Death to True Transformation

Hannah Robinson

After an unexpected accident and near-death experience, Hannah Robinson found herself radically transforming her life, while a remarkable new insight altered her relationship with her father, a practising Catholic priest.

Paperback: 978-1-78535-254-6 ebook: 978-1-78535-255-3

**The Ecology of the Soul**
A Manual of Peace, Power and Personal Growth for Real People in the Real World
Aidan Walker
Balance your own inner Ecology of the Soul to regain your natural state of peace, power and wellbeing.
Paperback: 978-1-78279-850-7 ebook: 978-1-78279-849-1

**Not I, Not other than I**
The Life and Teachings of Russel Williams
Steve Taylor, Russel Williams
The miraculous life and inspiring teachings of one of the World's greatest living Sages.
Paperback: 978-1-78279-729-6 ebook: 978-1-78279-728-9

**On the Other Side of Love**
A woman's unconventional journey towards wisdom
Muriel Maufroy
When life has lost all meaning, what do you do?
Paperback: 978-1-78535-281-2 ebook: 978-1-78535-282-9

**Practicing A Course In Miracles**
A translation of the Workbook in plain language, with mentor's notes
Elizabeth A. Cronkhite
The practical second and third volumes of The Plain-Language *A Course In Miracles*.
Paperback: 978-1-84694-403-1 ebook: 978-1-78099-072-9

**Quantum Bliss**

The Quantum Mechanics of Happiness, Abundance, and Health

George S. Mentz

*Quantum Bliss* is the breakthrough summary of success and spirituality secrets that customers have been waiting for.

Paperback: 978-1-78535-203-4 ebook: 978-1-78535-204-1

**The Upside Down Mountain**

Mags MacKean

A must-read for anyone weary of chasing success and happiness – one woman's inspirational journey swapping the uphill slog for the downhill slope.

Paperback: 978-1-78535-171-6 ebook: 978-1-78535-172-3

**Your Personal Tuning Fork**

The Endocrine System

Deborah Bates

Discover your body's health secret, the endocrine system, and 'twang' your way to sustainable health!

Paperback: 978-1-84694-503-8 ebook: 978-1-78099-697-4

Readers of ebooks can buy or view any of these bestsellers by clicking on the live link in the title. Most titles are published in paperback and as an ebook. Paperbacks are available in traditional bookshops. Both print and ebook formats are available online.

Find more titles and sign up to our readers' newsletter at http://www.johnhuntpublishing.com/mind-body-spirit

Follow us on Facebook at https://www.facebook.com/OBooks/ and Twitter at https://twitter.com/obooks